The Practice of Law

The Practice of Law

Tang Hang Wu
PhD, LLM (Cambridge), LLB (NUS)
Advocate and Solicitor (Singapore),
Solicitor (England and Wales),
Associate Professor, Faculty of Law,
National University of Singapore

Michael Hor
LLM (Chicago), BCL (Oxford),
LLB (NUS), Advocate and Solicitor (Singapore),
Professor, Faculty of Law,
National University of Singapore

Koh Swee Yen
LLB (NUS), Advocate and Solicitor (Singapore),
Solicitor (England and Wales),
Partner, WongPartnership LLP

LexisNexis
Singapore • Malaysia • Hong Kong • India
2011

The Members of the LexisNexis Group worldwide

Singapore	LexisNexis, Singapore
	3 Killiney Road #08-08 Winsland House I
	Singapore 239519
Malaysia	LexisNexis Malaysia Sdn Bhd
	T1-6, Jaya 33
	3, Jalan Semangat, Seksyen 13
	46100 Petaling Jaya
	Selangor Darul Ehsan
Hong Kong	LexisNexis, HONG KONG
	39/F, Hopewell Centre,
	183 Queen's Road, East
India	Butterworths Wadhwa Nagpur
	14th Floor, Building No 10, DLF Cyber City,
	Phase-II, Gurgaon, Haryana,
	India 122002
Argentina	LexisNexis Argentina, BUENOS AIRES
Australia	LexisNexis Butterworths, Chatswood, NEW SOUTH WALES
Austria	LexisNexis Verlag ARD Orac GmbH & Co KG, VIENNA
Canada	LexisNexis Butterworths, Markham, ONTARIO
Chile	LexisNexis Chile Ltda, SANTIAGO DE CHILE
Czech Republic	Nakladatelství Orac sro, PRAGUE
France	Editions du Juris-Classeur SA, PARIS
Ireland	Butterworths (Ireland) Ltd, DUBLIN
Italy	Giuffrè Editore, MILAN
New Zealand	Butterworths of New Zealand, WELLINGTON
PRC	LexisNexis Beijing Representative Office, BEIJING
Poland	Wydawnictwo Prawnicze LexisNexis, WARSAW
South Africa	Butterworths SA, DURBAN
Switzerland	Stämpfli Verlag AG, BERNE
United Kingdom	LexisNexis Butterworths Tolley, LONDON and EDINBURGH
USA	LexisNexis, Dayton, OHIO

ISBN 978-981-236-903-1

Printed in Singapore

List of Contributors

ADRIAN TAN, LLB (Hons) (NUS); BSc (Computer Science and Psychology) (NUS); Advocate and Solicitor (Singapore); Director, Drew & Napier LLC.

ALFRED DODWELL, LLB (Hons) (Warwick); Advocate and Solicitor (Singapore); Dodwell & Co.

ALVIN YEO, SC, LLB (Hons) (London); Barrister-at-Law (Gray's Inn); Advocate and Solicitor (Singapore); Senior Partner, WongPartnership LLP.

ANAND NALACHANDRAN, LLB (Hons) (NUS); Advocate and Solicitor (Singapore); Partner, Braddell Brothers LLP.

BENJAMIN TAN, LLB (Hons) (NUS); LLM (London); Advocate and Solicitor (Singapore); Solicitor (England and Wales); Attorney (New York); Senior Partner, Sichenzia Ross Friedman Ference LLP.

CHAN LENG SUN, SC, LLB (Hons) (Malaya); LLM (Cambridge); Advocate and Solicitor (Singapore); Advocate and Solicitor (Malaya); Solicitor (England and Wales); Co-Head, Disputes Practice Group, Baker & McKenzie.Wong & Leow.

CHONG IK WEI, LLB (Hons) (NUS); Advocate and Solicitor (Singapore); Solicitor (Hong Kong); Solicitor (England and Wales); Resident Partner and Chief Representative, Clyde & Co (Shanghai).

CONNIE HENG, LLB (Hons) (NUS); Solicitor (Hong Kong SAR); Advocate and Solicitor (Singapore); Partner, Clifford Chance (Hong Kong).

CYRIL CHUA, LLB (Hons) (NUS); Advocate and Solicitor (Singapore); Partner, ATMD Bird & Bird LLP.

DAVINIA AZIZ, LLB (Hons) (NUS); BCL (Oxford); LLM (NYU); Deputy Senior State Counsel, International Affairs Division, Attorney-General's Chambers.

GREGORY VIJAYENDRAN, LLB (Hons) (NUS); Advocate and Solicitor (Singapore); Partner, Rajah & Tann LLP.

GUY SPOONER, LLB (Hons) (Southampton); Solicitor (England and Wales); Solicitor (Hong Kong SAR); Barrister and Solicitor (Australia); Partner, Norton Rose LLP.

HO SENG CHEE, LLB (Hons) (NUS); LLM (NYU); Group Chief, Corporate Services, Mapletree Investments Pte Ltd.

JACK TSEN-TA LEE, LLB (NUS); LLM (London); PhD candidate (Birmingham); Advocate and Solicitor (Singapore); Solicitor (England and Wales); Assistant Professor, School of Law, Singapore Management University.

JEYENDRAN JEYAPAL, LLB (Hons) (NUS); LLM (Harvard); Assistant Registrar, Supreme Court of Singapore.

JOEL LEE, LLB (Hons) (Wellington); LLM (Harvard); Barrister and Solicitor (New Zealand); Advocate and Solicitor (Singapore); Associate Professor, Faculty of Law, National University of Singapore.

LEONARD NG, LLB (Hons) (NUS); LLM (Chicago); Solicitor (England and Wales); Partner, Sidley Austin LLP.

LIM HUI MIN, BA (Jurisprudence) (Oxford); BCL (Oxford); Barrister-at-law (Lincoln's Inn); Advocate and Solicitor (Singapore); Deputy Senior State Counsel, Attorney-General's Chambers.

LOW SIEW LING, LLB (Hons) (NUS); LLM (Harvard); Advocate and Solicitor (Singapore); Deputy Senior State Counsel, Civil Division, Attorney-General's Chambers.

NORMAN HO, LLB (Hons) (NUS), LLM (London); Advocate and Solicitor (Singapore), Solicitor (England and Wales); Senior Partner, Rodyk & Davidson LLP.

RAJAN CHETTIAR, LLB (Hons); Barrister-at-law (Middle Temple); Managing Partner, Rajan Chettiar & Co.

RUBY LEE, LLB (Hons) (NUS); LLM (London); Advocate and Solicitor (Singapore).

STEFANIE YUEN THIO, LLB (Hons) (NUS); Advocate and Solicitor (Singapore); Joint Managing Director, TSMP Law Corporation.

SYLVIA LIM, LLB (Hons) (NUS); LLM (London); Advocate and Solicitor (Singapore); Member of Parliament, Aljunied GRC.

THIO YING YING, LLB (Hons) (NUS); Advocate and Solicitor (Singapore); Senior Partner, M/s Kelvin Chia Partnership.

VALERIE THEAN, LLM (Harvard); MA (Cambridge); Director-General, Legal Group, Ministry of Law.

Acknowledgements

The editors would like to thank the Attorney-General, Mr Sundaresh Menon SC, for agreeing to write the foreword of this book. Mr Menon is certainly a role model to our readers as to what is possible in the practice of law having been an international leading expert in the fields of commercial litigation and arbitration, insolvency and construction law and a Judicial Commissioner of the Supreme Court before his current appointment as Attorney-General. We are also grateful to all the authors for contributing excellent chapters in their respective fields despite their busy schedules. Eleanor Wong was instrumental in helping us bounce some ideas about the concept of the book and introducing us to some of the authors. The generosity of WongPartnership LLP and the Attorney-General Chambers is also much appreciated. Through their generous contributions, we are able to donate copies of this book to every secondary school, polytechnic and junior college library. Our appreciation also goes out to Christopher Ong Siu Jin for assisting us in the launch of the book and to Lilly Oh for providing administrative support. As ever, we are indebted to Dr David Tan for taking the photograph on the cover and designing the cover. The photograph, 'Into the Light' was taken at Maxwell Chambers, and we thank Maxwell Chambers for allowing us to take photographs of the facility. Finally, we are grateful to our publisher, LexisNexis, namely Joanna Yap and Abigail Kway.

Tang Hang Wu, Michael Hor and Koh Swee Yen

Foreword

Among all professionals, lawyers seem to score the highest in terms of the number of jokes there are about them. At least, some of these are quite funny. But too many are the inventions of outsiders looking in and seeing something they do not entirely understand or cannot easily relate to. For some of them, it is difficult to see why the lawyers say that theirs is an honourable profession.

Herein lies the beauty of this book. In the space of 25 highly interesting and extremely readable chapters, the authors, under the superb guidance of the General Editors, have given an account of what the practice of law means to those of us on the inside. The result is a very informative guided tour through some of the more common (and sometimes less common) ways in which lawyers practise their craft. Between them, the authors include lawyers in the public service as well as in the private sector; lawyers who are principally advocates as well as those who are mainly concerned with transactional work; lawyers who work here in Singapore as well as those who work abroad; and even one who works in an international organisation.

This tremendous breadth provides a valuable insight into the wonderful opportunities that are available to lawyers in Singapore. It also hints of the growing complexity of the practice of law.

The Practice of Law in the final analysis is a celebration of sorts. Those who have found deep meaning, purpose and relevance in their calling as lawyers have shared some very personal insights into what the law has given them. And in sharing these insights, it is hoped that those on the outside, and perhaps especially those thinking of coming inside, will be better informed and ultimately inspired to be a part of this wonderful profession.

I congratulate the Editors and Authors on completing this work. I am delighted to recommend it to all who want to get an insider's perspective on practising law.

Sundaresh Menon, SC
Attorney-General
Singapore

Preface

The Practice of Law is a sequel to Hang Wu and Michael's earlier book, *Reading Law in Singapore*. After the latter came out, they thought that their work was done in this regard – having introduced aspiring law students to what it means to study law. Then they started getting calls from secondary schools and junior colleges to give presentations during their career fairs. During these presentations, they found that recurrent questions from the students often revolved around the practice of law especially in the field of litigation, corporate and criminal practice. They would also get unsolicited emails from aspiring lawyers asking them about various areas of practice. It was then that they decided that perhaps the work was not done after all – a sequel to *Reading Law in Singapore* covering the major areas of practice was needed. While they have spent some time in practice (Michael for three years in legal service and Hang Wu as a commercial litigator for three years), their practice experience was relatively short and took place a long time ago. They decided to rope in their former student, Koh Swee Yen, a litigation and dispute resolution partner at WongPartnership LLP to be a co-editor. Swee Yen comes to this project after wearing many hats: a former Justices' Law Clerk, adjunct tutor at the university, young *amicus curiae*, law clerk to the Competition Appeal Board and partner at a major law firm. Her energy, enthusiasm and experience in legal practice have been instrumental in getting this project off the ground. All royalties of this book will go to the Special Needs Trust Company.

***

In *The Practice of Law*, we have assembled some of Singapore's most exciting lawyers to write a 'taster' chapter on their area of practice to give our readers a flavour of what their professional life is like. True to two of the editors' academic background, we have also included two chapters on a career of teaching law, in the university and at the polytechnic, written by Jack Lee and Sylvia Lim respectively. The brief to our authors was simple: Tell us about your typical day, what do you enjoy about your job, what do you find challenging about your job, what do you wish you were told as an aspiring lawyer? We urged the writers to give the reader 'a realistic and honest account – warts and all'.

In line with our philosophy of full disclosure of warts and all, the narrative in *The Practice of Law* begins, perhaps unusually, with the frank reflections of a rookie lawyer in his or her first year of practice.

To encourage candour, we offered anonymity to the author, which after some discussion was accepted. We hope that senior lawyers and judges who might read this piece will have some sympathy for this young lawyer's plea for some kindness, patience and civility in the legal profession. Too often in the newspapers, we read about the high attrition rate of lawyers in Singapore and elsewhere. Also, stories about lawyers finding fulfillment as chefs, building food and beverage empires, being successful actors and actresses seem to capture media attention these days. We applaud them and are very proud of their success as (originally) lawyers inhabiting other professional worlds. Yet the impression should not be created that you can only find happiness if you *do* not practice law. We have encountered not a few students and legal associates who tell us that they are determined not to practice law. It seems to us that the legal fraternity is facing a crisis of sorts in retaining enough young talent to sustain and grow the profession. The seemingly unrelenting pace of modern legal practice has the potential to conflict with an understandable desire to maintain a healthy work-life balance and a yearning for a greater sense of purpose beyond amassing material wealth. This spiritual crisis is not unique to Singapore. In this book, we do not pretend that our contributors are able to offer any definitive solution to these difficult problems. However, we think that our authors show by example, in the lives that they lead and the humanity that they display in discharging their responsibilities, that it is possible to do noble things and maintain a sense of purpose while practicing law and juggling the demands of family. We are struck by the recurrent theme in the chapters by Low Siew Ling, Jeyendran Jeyapal and Lim Hui Min on how public service provides them with a sense of purpose and fulfillment. Hui Min's essay also demonstrates certain nobility in serving the needs of the humble man or woman through her work as a family lawyer at the Legal Aid Bureau. Hui Min teaches us that it is 'within the power of almost every person to help another, if he [or she] has the will to do so'.

Valerie Thean's and Davinia Aziz's pieces illustrate an entirely different kind of purpose and fulfillment. Valerie provides us with a fascinating insight into how law and policy relate to each other in her work at the Ministry of Law whereas Davinia explains to us how international law affects Singapore. Beyond the legal service, Gregory Vijayendran is well-known as both a busy commercial litigator and an award winning pro-bono lawyer who is recognised for his work with Club Rainbow, an organisation which helps children and youths suffering from a range of chronic and potentially life-threatening illnesses. A desire to give back to society is also evident in Rajan Chettiar's piece on starting a small firm practice. While most lawyers are attracted to the glitz and glamour of Biglaw practice, Rajan's primary motivation in setting up his own firm was to follow his father's simple principle that: 'You can help people by being a lawyer.' His story tells us that sometimes the simplest advice is also the wisest.

Work life balance is a perennial struggle for many working professionals and we know of no one more qualified than Thio Ying Ying to write this chapter. We are in awe of Ying Ying – head of litigation in her firm, married for more than 26 years and bringing up six children. Most people cannot even manage to do one of these things right! We are moved by Ying Ying's honest account of how it is a struggle to juggle being the best lawyer that she can be with the demands of being a spouse and a devoted mother. Her story comes full circle as her sons are now in law school with a mother's hope that her sons will become loving husbands, good fathers and competent and fair lawyers. What then sustains remarkable lawyers like these? One thing that struck us about the essays from our contributors is their obvious love and passion for their jobs. Norman Ho, who like property mogul, Donald Trump, is truly excited about real estate after 30 years of practice. Ruby Lee who as a legal counsel for a company has traversed the globe with vim and vigour doing diverse work such as managing litigation in various jurisdictions, handling labour disputes and even assisting her company acquire hotels all over the world. Stefanie Yuen-Thio shows us how one can maintain sanity while being both a corporate powerhouse and retaining a wicked and irreverent sense of humour. Another theme which emerges from these essays about the motivation of lawyers is the desire to help people. Anand Nalachandran who is in criminal practice is sustained by the knowledge that his efforts allow him to help people in their darkest hour. And Joel Lee reminds us that litigation is not the only way to resolve disputes preferring to use other means such as mediation and negotiation. Finally, the practice of law is always interesting and intellectually stimulating. For example, Chan Leng Sun, SC sees his practice almost like an intellectual puzzle and weaves an entertaining story about shipping practice which challenges the readers.

To reflect the global reach of Singapore's legal profession, we are delighted to be joined by Singapore-trained lawyers who have successful practices elsewhere. We can almost feel the crispness of the air as Leonard Ng cycles to work 'on a beautiful spring morning' in London. We sense the adrenalin pumping as Connie Heng works hard, plays hard, and of course shops equally hard in Hong Kong. We rejoice with Benjamin Tan who has found a niche in New York bridging the legal gap between investors and enterprises in mainland China and the United States, and with Chong Ik Wei in Shanghai, who has become part of China's international resurgence. On a slightly different plane, we read of Ho Seng Chee's work with the International Monetary Fund, designing policies which may potentially make or break governments around the world. Far from seeing all of them as lost to the Singapore legal profession, we consider them as our bridges and ambassadors around the world. Even in the context of a 'domestic' legal practice, the international element is evident. For example, we follow Cyril Chua's exciting journey in his battles with modern day (intellectual property) pirates found in diverse places such as the air-conditioned environment of Sim Lim Square to the backstreets of Penang and New Delhi and the borders of Vientiane into Nong Khai. Just as we have Singapore trained lawyers based elsewhere, we are delighted with the contribution of Guy Spooner who is a foreign lawyer based in Singapore with a thriving practice in international arbitration.

We would sound a word of caution for aspiring lawyers. A career in law practice is hard work. As one of the pre-eminent litigation and dispute resolution lawyers in Singapore, Alvin Yeo, SC, tells us that success in law is '1% inspiration and 99% perspiration'. This is not limited to the area of commercial litigation and arbitration as Alfred Dodwell's piece on family law practice describes the relentless demands of clients on their counsel. Unlike John Grisham's novels, no fresh graduate steps out of law school and then has the immediate opportunity to argue a ground breaking case as lead counsel before the highest appellate court. It is also almost unheard of for new graduates to start their career by negotiating multi-million contracts by themselves. Reality is usually more mundane – new lawyers must learn their craft by doing more menial and painstaking tasks such as discovery, interlocutory applications, due diligence and proof reading before they are ready to represent clients on more complex matters. Adrian Tan reminds us in his closing epilogue of this book that one of the most important qualities a lawyer must have is tenacity, ie the ability to keep pushing on and chipping away on behalf of his or her client. For Adrian, 'great lawyers never surrender. They soldier on, making argument after argument, asking question after question, trying to push back the darkness and uncover some small spark of light that may reveal their case to the judge. They do this day after day, trial after trial, until optimism becomes a habit.' Despite the hard work that law practice entails, we are gratified that a seasoned lawyer like Adrian finds that ultimately law practice is rewarding and has taught him much in life.

We are reminded by Guy Spooner of the wise words of the well known barrister, author and playwright, Sir John Mortimer, who said: '*No brilliance is needed in the law. Nothing but common sense, and relatively clean finger nails*'. After reading the essays from these interesting and accomplished lawyers, we believe what was said by two of us in the preface in *Reading Law in Singapore*, still rings true. There will always be a place in the legal profession for a young man or woman who has common sense and is willing to work hard. Just remember to keep your sense of humour. And we hope to see you out there doing great things after your law degree.

Tang Hang Wu, Michael Hor and Koh Swee Yen
October 2011

Contents

OVERSEAS PRACTICES

PROLOGUE

REFLECTIONS OF A YOUNG LAWYER – FINDING MY NORTH STAR

The Anonymous Lawyer

As I celebrate my birthday this year, I also mark one year as a legal associate. I write these reflections from a position of weakness, knowing that the comments and observations I make apply likewise to me. Nonetheless, I think it is crucial for us as young lawyers to think about the profession we love, and think 'highly' of it, to hold it in high regard and to mould it in that fashion.

I work in a big firm. The salary is marginally better than my friends elsewhere. But the hours are horrendous. Part of the reason is that the people who run big firms are highly profit driven. A senior partner takes home a few million dollars a year. The aim of increasing one's share of the equity pie also drives one to take on as many new files as possible. Rarely is it one too many. Overtime and burnt weekends (for the associates) are often commonplace.

But money isn't everything, and I consider myself blessed to have done my bit for society. You see, I work for several bosses, but two of them, whom I consider myself privileged to have worked for, stand in stark contrast. I respect them both and have learnt (and continue to learn) much. Yet, their difference in style has made me think deeply about how I want to practice.

One boss is a high flying corporate litigator. All his clients are institutional clients. They can pay. He lives in an expensive area and drives a sports car. He brings the clients (and sometimes us juniors) for meals in fancy restaurants, costing sometimes a hundred dollars a person (which to us juniors is quite a sum). He jet-sets and bills.

My other boss is equally capable. Yet, it is fortunate for me that he has a fair bit of clients who are 'common folk' – individuals, contractors, lay people, etc. His drafting is immaculate. He will say clearly what he means in the shortest possible sentence. Working for him is a breeze, not only because of his succinctness. I shall mention another two of his traits which deserve merit later.

Working for my first boss is heavy-going. Drafts are amended several times, each time with a plethora of changes, both in style and in content. He floats from file to file which often leaves us without clear direction, which in turn causes us to react. But reacting is not good for us – it costs us precious time away from family and friends. Worse still, it costs the client. I was embarrassed on one occasion where a client complained that an interlocutory application cost him over S$20,000. This boss did give me feedback that I had spent too much time on the file. Eventually, out of professionalism, this boss of mine did give a fair discount. Whilst as a junior I was probably slower and expended more time than necessary, I do wonder if inflated bills are common because of his (overly) rigorous working style.

Working for the second boss is more pleasurable. He deliberately questions us and discusses our thought processes with us. This hones our thinking skills, which is crucial in lawyering. As a boss, he respects our time. He demands a high standard of work but never makes the associates or staff stay beyond what is necessary. He once told me 'the benefit of a secretary's job (and their lower pay), is the promise of stable working hours. Paying them overtime for working overtime robs them of this. We must respect that everyone has their role and place.'

What I respect most about the second boss is that I have seen compassion in his practice of law. This was best demonstrated when he took on an estate matter, despite the client being jobless and having real issues with payment. It was unfortunate that for many years, because this client was impecunious, he could not afford legal recourse against his sibling executors who refused to distribute his share of the estate. When we took on the file, we only took $2,000 as a deposit for him (which is extremely low for a contentious file in a big firm). Away from the client, this boss told me he would only bill the client for my hours, because this was his way of 'giving back to society'. I have seen this boss argue in Court and know that he is worth his salt and he is also one who bills accurately. Yet, in my first year alone, I have also seen him delay or discount billings for clients who deserved legal representation but had real issues with payment. This gave me courage to know that I could practice with compassion as well.

I never started practice with dreams of justice. I never told my law school interviewer that I wanted to do justice. I was a simple history and general paper enthusiast which thought that my love for argument would make me interested in law. Yet, being in practice has made me realise it must be about justice. People all over the country, rich or poor, will have injustice visit them. And in many cases, the tool of the law is only available through us, their lawyers. If all we are about is bringing in the money, I am afraid concerns of justice, ethics and a sense of righteousness on behalf of the client will be lost to practical and commercial considerations and cutting corners.

Apart from justice, I think what the profession sorely lacks is a sense of fairness and courtesy. I worked on a file where a sole proprietor had instructed us as Counsel. Lamentably, through correspondence, the big firm on the other side was consistently using harsh words, trying to corner our instructing solicitors, setting unreasonable deadlines. The truth is, if we did not come on board, the case may have been lost by the sheer overwhelming efforts of that big firm. Imagine a boutique firm facing the machinery of an army of lawyers, research, drafting nasty letters, having a full range of legal resources at their beck and call. I find it absolutely unacceptable and ridiculous that such nasty letters have to be written. It is never just about winning the case but fighting in a way that is fair, humane, and that brings honour to the profession. Unfortunately, impressing the client with big words and stealing a march on the opponent seems to be the trend.

Lastly, I wish to say a word about our Judges. I have immense respect for the bench who through many years, even before I was born, had roughed it out and learnt their trade under hard taskmasters. Yet, as a new lawyer and in some ways an 'outsider' to the Court system, I realised from times I attended Court that it was common for the Judges to make some disparaging comments about Counsel. Obviously there are black sheep – lawyers who try to hoodwink the judges and steal a march. However, in all of this, the love for our profession behooves us all to treat each other with respect. Practitioners face the pressures of needing to serve our clients' interests, and yet fulfill our duty to the Court. We are often 'hard-pressed' on every side. In this regard, I only hope that the Bar could be accorded a little more respect. In my humble view, I do wonder at times if lawyers treat each other unkindly because we have lost the respect of each other and the Judges as well. With the likely influx of foreign lawyers, and the lack of encouragement of local Counsel, will we be unwittingly narrow the path for our own litigators? I recall, in some casual discussions with the senior lawyers in my own firm, that it was a kind word or two from a Judge in their day which helped raise their confidence and gave them the needed assurance that they were on the right track. Hopefully the Bench and Bar would foster some mutual and natural respect for each other which would boost the love and regard for our Honourable profession.

Obviously, the path gets tougher as one climbs higher. Not only will I face different challenges but be measured by my own criticisms above. I only pray that the goal of being a member of an Honourable profession would somehow be my North Star.

PRIVATE PRACTICE

CHAPTER 1

LITIGATION – A PERENNIAL BATTLE OF WITS

Alvin Yeo, SC

Bearing the distinction of being the youngest lawyer to be appointed to the position of Senior Counsel, Alvin is widely recognised as a leader in litigation and arbitration and has shown excellence in navigating banking and corporate disputes, insolvency and restructuring, and construction and civil engineering matters, all of which form the core of his practice.

Alvin is also actively involved in various Committees for Arbitration ranging from sitting in Singapore's own International Arbitration Centre's Council of Advisors to being a member of the Korean Commercial Arbitration Board and the Kuala Lumpur Regional Centre for Arbitration. An elected Member of Parliament, he has also served on various public committees for reviews of the legal services sector and is a member of the Appeals Advisory Panel of the Monetary Authority of Singapore (MAS).

So what is litigation *really* like? The television usage of advocates (typically tall, sometimes handsome but predominantly male), dressed regally in black robes, presenting silver-tongued arguments to the Court or breaking down a witness in cross-examination, springs readily to mind. But is the reality anything close to that dramatic vision? Allow me to share some thoughts about life as a litigator, and you can draw your own conclusions.

1. You Win Some, You Lose Some

Unlike other areas of law where the parties are agreed on the main object, litigating parties are poles apart. Typically, what one side wishes to obtain in Court is directly at the expense of the other side, one party's gain is the other party's loss. It is a stark conflict, and in a sense, the successor to duels from days of yore when two sides fell out with each other.

So into this arena ride the litigators, armed with their bundles of authorities, the affidavits of their client, and that most deadly of weapons – their written submissions. But when they ride out again, only one of them (absent a really ingenious judgment) will be happy. The other advocate will be consoling him or herself that the outcome could have been worse, or trying to do the same with his or her client. Every litigator goes through that experience of losing his or her case, and this goes on throughout your career! It can be such a sinking feeling that can affect your mood for days and sometimes weeks after. And true litigators never lose that sense of hating to lose their case.

So you do need a certain sense of sangfroid, resilience or just plain thick skin, to absorb the disappointment and to move on. Truth be told, it would be difficult if not impossible to survive a career in litigation if one could not get over the (hopefully occasional) loss. However, losing has to hurt a little (at least), because that is where you get your 'edge' as a litigator. It is an adversarial contest, and the competitor in you has to want to win, and correspondingly, hate to lose.

Which brings me to why we litigators carry on. The sheer adrenaline rush, sense of satisfaction, the look of gratitude in your client's eyes after a hard-fought victory, somehow make all those long hours of toil and set-backs along the way seem worthwhile, and give you renewed vigour to soldier on.

2.   1% Inspiration, 99% Perspiration

That was how Thomas Edison defined 'genius', probably by modest reference to himself. But it could equally be applied to what it takes to be a good litigator, even a great one. The nature of a court-room battle, with the human factor of the Judge and the witnesses on both sides (yes, sometimes you get surprised by what your own client says on the witness stand), and your opponent doing his or her level best to put one over you, means that you have to expect the unexpected. Those that crave a life of predictable outcomes will not find it in litigation. There are cases when everything goes according to plan, or as you had called it. But this is the exception, not the rule.

So how does one prepare for the twists and turns of litigation? Simply by being prepared, and very prepared at that. You can get by at a particular hearing or on a particular aspect of the case by 'winging' it, but sooner or later you will get found out. While you will be better able to navigate an unexpected turn of events if, knowing the material in your case thoroughly, you can make a tactical decision to switch tracks. This could be to downplay a particular witness' evidence if the witness came across poorly on the stand, or changing emphasis from a line of argument that the Judge seemed less than impressed by, to even opening a new line of attack (or defence). These forks in the litigation road

6

are encountered with surprising regularity, and it is the well-prepared advocate who negotiates them more adeptly than others.

It also means that one cannot generally follow a set script in court, because one has to react to what is going on around you. So the best litigators are thoroughly familiar with the facts and law, have a general plan of action – and yet are flexible enough to depart from the plan when the circumstances warrant it. This is also why litigators, even the very experienced ones with the strongest nerves, are all keyed up before the big day. Like a modern-day gladiator, no matter how much training one has put in before, it will come to naught if you do not perform on the day itself.

It adds to the challenge of being a litigator. But also to the sense of satisfaction and achievement when you have gotten the job done.

3. Single-minded, But Keep Your Balance

When you enter the courtroom, you set out to persuade the Judge that your client is right, his cause is just and that your witnesses are telling the truth. While cross-examining the other side's witnesses, you are seeking to elicit answers from them which are, often reluctantly or even hostilely given, to support your case. And even before you get close to the trial, you would need to convince your client that he has a case (although some do not need persuading but rather moderating!) and that you are the right advocate to get him the result he deserves.

In short, the role of the advocate is to persuade others to come around to his or her view. To achieve that, you need to be thorough, clever, eloquent and all that. But most significantly, you need to be single-minded about that objective. A good advocate, I believe, manages to (almost) convince him or herself of the merits of his or her client's case, no matter the odds. After all, if one cannot persuade oneself, what hope is there to persuade others? This is not an invitation to be dishonest in presenting your client's case, but rather a stricture against going into court half-hearted or unconvinced about your client's case. That will surely show on your face or in your opening remarks, and it will get even more difficult after that.

I said a good advocate manages to 'almost' convince oneself, because paradoxically, you will not serve your client by not being objective about his or her case. At the outset when you review your instructions, you need to objectively assess the strengths and weaknesses and advise your client what options he or she has and the best way to pursue those options. It might be best never to start proceedings but to try reaching an accommodation with the other side, or to bring a limited claim according to your view of the merits of your case. Or even to start an action for tactical reasons with a view to using that as leverage for a settlement or other concessions. That sense of balance, of knowing how good or bad your case is and of remembering just why you started the claim in the first place, needs to be maintained right up to the trial. But somehow, when the trial begins with no settlement in sight, one has to present your case with conviction, trying your best to win it notwithstanding your misgivings but without ever being misleading. At the same time, if an offer for settlement comes up during the trial, or the Judge gives an indication of how he sees the case going, you have to take a step back to coolly assess the implications and to advise your client accordingly. It is this 'Jekyll and Hyde' quality that allows an advocate to be both persuasive, and yet objective, in representing his or her client.

4.   Conclusion

I have tried to set out some personal thoughts on what it means to do litigation, and what goes into the make-up of a litigator, in the hope it allows you to better make an informed choice of the career you pursue. The challenges it presents, and the qualities it demands, are not for everyone. But for those to whom it appeals, it is a richly rewarding career where one can fight for causes one believes in, engage in eloquent advocacy, searching cross-examination and a tactical battle of wits. And perhaps come closest to what *truly* being a lawyer is all about.

CHAPTER 2

CORPORATE – RAIDERS OF THE LOST ART OF NEGOTIATION AND WHERE THE DEVIL DOES WEAR PRADA

Stefanie Yuen Thio

Stefanie Yuen Thio is the Head of the Corporate Department of boutique firm TSMP Law Corporation, where she is also a Joint Managing Director. Having had her childhood dreams of becoming a movie star or a TV journalist thwarted early on, she studied law at the National University of Singapore and became a corporate lawyer upon being called to the Singapore Bar in 1994. In addition to her corporate work, Stefanie also actively volunteers in VWO and does charity work on issues she feels strongly about.

1. Why Corporate Practice?

There are many good reasons to become a corporate law practitioner. It is an exciting practice area, which will stretch your legal and intellectual capabilities. It is multi-disciplinary, as many areas of law will come into play – from company and securities law, to banking and international trade principles, and intellectual property and insolvency concepts. A top-notch corporate lawyer will be able to advise his clients on all of these issues as may be relevant in the context of the specific transaction. Corporate legal practice is also boundlessly interesting because every transaction and every client is different. A good corporate lawyer will not just have a good grasp of the transaction terms, but will be able to navigate the waters around the spoken and unspoken requirements of the client. These, and other factors, are fantastic reasons to go into corporate practice.

Unfortunately, none of these were reasons as to why I became a corporate lawyer. I wanted to be an actress, a TV journalist or a writer. However, those jobs required real skills – like the ability to act, a knowledge of world affairs and the ability to string two sentences together. Skill sets that were way beyond me. My parents wanted me to become a doctor (whose parent doesn't?) but my ability to memorise long Latin names of diseases and body parts was limited at best. Nor did I do too well cutting up Kermit the frog in my Secondary Three Biology class, so that plan was a wash as well, and my parents had to resign themselves to hoping I married a doctor (another area in which I was to be a crashing disappointment).

So I kind of fell into the law.

Like any law student worth his salt, I wanted to be a litigator. The glamour of standing up in a courtroom, all eyes trained on me, presenting my closing arguments to a hushed and awed audience, all the while dressed in the most traffic-stopping Manolo Blahniks – that was my dream. A dream that came crashing down when (a) I discovered you could only wear black and white to court, the white being a shirt buttoned all the way up to your chin (and I did not study for five years just to dress like a waitress), (b) the bulk of my litigation time was spent in legal research or waiting outside the Assistant Registrar's chambers for a mention, and (c) even if I could afford Manolos (what a laughable thought that was when I think of my first paycheque), I would have leg cramps from standing in four-inch heels in court all day.

But on a more fundamental level, I did not like the scrappiness of the litigation fight. I took it personally when I did not get a win for my clients; it hurt my feelings when the other side called me dishonest or expressed astonishment at my line of argument. You need to have an unquenchable fire in your belly for litigation and the ability to pick yourself up even when floored by the pithy put-down by a Judge. My husband (who redeemed himself somewhat for not being a doctor by becoming a Senior Counsel) loves the soapbox of the courtroom and the cut and thrust of the battle. Watching him live to fight another case another day, I know I made the right decision not to buy a court gown (plus I get to wear way cooler clothes as a corporate law practitioner).

But not liking litigation is not a good reason to drift into corporate practice. The latter is a demanding practice and an even more jealous lover than dispute resolution. The courts have a schedule for hearings and mentions; on the other hand, there's no limit on what a corporate client can require of you, especially in today's world where the internet has made 24/7 legal practice a reality. You have to love this job, or it will suck the life out of you, and leave you dry and broken, too tired to shop for Manolos when you can finally afford to buy them.

2. What is Corporate Practice?

When I first started in the corporate department, I thought it was going to be all proofreading and preparing of tedious verification notes for

Initial Public Offering ('IPO') (ie sale of shares by a private company to the public) meetings. It is easy for a young lawyer to be discouraged in the first few months of corporate practice, especially as he or she will feel out of their element at the start.

That is because nothing in law school quite prepares you for life as a corporate lawyer. In transactional work, unlike in litigation, the law does not define you or your work. Rather, the law sets the legal boundaries within which you (and your client) will operate; it is a tool of your trade rather than the product of your work. For example, you do not practise company law; company law sets the limits on the sorts of transactions Singapore entities can enter into. These transactions may also, variously, encompass intellectual property issues, fund-raising activities, mergers and acquisition financing.

So here is a list of the general areas of specialised corporate practice, and a short description of the kind of work involved:

Equity Capital Markets

Basically, 'ECM' is about listed company share deals. These would cover IPOs, secondary listings, rights issues and stock market related securities issuances for listed companies. It is relatively complex and draws more from practice than from legal statutes. In addition to legal principles, the rules and practices of the Singapore Exchange Securities Trading Limited ('SGX-ST') are important, and not all of them are published helpfully in a manual. For this reason, it is seen as a higher barrier-to-entry practice area. Practitioners in this area can be identified by their specialised language references (such as 'Is that a Rule Ten-Fifteen transaction?', referring to the Listing Manual provisions on Reverse Takeovers).

Debt Capital Markets

'DCM' deals with debt instruments. This area of practice is usually for large debt issuances, such as bonds, notes and medium term note programmes, which are very often listed on a securities exchange. Practitioners in this area can be identified as being the only people on the planet, other than bankers, who know what *Euroclear* is.

Mergers and Acquisitions ('M&A')

'M&A' is a strange term in the corporate world. To those of us who handle mergers and acquisitions, it means 'mergers and acquisitions'. To general corporate practitioners, it means 'memorandum and articles'. To truly show that you are a high end specialist in this area, you should always refer to the constitutive documents of a company as the 'Mem and Arts' because the cool kids all know that 'M&A' is about buying and selling big stuff.

Banking and Finance

Needs no introduction. All banking and finance transactions boil down to this: Bank lends money to borrower, who pays it back with interest. Because it is so simple, banking lawyers have to make it sound more happening by using words like 'spread' and 'margin' (things that banks like; not to be confused with 'margarine spread' which bankers will eschew in favour of French butter). It is also important to know which Reuters page the Singapore Interbank Offered Rate ('SIBOR') can be found on, and what a Loan-To-Value ('LTV') ratio is when talking about financial covenants. The real complexity in banking and finance transactions lies in the security package, where the law is constantly developing and very complicated. For example, the nature, rights and obligations surrounding derivative financial instruments, and issues surrounding crystallisation, de-crystallisation and re-crystallisation of security interests make this a fascinating study for the intellectual lawyer, and a landmine ridden field for the practitioner.

Real Estate Conveyancing and Corporate Real Estate

Conveyancing as a practice area had lost popularity in the late 90's due to the tanking of the real estate market in Singapore. However, with land being the most high-value commodity in Singapore, a lot of banking and finance transactions here will have a land law element. Also, with land prices having adopted a stratospheric trajectory, real estate is to the law what the colour black is to the fashion industry, ie, it's back, baby.

In the past decade, with the rise of real estate investment trusts ('REITs') and business trusts, the area of 'Corporate Real Estate' has taken off in popularity. Collective investment schemes are a new twist on the traditional structures of trusts and unit trusts, and are a specialised structure used to maximise returns to shareholders in specific asset classes. Because it is a relatively new area of law, market participants have been very innovative in developing new structures. For example, REIT sponsors have recently started offering 'stapled securities' comprising a combination of REIT units and business trust units. The management and governance of these structures are necessarily different from companies and continue to evolve, with market participants creating new product offerings and regulators coming up with re-calibrated regulations to meet the challenges of these changes.

Take-overs of Public Companies and Privatisations

Public take-overs are my personal favourite because of the adrenaline rush these deals necessitate. These are invariably extremely urgent transactions, and require some fancy footwork from the lawyers who need to juggle the requirements of the underlying M&A transaction, the takeover documentation, coordinating with the regulatory authorities and securing financing for the bid, all within a short time frame because of the fear of an information leak, given the highly price sensitive nature of the information. A hostile take-over is often even more nail-biting, with professionals needing to have the ability to analyse the opposing bidders. Meetings will cover the gamut – from due diligence issues, to questions of how the ego of the major shareholder is likely to be affected by the bid.

Asset Finance

This includes ship financing and aircraft financing – specialised financing requirements and laws that are specific to the type of asset being financed. Ship financing lawyers have terrific gigs – they get to fly to exotic countries to close the deal. Even a second year ship financing lawyer would have developed a jaded sigh as he tells you about yet another trip he has to make to Tokyo for a closing, shrugging with faux boredom over the copious amounts of champagne he had to imbibe. The IPO lawyer, who just spent two months camping in a fish-feed plant in Fuzhou, People's Republic of China, doing due diligence and learning to be grateful for basic plumbing back home, will curse and swear behind his colleague's back, while pretending sympathy for his ennui.

Securities and Regulatory Law

This is real lawyers' work. These practitioners know the ins and outs of the securities law statutes and all the related regulations and notices and rules issued by the Monetary Authority of Singapore. They will be able to advise fund managers on their detailed licensing requirements and investment banks on selling restrictions. They are the unsung heroes of the corporate corridors because anyone who can understand the convoluted maze of securities and regulatory statutes deserves an ovation.

Funds

In recent years, more and more funds have been set up. These span hedge funds, to special situation (read 'distressed') funds, to private investment funds. Lawyers have to be able to set up these fund structures, which requires some knowledge of international tax law, and advise on licensing and regulatory requirements.

General Corporate ('Gen-Corp') and Commercial Transactions

Not the most sexy of practice areas but one of the most interesting because of the different types of transactions that could be involved. The humble and ubiquitous joint venture agreement is one of the hardest to draft – because of the many possible permutations of personalities, businesses and relative contributions that the parties will bring, and also because the document needs to cater for possible future changes to shareholdings and shareholders. No corporate lawyer should enter an uber-specialisation without a stint in Gen-Corp because the breadth of the exposure, simply put, will make you a better lawyer.

Financial Derivatives

Esoterica. Enough said.

3. What does a Corporate Practitioner look like?

So what do you need, if you want to be a corporate lawyer? Do you need to be a bookworm or a social butterfly? What skills are must-haves, which are good-to-haves?

Firstly, there is no one template corporate lawyer. This is mostly because it is such a varied field. Quiet, considered types do well in certain areas of practice, especially in practice areas which are documentation heavy and require a meticulous mind. On the other hand, outgoing lawyers who are good people-persons will excel in negotiations and in managing client expectations.

Let me introduce you to some boardroom warriors I have come across in my almost two decades of practice. Names have been changed to protect the guilty (actually, mostly to protect me and the publishers from defamation suits).

All-Rounder Allison

This is the one you want to beware of. Allison is the kind of corporate lawyer that made the general public call us 'sharks'. Seemingly pleasant, she is a tough negotiator and gives no quarter. The Allisons of the world are workaholics and all have some kind of super power – usually a photographic memory or the ability to work for weeks on only three hours sleep a night. They spot the smallest mistakes, and yet are very good in understanding and identifying the big picture on the commercial deal. Allisons are uber successful but have no patience for the frivolity of branded handbags or shoes. Which is very annoying as you cannot

14

even make yourself feel better by castigating them as frivolous and spendthrift in your head even as they tear your draft apart. You will recognise them by the staccato rat-a-tat-tat of their speech pattern, their piercing eyes and the fact that their Blackberries are surgically attached to their hands. Also by their ugly handbags.

Business-minded Ben

Ben is only interested in the business and commercial aspects of the transaction. A wannabe investment banker, he gets excited about the numbers and the structure of the deal, but drops the ball when it comes to crossing the T's and dotting the I's, which are a big part of what corporate lawyers are required to do. Ben is the guy who will show up at a signing meeting and suddenly suggest another way to structure the profit sharing mechanism, which will involve a total change in the entire transaction. He is the guy you want at the table when the deal is being structured at the start, and the guy you want to keep away from the room when it is near completion. His junior lawyers are the ones trying not to roll their eyes when he shows up at the signing ceremony and starts to casually leaf through the execution copies of the agreements.

Charming Charlie

It is not much of an overstatement to say that Charlie owns the boardroom. His personality is larger than life; he is friendly to client and counterparty alike, and even has a kind word for the most junior lawyer of the other team. His charm is sincere and well-meant. He sees his main contribution as facilitating smooth negotiations. His weakness is that he is often not the lawyer that did the legal work so he may not be able to make a detailed contribution. Allison hates Charlie and will try to destroy him with a glare from her piercing eyes; a look Charlie will completely miss as he chats with clients and sips from his skinny Macchiato, which he bought as part of his coffee run for all the attendees at the meeting.

Dogged Dorothy

To say Dorothy has staying power is an understatement. She is a woman who is tireless in quietly and doggedly fighting for each point for her client, whether it is inserting the qualifier 'reasonably' into 500 covenants or asking for grace periods to cure breaches. What she lacks in creative new arguments she makes up for in sheer will power and the ability to repeat her amendment request as if she is not saying it for the 40th time. The ability to steadily push back with the same arguments, one clause at a time, should not be underestimated, as parties develop negotiation fatigue after ten hours locked in marathon meetings. Dorothy is not fazed by hunger and, as she attended a Singapore girls' school in the 70s when no toilet paper was provided, she only needs to visit the toilet once in any 24-hour period. She may not be the most articulate or persuasive lawyer in the room, but her clients stay fiercely loyal to her because they feel that she will stop at nothing to protect their minutest interest.

Egomaniac Egbert

This guy is, almost invariably (a) at a big corporate firm currently or (b) formerly a corporate practitioner with a big firm (to be clear, not all lawyers in big corporate firms are like this guy). You will recognise him because his ego enters the room about 20 seconds before the rest of him does. For him, every meeting is an opportunity to show his clients what a champion lawyer they have hired, and a chance to show up the other side. He will fight just to score points. Egbert used to be an up-and-coming corporate lawyer but started to believe his own press and let his sense of self-worth get too big for him. While possessing a fine technical mind, Egbert's failing is that he misses the wood for the trees and lets his ego take precedence over his clients' interests.

These are obviously caricatures and are not indicative of real people (except for a few lawyers out there – you know who you are).

Whatever personality type you are, the best corporate lawyers will need the following skill sets:

i)   Firstly, you need to have a good grasp of the law. There is usually very little time to do in-depth research when you are doing a deal, so you need to have a handle on the important legal principles, and know where to look for answers quickly and effectively.

ii)   A good corporate lawyer never starts work on a project by wondering which precedent she should use as a base. There is a predisposition for junior practitioners to ask for relevant precedents. This often blinds them to the need to understand the essence of the deal. Precedents are there to help you; they should not define the nature of the transaction. It's your clients who should do that.

iii)   People skills are essential. Every client you will ever deal with is going to be a person. He may be a junior in-house counsel of the bank, newly joined and not wanting to make any mistakes in front of his superior, or a jaded hedge fund manager who has seen more deals go south than you have eaten Subway sandwiches at your desk while proofreading an Offering Memorandum. The ability to process communication, some of which will be express and some of which will be unspoken, is important. The ability to convey not just a knowledge of the law and the issues, but also a sense of confidence and that you have your client's back, will make all the difference in whether that client comes back to you.

iv) This next one is a no-brainer but it bears repeating. There is no substitution for hard work. Quality comes from experience and thorough ground work. The top corporate lawyers are not those who were born with a sharper mind, or who are blessed with a more engaging personality. Meet any top corporate lawyer in Singapore and you will be amazed at how au fait he or she is with latest developments in the law, the regulations and the latest transactions.

v) Finally, every transactional lawyer needs to understand what his role is, that is this: to make a good deal for their client. And the only lasting good deal is one where everyone leaves the room with something. Some corporate lawyers think that if they browbeat the other side into snivelling submission, or score points like in a basketball match, they have done their job. This is not the case. It truly is in everyone's best interest to create a win-win situation, so there is incentive to make the deal work and not to look for potholes with which to trip up the other side. Even where your client has the clear upper hand, the counterparty should be treated with respect so that they end the negotiation with their dignity intact, and a sense that they hammered out the best deal they could. It's our job to make this happen.

Every generation will have its share of a few top notch corporate practitioners. These are lawyers I look up to and try to emulate in their areas of greatest ability. I hope this chapter has given you a sneak peek into the charming and often chaotic corridors of the corporate world.

CHAPTER 3

INTELLECTUAL PROPERTY –
AN ANTI-COUNTERFEITER'S TALE

Cyril Chua

Cyril started his practice in 1996 and has been in the same firm since. His practice mainly involves the management of anti-counterfeiting portfolios for multinational clients as well as brand protection advisory work. He enjoys chess, computer games and charity work. Cyril believes in a work-life balance and spends his time between his family, professional work and various engagements in the charity sector.

1.   Introduction

I try not to work on Sundays because it often reflects bad time management. However, as my practice involves intellectual property enforcement, there would be times where my weekends are taken up by anti-counterfeiting operations. It was not too long ago when I received a call from a senior enforcement officer from the Malaysian Ministry of Domestic Trade and Consumer Affairs ('the Ministry') on a Sunday morning. We had been tracking a counterfeiter for some time and we had finally located some premises used by this counterfeiter to manufacture and store counterfeit goods. While I was looking forward to a lazy Sunday, the opportunity to shut down a large counterfeiter had my adrenaline pumping. It has always been the chase that kept me going in this profession.

I packed some clothes and headed off to the airport in search of a flight to Penang on a Sunday afternoon. By 7am the next day, the senior enforcement officer had assembled her raiding team. I was told that we had to conduct raids at thirteen premises and the raid might 'get complicated'. It meant that we might encounter physical resistance or violence in some of these locations. After a brief analysis of the locations, we decided to raid only eleven of thirteen premises as it would be unwise to spread our manpower too thinly on the ground.

After a long drive to a neighbouring state, followed by a further wait for the search warrants, we finally started the raid sometime in the late afternoon. As there were a lot of counterfeits, the inventory process was back breaking. It was not too long before we reached midnight. The raiding teams were then surrounded by thugs. Some just stood menacingly while others were practising their camera skills at me. It was obvious that they had singled me as the initiator of the raids. The officers of the Ministry were neither armed nor ready for any violent confrontation. The local police was contacted. The police arrived within 20 minutes but seemed hesitant in taking any action as they were of the view that the thugs had not committed any criminal intimidation. The senior enforcement officer requested that I leave the raid location so as to reduce the 'temperature' at the raid site. It was sound advice.

It was well after midnight when some officers from the Ministry bundled me into a car. We were followed by two cars belonging to the counterfeiting syndicate. The drive back to Penang was harrowing. They chased us down the North-South Highway. Had it been that we were not able to evade them, I would have been quite satisfied spending a night in any police station in Penang. I was quite glad that we lost them somewhere around Butterworth before crossing the Penang Bridge. I figured that the airport was the safest place to wait before taking the first flight back to Singapore. So there I waited in my grimy clothes with ink and toner stains, as the minutes peeled away.

The remaining officers from the Ministry took two days to move all the items into a warehouse. I only managed to inspect the seized items once after the raid before the warehouse was set ablaze. All seized items were destroyed, leaving me with very little evidence to proceed on a claim against the counterfeiter. A senior enforcement officer said that we should have deployed a security guard within the warehouse. It probably did not matter as the counterfeiters would have torched the warehouse together with the security guard.

It is disappointing to see your evidence go up in flames after all the effort of putting together an investigation and conducting a successful raid. On a brighter note, the counterfeits were destroyed and no one was injured. It was not so bad after all. We all lived to fight another day.

This was, but a snapshot of anti-counterfeiting practice.

2. The Beginning of Practice

I never thought that I would be a lawyer, let alone an intellectual property rights practitioner. I was brought up in a different time, in a different place. Pirated software in floppy discs was ubiquitous. After school, kids would run down to the local computer shop for a copy of the latest game for their Apple II compatible PC. For two dollars a copy, each kid would gleefully return home with anticipation of the hours of fun embedded within the floppy disks. The more entrepreneurial ones would make copies of the game and sell them to their friends in school.

The copyright notice on the boot-up screen of a game meant it was time to get some snacks before the start of the game (though I suspect some geeky kids bothered to check out the definition of copyright in their mini dictionary). Their parents would happily visit the neighbourhood video rental shop for recent releases of movies. There was no thought of copyright piracy. After all, it was presumed to be a victimless crime, if at all a crime.

It was probably fortuitous that I became an intellectual property practitioner.

I took up law because I had very little interest in reading other subjects. I took up intellectual property because Professor George Wei made it interesting. In my fourth year, I sought Professor Wei's opinion on the prospects of practising in the field of intellectual property litigation. He said that I should speak with Alban Kang. I have been working with Alban since.

I joined the firm of Alban Tay Mahtani & de Silva as a trainee and then a lawyer. The transition from a law student to a junior lawyer required some adjustments. A fifteen-hour school week allowed for lazy walks in the park or endless hours mulling over a script for a new play. A sixty to seventy-hour work week was no lazy walk to anywhere. No amount of good grades in law school prepares you for the rigours of the practice of law. I found myself making mistakes almost at every juncture. It was demoralising but essential. I found myself learning the law from scratch, this time, as a practitioner. In the process, I also learned how to operate the fax machine as well as make a good cup of coffee. Humility is a virtue.

I was however fortunate to have very patient bosses and colleagues. They understood what it meant to be starting out as a practitioner and always had a kind word whenever I was down. Peer support was also important. My classmates in other law firms and I would often get together to discuss the various pitfalls of the practice. As such, we not only learnt from our own experiences but also from that of one another. What was essential was to be able to keep an open mind. There is always room to improve on one's practice.

As A Litigant

In my first few years of practice, my work consisted mostly of trademark prosecutions, intellectual property litigation, which involved civil litigation as well as anti-piracy. Litigation was enjoyable as I am not one who could sit still in my room. I loved the courts and enjoyed meeting up with fellow litigators. You will often encounter many highs and lows in litigation: A sweet victory over a point of law could be followed by a bitter blow in the next application before the Registrar. Every trial is a steep learning curve as there are always new surprises lurking around the corner. You never quite stop learning whenever there is a trial.

While the practice was enjoyable, managing litigation deadlines was always stressful. The then Registrar, Mr Chiam Boon Keng, taught us well on managing our deadlines and ensuring that all court documents were filed on time. I recalled an incident where my client was issued with an 'unless order' to file and serve eight affidavits within four weeks. It was particularly challenging as it was a very old case which I inherited and tracking down the witnesses was not terribly easy. The sheer fear of having the case struck-off spurred me on to ensure that the affidavits were filed and served before the deadline.

I was also involved in an intensive and high-profile litigation matter where the litigation team had to work around the clock for a period of two months. I was one of the many junior lawyers involved in research, fact finding and formulating clever arguments. I was alternating between twenty to thirty-six-hour shifts. There was neither night nor day in our work. Our body clocks were totally out of synch and our cadaverous faces would not look out of place in the Addams Family. Notwithstanding all the work, we were resoundingly crushed by the opposing team of lawyers. Litigation can be physically and mentally devastating.

At the end of every battle, there is always the Bar Room which you could adjourn and seek solace from your fellow battered litigators. The little stories which Mr Choo (the barman) shared with us over a cup of tea would warm our hearts. There is always another battle in the next turn and you would win that one. Deep down, litigators are optimists.

As an Anti-Piracy Practitioner – The Local Arena

My other key practice was battling software piracy in Singapore. While it was far easier than battling pirates in the seas around Somalia, the software pirates were no pushovers. In the late 90's, I would be queuing at the Crime Registry almost every other week to make applications for search warrants against software pirates. My colleagues and I would then make elaborate plans to conduct raids against these pirates located in Sim Lim Square. Planning was important as the pirates would engage lookouts stationed at strategic points around the mall. Syndicates would also engage 'lookouts' to track or monitor right owners representatives who were combating piracy. The first sight of police or the raiding party would trigger an immediate closure of the premises selling pirated software within the mall. Hence, we spent much time weaving through the car park and stairways to circumvent the lookouts. There was a raid in Sim Lim Square where I found a photocopied picture of myself and my name card in one of the drawers in a pirated software retail shop.

As a junior lawyer, I found anti-piracy work to be more exciting than deskbound solicitor work. However, the software pirates were a resilient lot and it soon became a war of attrition. Rights owners would step up the number of raids conducted against these pirates but the impact appeared to be minimal. These pirated software syndicates were able to re-stock the seized software within twenty minutes after each raid. They would employ 'fall guys' to claim ownership of the pirated software whenever their shops were raided. This effectively shielded the actual proprietor of the pirated software business from criminal prosecution.

It was a difficult battle for the rights owners. Rights owners, unlike the police, are not vested with the powers of investigation under the Criminal Procedure Code. Back then, during a raid, the police would only enter the premises, explain the search warrants to the shop operators and note down the items seized. Apart from taking down the name of the person who acknowledged the seizure, the police did little else to assist in the investigation of such cases. The investigations were left to the private investigators. Unfortunately, the power of observation by the private investigator alone is usually insufficient to turn a case against syndicated software piracy.

For a good part of the 90's, the rights owners were on the receiving end of the battle against software pirates. It appeared that the raids and prosecutions were not terribly effective in curbing software piracy. Loss of inventories arising from raids was merely treated as acceptable business losses by software pirates, as the manufacture of pirated CD-ROMs cost next to nothing. The use of 'fall guys' by these syndicates was factored as a business cost for the pirates. It was apparent that raids by rights owners alone were insufficient. The police had to play a more proactive role and that was precisely what they did.

The tables finally turned on 18 July 2000. On that Sunday afternoon, the police organised a massive sweep against the pirates in Sim Lim Square. The retail pirates were cuffed and driven off in Black Marias. They were thoroughly interrogated. Their shops were sealed. Pirated software was seized together with cash registers, display racks and other equipment. A syndicate which was supplying to Sim Lim Square was also raided over the weekend. All were remanded and charged in court within a few days. The syndicate leaders were given lengthy imprisonments. The software pirates never quite recovered from that day.

For the next few months, the police pursued software pirates relentlessly. Raids were conducted from Orchard Road right to the heartland malls. For some pirates, they knew that it was 'game over' as the police crackdown was quite unlike the earlier raids. Some hardcore software pirates remained in Sim Lim Square but were quickly removed by subsequent police raids. Those who remained in business started setting up in neighbourhood estates or moved to a neighbouring country to continue the trade. Those who remained were completely eradicated by police raids and prosecutions. Retail optical piracy was eradicated in Singapore by a combination of aggressive police action and internet piracy, which soon caught up.

It was an exciting time for an intellectual property lawyer specialising in anti-piracy. Over a period of seven years, the once ubiquitous pirated CD-ROMs disappeared from the streets of Singapore. It was a great learning experience to be involved in the strategic planning and execution of enforcement actions which ultimately lead to the demise of the CD-ROM software piracy.

As an Anti-Piracy Practitioner – The Regional Arena

In 2001, my anti-piracy practice took on a regional dimension. My clients were hoping to replicate the successes in battling piracy in Singapore to other countries in the region. I was not confident that this would be possible as the law and enforcement regimes in other countries are quite different from Singapore. However, it is a challenge of this sort that keeps my interest in the practice.

While the experience gained combating software pirates in Singapore was useful, the strategies used in Singapore were not so easily adaptable in a regional context. In the beginning, months were spent on just meeting up with clients and their distribution partners merely to understand the complexities of a product supply chain. To formulate an anti-piracy strategy, it is vital to comprehend how counterfeits enter the channel of trade. After many meetings, we devised strategies and implemented processes that would help to battle counterfeits. The next step was to execute enforcement raids against the counterfeiters.

What was essential was to understand the gap between the theory and practice of law in the region. Reading the various statutes relating to intellectual property rights would not be helpful in understanding what enforcement of intellectual property rights entailed. During that time, I found it useful speaking with enforcement officials in a country to learn about the mechanics of an enforcement action.

The demands of managing regional anti-counterfeiting portfolios are quite different from the local practice. Having to work with lawyers and investigators from different language and cultural backgrounds was a challenge. The same English word may have a different meaning to a lawyer depending on his country of origin. In addition, different cultures have differing respect for deadlines.

The work has been interesting, rewarding and sometimes infuriating. There was once where our power of attorney was rejected by a court in a neighbouring country on the basis that it was executed by the company secretary. The court official was of the view that a secretary, who serves coffee, would not have the authority to execute a power of attorney. As the document was legalised by the Secretary of State of the United States of America, I wondered if Hillary Clinton would make a good cup of latte for President Obama.

The regional enforcement work can be physically challenging as it sometimes takes you from the mountains of Laos to the backstreets of New Delhi. I was once asked to devise a strategy to stop counterfeit mobile phones from entering Thailand from the Laos border. Based on the reported quantity of counterfeits entering Thailand, I was of the initial opinion that there were probably trucks and vans smuggling counterfeits from Vientiane into Nong Khai. I then travelled to Vientiane and visited the markets where such phones were sold. I also took a short ride to the Friendship Bridge which connected Laos with Thailand across the Mekong River. After some observations, it was easy to conclude that the counterfeit phones were simply hand carried by the streams of people crossing the bridge on a daily basis. Each would just carry four to eight mobile phones across the bridge and would sell them once they reached Thailand. Being on the ground is sometimes the only way to understand the counterfeit trade.

I have been in practice for the last fifteen years. As a child, my naive view of the practice of law was shaped primarily by the media. The image I had of a lawyer was personified by Atticus Finch, a swashbuckling litigator fighting for the individual against the oppressive system (and Gregory Peck made it so believable). I would never have envisaged that the practice of law would entail chasing pirates in the jungle of Laos or advising policy makers on trade related aspects of counterfeiting. I would never have looked or spoke as well as Gregory Peck even if I tried. Atticus Finch lived in a different world at a different time. I am merely a commercial lawyer providing a solution to my clients' business problems. While I am not fighting for the life and liberty of the downtrodden, I still hope to provide the best legal and commercial solution to my clients.

3. Conclusion

In closing, I am still enjoying my journey. While I continue to build my practice around anti-counterfeiting, what I truly enjoy is to see the junior lawyers emerging from the ranks. I appreciate the issues they face as I was once there. I admire their energy and hope that they will one day truly emerge as the leading practitioner of their area of interest. I hope that they will enjoy the journey as much as I do.

CHAPTER 4

INTERNATIONAL ARBITRATION – A CIVIL END TO CIVIL DISPUTES

Guy Spooner

Guy Spooner is a partner and head of the Singapore dispute resolution practice at Norton Rose (Asia) LLP. He specialises in all forms of litigation and arbitration, with particular experience in shipbuilding, energy, international trade, commodity, insurance, infrastructure, transportation and FPSO disputes.

Guy has considerable experience in arbitrations in Asia, having practised in Hong Kong and Singapore for a number of years. He is named as a leading individual for international arbitration in the Legal 500 in which he is described as having 'top-notch arbitration expertise' whose 'vast experience of both the Singapore and Hong Kong markets stand him out as a skilled operator in an exponentially growing area.'

Guy is qualified to practice in England, Hong Kong and Australia. He was admitted to the Singapore International Arbitration Centre's Panel of Arbitrators in 2009 and was appointed as a director of the board of Singapore International Arbitration Centre from October 2010.

1958 was a bad year for British motorists. On 10 July, parking meters were installed for the first time on English roads, marking the end of uninhibited free parking and, perhaps, the start of what has now become the vilification of motorists the world over. On the other hand, the year was apparently a good one for French wine makers and for astronauts (with the formation of NASA in July). 1958 was also a good year for music. The Beatles made their first recording as The Quarrymen and Michael Jackson was born – and although neither event made much of a splash at the time, they certainly proved to have a lasting impact. One event which also passed relatively unnoticed at the time, but which was to have a fundamental effect on global trade and investment, was the adoption by the United Nations of the Convention on the Recognition and Enforcement of Foreign Arbitral Awards on 10 June in New York ('the New York Convention'). As it turns out, 1958 was a very good year for Singapore arbitration.

What the New York Convention did, in a nutshell, was to help level the playing field for developing countries by reducing the risk, or at least the perceived risk, of making and funding developments in foreign countries and trading across borders. It achieved this by requiring countries signing the Convention to respect commercial agreements which called for disputes to be referred to international arbitration, and then to enforce those arbitration decisions (or 'Awards') made by international arbitration tribunals in countries which had also ratified the Convention. In short, this meant that parties to a contract could avoid the prospect of finding themselves in an unfamiliar court if things went wrong, and as a result, have more confidence in what they were doing in a foreign jurisdiction. It is sometimes said that arbitration is a neo-colonial device which is somehow unfair or disrespectful to local courts and for a time, countries were slow to adopt the terms of the Convention and were reluctant to introduce the necessary legislation to give effect to its terms. However, that perception has largely passed, and it is broadly recognised that the Convention has been one of the most successful tools ever devised for promoting trade and development. Building confidence amongst foreign traders and investors that their contracts will be impartially decided and then enforced, if necessary, is critical to any country when it comes to building basic or even complicated infrastructure. By reducing the perceived risk of an investment, a country opens up opportunities for dams to be built, power stations to find outside funding, raw materials and commodities to be traded or exported. It is perhaps for that reason that over 143 countries have now signed up to the Convention, most of which have also given legislative effect to its terms.

The reason 1958 was a good year for Singapore arbitration is that with the widespread adoption of the Convention, the commercial world needs, and gravitates towards, arbitration venues which are seen as impartial, consistent, non-partisan and where (most importantly) the local courts will not interfere with the decision. For many years, the principal international arbitration centres were widely regarded as being London, Geneva, Paris, Stockholm and New York. However, it can readily be seen that nowhere in Asia appears on that list. Things have now changed, dramatically so. Major arbitration centres have now developed in Hong Kong, China and, not least, Singapore. Whilst Hong Kong and China have largely developed on the back of China trade and investment, Singapore has successfully positioned itself as a centre for arbitration between parties who have nothing to do with Singapore at all. It is now common for contracts between, say, an Indian importer and Indonesian exporter, to provide that if they have a dispute, it will be referred to arbitration in Singapore. The reason is simple. Neither party wishes to end up in the other party's courts. Arbitration therefore provides a mutually acceptable solution and Singapore fits the bill as a venue. The net result of this is that there are now opportunities for lawyers who specialise in international arbitration in Singapore to work on a wide variety of cases from around the world, which in the past may have only been heard in London or Paris. It is this sheer variety which makes the practice of international arbitration in Singapore so appealing.

So what is involved? The process of arbitration is in many ways similar to court litigation – at least at a basic level – in that both parties argue their case in writing and then bring evidence before a Tribunal which can either be a sole arbitrator chosen by the parties (or by an arbitral institution they both trust), or three arbitrators where usually each party gets to pick one and the third is picked by those two. Things can get interesting when the two arbitrators cannot agree on who the third person should be but this is typically resolved amicably, or by the appointing authority of an arbitral institution.

One major feature of arbitration is that it is conducted in private and cannot (with some exceptions) be reported without the parties' agreement. This is a fundamental attraction of the process to the commercial world. Another attraction is that the winning party is usually awarded its legal costs on a sensible basis rather than having them significantly reduced by a court due to its taxation policy or other policy grounds such as access to justice – a feature in many jurisdictions which can result in the winner feeling like anything but that. Where the arbitration process itself starts to differ from court proceedings is that the arbitrators are relatively free to decide on the procedure and timetable for the case, even when institutional rules such as those of the Singapore International Arbitration Centre (SIAC) are written into the contract. The arbitrators are also relatively free to decide on the 'admissibility' of certain evidence with the result that practitioners and lawyers who are used to court proceedings can find themselves having to adopt rather different techniques than that they are used to. Since a party can generally choose anyone to act as its arbitrator (provided they do not have a connection which could lead to them being biased), lawyers also need to be able to adapt to arbitrators who may come from a very different legal system where, for example, it may be common for an arbitrator or judge to be much more active and inquisitorial in the process than listening relatively passively to the cross examination of a witness – which is often the way in many common law jurisdictions.

I remember a case where the Tribunal consisted of an English QC, a US State Supreme Court Judge and an eminent Swiss lawyer as the panel of arbitrators. Having made a conscious decision to only ask a particular witness three or four (in my mind brilliant) questions in cross-examination (so as to not give the witness the opportunity to try to introduce fresh evidence on the hoof which had not been covered by his last-minute witness statement), I was somewhat concerned (livid in fact) when one of the arbitrators then decided to ask a series of what I thought were sympathetic and leading questions designed to fill in gaps in the other side's story. In fact, no harm was done, and that was not the arbitrator's intention but what this showed was that the process of arbitration can sometimes be different and more flexible in its approach and those who are used only to court procedure do sometimes need to leave a number of preconceptions at the door. That said, anyone who is interested in pursuing a career in international arbitration should consider starting out with a decent grounding in traditional litigation. Apart from learning good skills such as advocacy and preparing a case theory, a basic grounding in court litigation (even in simple cases) sharpens the instincts for a dispute and identifying what actually matters in a case.

John Mortimer, the English barrister and author of the popular TV series Rumpole of the Bailey once said 'No brilliance is needed in the law; nothing but common sense, and relatively clean fingernails.' Much as law firms might nowadays seem to set the bar almost impossibly high for new entrants to the profession, he had a point. Ultimately, the law is essentially common sense codified even if it appears at first blush to be bewildering and full of arcane concepts to the lay person. Of course, there are legal rules and pitfalls such as the concept of 'accepting a repudiatory breach' (which I will not go into here) where the unwary can come unstuck, but by and large, the flexibility of the arbitration process, coupled with the fact that many arbitrators are chosen for their particular industry experience, means that a result which also happens to accord with common sense is often achieved. That does not mean you do not have to be on top of the law, you most certainly have to be, but arbitrators are not generally interested in lawyers scoring points off each other or moaning about petty points of procedure. In a hearing, it is very rare to see counsel jumping up with 'objections' and I have yet to hear the phrase 'move to strike' in any case except on American TV shows. In fact, whilst the issues in an arbitration may be serious and significant amounts can be in dispute, hearings are conducted with relative informality. Nobody wears a gown and wigs are reserved only for those who are follicly challenged.

So how does one become an arbitration lawyer – and why would you want to? In my own case, the decision was made for me by virtue of the fact that the firm I decided to join after law school in London specialised in shipping and international trade, both of which rely heavily on arbitration to resolve disputes. Although the firm (then) had offices in a particularly dreary 1960s building, it somehow felt that we were at the centre of the commercial world. My first case was about a ship which had run aground on the Orinoco River in South America and the issue was who was liable for the lengthy delays. Reading the file with Captain's reports, witness statements and photos, one could not help being at least momentarily transported from the grey cold of central London to somewhere altogether more exotic. To me, this was far more exciting than being the sixth most senior lawyer on a merger and acquisition transaction and from that point onwards, I was hooked. I think the opportunities I first saw in London to get involved in resolving disputes from around the world now begin to present themselves to young lawyers in Singapore. Nothing gets built in a day but over the last decade, Singapore has carefully positioned itself as a leading centre for arbitration. It now has the best purpose-built facility in the world for holding arbitration hearings (Maxwell Chambers, pictured on the cover), panels of leading arbitrators from around the world have signed up to sit and hear cases here, and the courts have consistently taken a non-interventionist stand in disputes. As a result, Singapore has achieved acceptance as an impartial, neutral and reliable arbitration venue by, for example, Korean industrialists, Japanese commodity traders, European banks, Chinese shipping companies, Middle Eastern property developers, airlines, Indian film makers, American oil companies and many multi-national corporations and even (some) governments. The list goes on, but these are just some examples of the type of clients who have come to arbitrate their disputes in Singapore.

As the region develops and as arbitration is increasingly recognised as a way of managing contract risk, I suspect that the list is set to grow. Whilst it always pays to have a good understanding of specific industries (clients expect this), the sheer variety of work that is likely to pass through Singapore in the coming decades makes it, in my mind, a good place for a young lawyer with aspirations to pitch his or her tent. The best way to get started is to join the mooting competitions at universities where students have to prepare for and then present a client's case in a mock arbitration moot. Whilst the timelines in such hearings are a little unrealistic, the discipline of researching and creating written submissions from a set of facts gives students a very good idea of the process and whether it suits them. Many of our best young arbitration lawyers were mooters and having endured (and enjoyed) that baptism, all that remains to be done by anyone who wants an interesting legal career is to obtain a decent degree, display common sense at an interview and keep one's fingernails, relatively, clean.

CHAPTER 5

SMALL FIRM PRACTICE – BEING AN ENTREPRENEUR AND LAWYER

Rajan Chettiar

Rajan Chettiar's greatest love is helping people. He started his working career as a law clerk in a family law boutique firm, where he had the opportunity to delve into his interest in family law. Realising that lawyers can make an invaluable contribution to the betterment of our society, he then went on to study law.

Having qualified as a barrister-at-law in England with admission into the Singapore Bar in 1997, Rajan worked in the General Litigation Department of a top local law firm for six years. Caught by the entrepreneur bug, Rajan set up Rajan Chettiar & Co in 2003, which has since grown into a seven-member team consisting of legal, paralegal and administrative staff.

Besides legal work, Rajan has actively involved himself in various voluntary welfare organisations such as the Tanjong Pagar Family Service Centre, Society For the Physically Disabled and Centre For Family Harmony. An active volunteer with the Law Society, he has served in its Council as well as in its various standing committees. An Associate Mediator of the Singapore Mediation Centre, he is a volunteer mediator in the Subordinate and Family Courts, and also authors the very well-read monthly column, 'Alter Ego' in the The Singapore Law Gazette.

His favourite past times are spending his weekends with his wife and cooking for family and friends.

It was the year 2001. I was then working in a large law firm. It took me five years to realise that a large firm was unsuitable for me. I was stressed and tired. When the weekend was coming to an end, I dreaded going into the office. My emotional state of mind transcended to physical symptoms – heart palpitations and constant flu symptoms. Every morning, I woke up dreading the workday.

At that point of time, I had an idea – running my very own law firm. I spoke to a colleague in my department about it. I recall her highlighting the financial aspects of the idea. The idea started to slowly brew within me for two more years. On hindsight, I am glad that I thought about it for that long. By mid August 2003, I decided to tender my resignation. I was 37 then. I had no idea what I was going to do next in my career. When I told my boss that I had no future plans, he was shocked. He said, 'How are you going to pay your mortgage and other financial commitments?' I smiled at him and replied that I had no such commitments. At that point of time, the only clear plan I had was a trip to North India, something which I wanted to do for a long time.

I told myself that I had to just rest my body and mind before I think about the next move in my life. To do this, I knew I had to travel alone to India. I left Singapore on 1 January 2003 – the beginning of the next phase of my life. Switching off my mobile and not taking any telephone calls from the office or clients was exhilarating.

In the last leg of my four-week trip, I started thinking about my future. I looked back to the reason why I wanted to study law. I have always wanted to help people from young. So, I was fascinated about being a doctor, a policeman and a social worker during my younger days. My father, who was then probably concerned that his eldest child was going to become a social worker, said to me, 'You can help people by being a lawyer.' The fact that I was fascinated about the study of law warmed me up to the idea quickly.

I was not able to really help people in my last job as I was doing banking and general litigation. Perhaps I could now fulfill my mission. I was also keen to be an entrepreneur. I was toying with the idea of running my own café (after all, it is fashionable for lawyers to dabble in the food and beverage industry). The practical side of me told me that I did not have the relevant skills and experience.

I returned to Singapore without a clear plan.

Back home, I attended a personal awareness and leadership programme, which was a turning point in my life. It made me examine my life inside out and to examine my values and beliefs. One of the activities in the leadership programme was setting and achieving three goals within three months. It was that exercise which crystallised my thought of setting up my own law firm. So, I achieved one of my leadership programme goals by setting up my own firm, Rajan Chettiar & Co in April 2003.

The firm started with just me and my father who was my secretary, despatch, office and finance manager. Today, we are a seven-member firm consisting of a junior associate, paralegal, administrative and secretarial staff.

I was prepared for the hard life ahead of me. The fact that I enjoyed all the various aspects of running a business such as management and administration, unlike most lawyers, made it easier for me to start off and build up my firm with little assistance.

Although I did not possess any knowledge about running a business, I had a deep sense of interest in how a business should be set up and run. Mission and vision statements were set up at the beginning. My goal was to be a top small law firm, which provides a personalised and friendly service as well as efficient and cost-effective solutions to our clients.

To be successful, a small firm must be a specialist. As family law was my favourite subject in law school, it was a no-brainer to choose that as my area of specialisation.

At the outset, I also embarked on a marketing campaign to inform the public about the firm. Besides setting up a website to promote the firm, I took out advertisements in newspapers and magazines. I was one of the pioneer lawyers to engage in internet marketing without any knowledge of the Google search engine.

I built contacts with social workers, counsellors, financial services professionals and the media. I also gave regular talks at law seminars, conferences and at voluntary welfare organisations.

I am always interested in client service models. I studied the service processes of fast food restaurants, Starbucks and the Ritz Carlton hotel. If I were a client of the firm, what would I expect? The answer forms the structure of our client service system. The service model is personal and friendly. We treat our clients in the same way we would like to be treated by any service provider. Basic qualities such as a smile, honesty, integrity, active listening and prompt service go a long way. My staff members are trained to handle telephone enquiries and to offer basic information to the callers. My basic knowledge in counselling and willingness to share my personal experiences gave an added edge to the practice. Telephone and email queries are promptly responded to even after office hours and during my vacations.

Work process systems were implemented early in the practice to ensure that all our clients received the same standard of client service. I give high priority to the role of information technology in delivering our services to our clients. An inexpensive practice management system is implemented in the firm. All our communication with our clients is done via the email system. To improve productivity and efficiency, an instant messing system was adopted throughout the firm. A video conferencing system, Justice OnLine, is being used in the firm to conduct hearings in the courts to cut down the massive waiting time in the courts. The EFS filing system was set up in the firm to increase the staff productivity.

Although the firm's goal is to grow into a medium sized firm, I was afraid of growth. Should the firm stay small and nimble or should we grow? This is always the dilemma faced by small law firms. Expansion meant growing business costs which will reduce the business profits. Staying small means that there is a limit to the number of instructions the firm can accept and the toll it takes on me. I would have to spend longer hours in the office and not take holidays.

It was only after seven years later in 2010 that I decided to grow the legal team by employing a legal associate and a foreign lawyer. Expansion of the business is a necessary evil as it will facilitate business growth in the future.

One of the difficulties I face in the firm is human resource management. It is difficult to recruit, retain and motivate staff in the firm. A different set of skills is needed to communicate with and manage the expectations of the younger generation of workers. I had to learn through experience and trial and error. This is still a work-in-progress.

The other important aspect of the business is client management. It is difficult to obtain a new client but it is easy to lose one. Therefore, it is important to have good people skills. It is important to establish clear and honest communication with the clients and manage their expectations clearly.

My persona as a lawyer is always on display to the client during my interaction with them. As I have a friendly disposition, I have been asked many a time whether I am a 'fierce litigation lawyer'. To them, such a personality is important to win their case. So, there is a need to show the hard side of my personality to the client to win his confidence.

Other clients often query about legal strategies I am going to adopt in their cases. During meetings, the strategies have to be outlined to the client. Some clients have their own strategies, which I am expected to adopt and fine tune.

The other important issue to clients is cost. Clients approach small law firms with a mindset that they can obtain legal services at a cheap price. Small does not mean cheap. Small firms must maintain the standard of legal fees and resist the temptation to undercut their fees to attract clients. Besides explaining it to them clearly, it is important for small firm owners to manage the firm's cash flow. It is crucial to ensure sufficient fee deposits are collected from the client and that periodic bills are rendered and collected promptly.

Even after eight years as a small firm owner, the journey is not easy. When I start to relax a little, challenges would crop up. Sometimes it can be as simple as a slowdown in new instructions, difficult clients or staff problems. I find that I am always on my feet.

Law practice is demanding and consuming. Being a small firm owner is challenging. I am not only a lawyer, but a business development manager, finance manager, human resource manager, IT manager and administrative manager rolled into one.

Personal management skills are important to lawyers like me. In a typical day, besides attending Court, meeting clients and working on client cases, I have to allocate time to answer telephone calls, emails and manage my staff. Sometimes, the substantial work such as drafting court documents is done after office hours or during weekends when there are no interruptions.

Like many, I thought that running my own practice means better work-life balance. I was proven wrong very soon. My working hours are equally long as in my previous job.

I often find that good temperament and a good dose of positivity is important in my work. Many lawyers ask me how I manage the emotional aspects of family law practice. Although I do not deny that it does drain me, I learnt to detach myself from my client's problems. It takes time and experience to do so. During such low moments, I remind myself that I am helping the client to overcome his or her personal problems and to live a happier life in future. It is also important not to bring the clients' problems home.

Patience is a virtue that cannot be over-rated in a family lawyer. When a client starts talking about his or her problem, I already know what this problem is and what the client ought to do before he or she finishes explaining his problem. I would have heard it many times. Yet, I have to be careful in not belittling the client's problems or feelings.

Family law is not one of the hot practice areas. It is fulfilling because it deals with the most important private aspects of a person's life. To me, it is the best way of helping people. When a client smiles at me at the conclusion of his case, gives me a warm handshake, sheds tears in gratitude, sends me an email or SMS to tell me how he or she is doing years later, money cannot buy the emotional satisfaction I receive then. The highest accolade that I get for being a good family lawyer is when a client refers his or her family and friends to me and when they tell me how he or she feels about me.

Should more lawyers run their own law firms? It depends on what they want out of their career. After seeing former colleagues taking the similar route I took and not being able to cope with the drastic change, I felt that I had made the right choice of taking two years to prepare myself for the rigour and vigour of sole practice. Mental preparedness is so important before a lawyer sets out to run his or her own firm. The substantial pay cuts and lack of administrative support can be very difficult and discouraging during the initial years.

Many lawyers only want to do the legal work and nothing more. A small firm owner is a lawyer and a businessman. He or she must be interested in the various aspects of the business especially the administrative work.

Putting aside all the difficulties and challenges that I have faced, I enjoy being an entrepreneur. Law is a service that I provide. I look forward to the week and the workday as it gives me another opportunity to work towards building a successful business. I enjoy the freedom to carve out my law practice and my future. The excitement of looking out for new ideas and opportunities to grow my business keeps the adrenaline running.

I do not think that life is harder for me now as compared to when I was working in a large law firm. The law firm has given me many invaluable opportunities to learn and grow in my personal life. I have learnt to take risks and many leaps of faith. I examine my weaknesses and find ways to overcome them.

The support of my parents, my wife whom I met in the first year of my business and my friends is why the firm and I are here today.

CHAPTER 6

REAL ESTATE – TANGIBLE. SOLID.
BEAUTIFUL. ARTISTIC.

Norman Ho

Norman is a partner in Rodyk & Davidson LLP's Real Estate Practice Group. A leader in corporate real estate work, he has extensive experience in a wide spectrum of property related transactions and regularly advises banks and financial institutions, property developers, statutory boards, property consultants, investors and purchasers in real estate matters. Norman has also acted for owners and investors in a myriad of developments both within and outside Singapore. In addition to representing clients in the acquisition, sale and leaseback of industrial developments, Norman also represents many financial institutions in Singapore and their facilities to small and medium enterprises.

A recognised leader in collective sale transaction, Norman was selected to make representations to the Select Committee, commissioned by the Singapore Parliament, on amendments to the Land Titles (Strata) Act in 1999 for facilitating collective sale. He was again consulted during a review of en bloc legislation and the ensuing amendments to the Act in 2007.

In addition to writing, Norman is also a regular in the speaking circuit and often gives talks and seminars at the invitation of recognised real estate bodies within and outside the country.

1.   Introduction

Real estate law, often also called 'conveyancing law' or 'land law', deals with all transactions relating to any type of real property. This chapter sets out to show the significance of this area of law to aspiring lawyers and law students, what the different areas of real estate practice are, and what skills an aspiring real estate lawyer should possess.

2. The Significance of Real Estate Law

Social Significance

To say that the topic of property ownership is close to the hearts of Singaporeans may very well be an understatement. With the exception of shopping, eating and queuing up for the latest white iPhone, few other things dominate the attention of our countrymen the way that property ownership does. In our land-scarce city state where a property is probably the most valuable investment to most, this phenomena of infatuation cuts across all races, ages and social classes — from couples getting married (in typical Singaporean no less with the five magical words 'want to apply for flat?', to the uncle in the coffee-shop, to the savvy sophisticated investor) — almost everyone has an opinion about land issues in Singapore. Every other day you can find property-related reports in the newspapers: the latest property prices, which estate has gone en-bloc, parties litigating over a property or which land parcel has been sold and allocated for some exciting usage. Home-ownership is also always one of the most fiercely debated topics at every general election in Singapore (together with the other perennial dilemma of how to increase our nation's birth rate). And if I may drive home the point, just take a look at your letter box — it will not be a surprise if you find it littered daily with brochures of new developments beckoning you to become the proud owner of a unit (or two) in the newest condominium addition in town!

Economic Significance

We are all familiar with Singapore's reputation (apart from banning chewing gum) as a resilient and fast growing financial centre. However, more than that, Singapore is quickly becoming the choice country for foreign property investors thanks to its focus on compliance and fiscal discipline, the growth in the global economy and the expansion of Asian markets in the last two decades. In the recent years, there has been a sharp increase in the number of institutional investors (although it would be wise to think twice about any fund bearing the name 'Madoff'), global property funds, public-listed real estate companies, government-linked companies and onshore and offshore special purpose vehicles purchasing properties in Singapore. Not only does this circumstance significantly enhance the value of land in Singapore, it creates new growth areas for our economy. This can easily be seen from the example of Real Estate Investment Trusts ('REITs'), the first of which made its debut appearance on the Singapore financial market in 2002 (which was also the debut appearance of a certain Kate Middleton in Prince William's life, breaking countless female hearts across the world). In a short span of time, we have seen the emergence of about twenty different REITs in Singapore, giving us the fastest growth rate in Asia. The real estate sector is at the very heartbeat of our economy as land continues to be considered valuable and profitable to acquire.

Practical Significance

Social and economic realities aside, any lawyer must arm himself (and the other arm as well, if it is free of encumbrances) with a solid knowledge of land law in order to be an all-rounded practitioner. This is essential regardless of the field of law he specialises in. Professor Tang Hang Wu sets this out very aptly in Chapter 6 of *Reading Law*, where he observes that this area of the law affects every aspect of our lives (do note that your neighbour may at this time decide to involve you in his life as well once he finds out you are a real estate lawyer by asking you to deal with his picky tenant or harassing you for the latest real estate inside news). More generally, the law of property forms the building blocks of difficult legal concepts such as the commencement and termination of general proprietary rights. As Professor Tang astutely points out, practically, real estate practice involves the transaction of land and interests in property – litigation lawyers commonly handle tenancy disputes and tussles pertaining to land borne out of contractual, insolvency or probate issues. With the increase of high profile and complex corporate deals, often involving transfer of real property in addition to corporate issues, corporate lawyers will also need to be well-acquainted with land law. One can also contemplate that similar issues of proprietary rights can come into play, even for an intellectual property lawyer! Practically, real estate lawyers are the most prestigious of the lot; we deal with royalty on a regular basis as many of our clients are landlords.

3. Areas of Real Estate Practice

Retail Conveyancing

Retail conveyancing involves acting for individuals and companies in the purchase of residential homes or commercial properties, often also encompassing assistance in property financing and mortgage arrangements. This area can be considered the bread and butter (and for many, the main course and dessert) of a conveyancing lawyer's work and is usually where his basic knowledge of real estate practice is first obtained. By handling more straight-forward transactions such as these, a lawyer gains a good grounding in the concepts and procedures of sale, purchase and financing arrangements which will be essential for later developing his skills in more sophisticated and larger deals (which interestingly enough, does not contain bread, butter nor food of any kind) such as those listed below. After all, one cannot learn to walk before learning to crawl!

There are many lawyers who have focussed their energies on building a niche practice in mass-market retail conveyancing. It is unfortunate that public perception of this has been rather negative. Comments such as retail coveyancing being routine, uncomplicated or even work that can be carried out by a secretary or a real estate agent call for grave concern, and are dangerously erroneous. Even for the simplest and most typical of transactions — that of an individual redeeming the mortgage for his property or selling/purchasing a property, the responsibilities and risks involved for the lawyer are numerous (contrary to popular belief, a mortgage cannot be redeemed with an 8 Days magazine cut-out coupon). His expertise cannot be replaced by that of an individual who is not legally trained. A good conveyancing lawyer will know how to look out for and deal with potential title issues, explain salient clauses in mortgage documents (the legal drafting of which is lost on most laymen (we have yet to conduct research on laywomen and are awaiting further evidence before we decide if they are as lost as the men)), and protect his client's interest against any unfair demands and/or late completion.

Further, due to the scarcity of land, the Singapore government is known to be highly interventionist when it comes to housing policies (for the moment, you may still choose your own furniture), both in allocating housing units to citizens and other residents and in often imposing new rules and regulations with regards to the sale and purchase of residential homes (which includes the financing thereof). This is particularly common when mass market housing prices are on the rise and cooling measures have to be introduced to prevent speculation and the formation of a property bubble. Such information is not always readily available or comprehensible to laymen, especially when housing agents conceal the same whether due to negligence or for self-interested reasons (another reason may be if the individual is suffering from a medical condition known as the 'blur sotong' phenomenon). One example is the introduction of a tiered seller's stamp duty. A conveyancing lawyer should be able to advise his client immediately when and how much (if at all) stamp duty (contrary to popular belief, this type of stamp duty is different from that of a postman's job) is required to be paid for the sale. Having a good conveyancing lawyer handle the sale and purchase transaction can therefore save a client from enormous legal and financial repercussions later.

Development Work

Generally, development work involves acting for institutional clients in acquiring land parcels or whole buildings for development in Singapore. These institutional clients are typically housing developers or global property funds who are interested in purchasing, amongst others, vacant land, commercial buildings, large numbers of office or residential units, warehouses, industrial plants, hotels and resorts.

Such projects are usually high-profile and more complex. In addition to the expertise of investigation of title and carrying out proper due diligence, the lawyer should come competently armed with an array of other conveyancing skills. This includes being familiar with regulatory requirements, deal structuring, drafting and negotiating management agreements, funding and divestment activities, land use and planning regulations, government land tender procedures and requirements and dealing with leasehold properties granted by government bodies (unfortunately, there is as yet no 'ten year series' textbook on these topics).

As one can imagine, work of such a scale often calls for multi-disciplinary legal knowledge for the delivery of an integrated solution to the client. This is where co-operation with other legal departments comes into play to deal with the wide-ranging legal issues that often arise. For example, in an acquisition of an uncompleted building, conveyancing lawyers will have to work closely (whether they like it or not, unfortunately) with construction lawyers to negotiate and draft the more technical aspects of the Sale and Purchase Agreement particularly with regards to terms like the appointment of project consultants, treatment of defects and assignment of various building works. A sale of a building from one global fund owner to another usually also entails a sale of shares or a share-swap. Corporate lawyers would have to be roped in to draft the share sale contracts and deal with all share sale compliance issues legislated under the Companies Act or the Listing Manual. Another example would be the assignment of intellectual property rights to a building's name, trademark and goodwill which would involve intellectual property lawyers. Such cross-disciplinary work is enjoyable, exciting and certainly widens the horizons, legal knowledge and expertise of the real estate lawyer.

REITs

As a brief explanation, REITs typically own shopping malls, office buildings, industrial buildings, carparks, serviced apartments or hotels. When a REIT buys a property, they will look at refurbishing it or changing its tenancy mix to boost yields. The rental collected from tenants of these properties is then mostly paid out to the REIT's shareholders (not unlike collecting rent on a Mayfair road hotel in a game of Monopoly). As REITs are traded like shares, they allow investors to 'own' a piece of property without actually buying one. Unlike buying an actual property, the capital outlay to buy a REIT is much lower and there is greater liquidity.

As mentioned earlier, the burgeoning REITS industry is widely regarded to be an important growth area, not just for Singapore but across Asian markets. This spells an urgent demand for legal skills in this area (please note, Monopoly skills are not considered legal skills). Unsurprisingly, REITs are governed by a complex regulatory framework governing the trustees and the fund, which includes the Securities and Futures Act, the Listing Manual of, the Code on Collective Investment Schemes, the Property Funds Guidelines, the Code of Corporate Governance and the Companies Act.

A real estate lawyer specialising in REITs will obviously have to be familiar with sale, acquisition and leasing of large-scale properties. Often, REITs also acquire industrial properties situated on sites owned by the Jurong Town Corporation ('JTC') or Housing Development Board ('HDB'). This means that various compliance requirements have to be met before the purchase is made. He or she would also have to be familiar with drafting the Put and Call Option Agreement and Lease-back Agreement. There are also usually extensive negotiations between the seller and the REIT in the preparation of these documents which the lawyer would have to handle.

Collective Sales

A collective sale (also commonly termed an en-bloc sale) is a combined sale by the owners of two or more property units to a common purchaser, usually a housing developer. The most common en-bloc sale is the sale of all the units in a strata or flatted development to a purchaser. The sale proceeds are then divided amongst all the unit owners. Other variations of en-bloc sales include the sale of all units in a development together with an adjoining development or landed properties. Due to Singapore's land constraints, collective sales are the main source of prime freehold land for developers (alas, we are still some years away from an underground Atlantis metropolis) and are a creative way of freeing up land and utilising increased plot ratios to realise the full developmental potential of such land. It would be of interest to note that due to its unique land situation, Singapore has one of the most sophisticated en-bloc laws in the world. It is therefore exciting for the real estate lawyer to be at the forefront of such a development.

The real estate lawyer acting for the seller(s) in this case would have to take his or her client through the entire sale process from the appointing of the property consultants, forming the sale committee and advising it of its responsibilities, drafting and negotiating the Collective Sale Agreement and Sale and Purchase Agreement with the owners, appearing before the Strata Title Board when necessary, to the successful completion of the transaction.

The sheer volume of the transaction should also be noted. As most projects consist of numerous units, the usual checks on title and bankruptcy/winding up searches done in one traditional conveyancing transaction have to be multiplied, and in some projects, several hundred times over (at the expense of considerable eyeball strain and increased caffeine sales). To raise the standards of governance and disclosure in such transactions, the government has over the last few years made numerous amendments to the en-bloc legislation. The collective sale lawyer must therefore have the legislative requirements under the governing Land Titles (Strata) Act at his fingertips (and preferably in his head as well) in order to ensure compliance and, more importantly, to avoid potential disputes and objections raised by minority owners. This can cause serious hostility, dissatisfaction and even financial losses amongst the owners which you will want to avoid at all costs as a lawyer!

Real Estate Financing

The practice of real estate financing has changed drastically over the years (yes, property did exist back when buildings did not have air-conditioning). No longer do conveyancers only deal with traditional mortgage securitisation relating to retail conveyancing. These days, there is a broad spectrum of securitisation and structured real property related financing transactions. This is closely tied to the increased servicing of institutional clients in recent years. Lawyers will increasingly represent corporate borrowers, domestic/foreign banks, finance companies or institutions in their acquisitions of buildings and land parcels. These clients usually require advice relating to syndicated loan facilities and the lawyer's expertise includes advice on bridging loans, compliance and regulatory issues, land and construction loans, loan structuring and restructuring and project management. The security documents that the lawyer will draft and negotiate are usually the Facility Agreement, Sale and Lease-back Agreements, Mortgage, Assignments of Rental Proceeds/Maintenance Contracts/ Insurance and others. Tax and revenue issues are addressed as well in a typical transaction.

4. Skills Required for a Real Estate Lawyer

Know The Law

Needless to say, any aspiring real estate lawyer should know his or her land law and relevant governing legislation thoroughly. This forms the basis upon which all other skills will be built. As such, if you are entering law school or still a law student, I would encourage you to read land law as a subject well (this may or may not be at the expense of your other subjects, let your professors fight it out!). This will no doubt put you in good stead for the future – many concepts will prove to be useful if you learn them well in school. For example, it will not be uncommon for you to have to go back to the fundamental principles of ownership and proprietary interests and rights, equity, caveats (particularly regarding priorities) and different trusts arrangements (and their respective implications) in the course of practice. A good understanding of legislation from the Land Titles Act, Conveyancing and Law of Property Act and Residential Property Act, to name a few, is also particularly important. While of course you will have textbooks and statutes at your disposal (pay attention, disposal does not mean you throw away your books) in practice, having the relevant knowledge at the back of one's head often makes the difference between a good and an average lawyer since the former will be better able to identify the issues to be red-flagged when preliminarily advising clients. This will be a great help in managing client's expectations.

Know The Practical Procedures

Unlike litigation and corporate practice, real estate practice and what it entails are usually very unfamiliar to the typical law student. This is perhaps the reason why very few law graduates even choose to enter this area of law – it is difficult to be attracted to the unknown (unless you fancy yourself a Bear Grylls thrillseeker). Whilst land law as a subject is being taught in law school, the practice of it is seldom addressed and is sometimes vastly different from or unrelated to academia. The study of land law lays a good foundation for a real estate lawyer to build his practice on, but this is insufficient. One can be armed with all the theory of land law, yet have absolutely no clue how to handle the most basic of conveyancing procedures – a redemption of a mortgage, or a straightforward sale and purchase of a residential home.

As such, the learning curve can initially be steep when one is thrown into the deep end of practice upon graduation. But I would encourage young associates (and the relatively young, or at least 'young at heart') to persevere – practical knowledge and skills will be honed and learnt in the course of practice and the pressure will ease once you have gained enough experience. It is important not to shy away from opportunities to handle files on your own, or to be on a team for a complex deal. These are the best ways to really learn and grow, of course together with your supervising partner's guidance and mentorship. Do not be afraid to ask questions, even if you think they sound silly. It is much better to clarify early than to struggle through it alone or worse still, find yourself facing a potential negligence suit if things go wrong!

Have A Keen Interest In The Property Market

Like any occupation in the world, you will do well to be passionate about the subject matter of your job. It is impossible for real estate law to be divorced from the landscape of the property market. To find relevance in your area of practice and to understand the full implications of your actions on a client's transaction, being in tune with the ebb and flow of market conditions and even familiarising yourself with the jargon and technicalities of the market will more than help your cause. For example, discussions on gross plot ratio will make no sense to you in development or collective sales work if you only concern yourself strictly with legal terms. I would strongly advocate aspiring (and current) real estate lawyers to make an effort to dive in and read up intimately on the industry (property watching is afterall, a national pastime, just behind our obsession with queueing up for Hello Kitty soft toys). Clients will always want their commercial needs to be met first and foremost, and to do that effectively it is crucial that a real estate lawyer must have keen commercial sense. Only with such a skill can you competently make decisions that will best assist the client in meeting his or her needs within the confines of the law. From this, you will also be in a better position to discern what items are deal-breakers in negotiations and what items are secondary. As an example, a REIT lawyer should be aware that sellers are usually obliged under the terms and conditions of the Lease-back Agreement to take up maintenance works to the building and should draft this into the document. This is because REITs often require that only buildings of a certain grade and quality be bought. A non-REIT buyer may not be as concerned about this requirement.

Have People Skills

Last but not least, a real estate lawyer meets people from all walks of life on a daily basis. It will not be surprising to meet with the man in the street for your retail conveyancing matter, and then move into the next meeting with the astute and perceptive director of a global fund for development work. Having good public relations skills and effectively managing client expectations are crucial to becoming a good real estate lawyer.

One obvious example will be in the area of collective sales. A special feature of such transactions is that they can become particularly acrimonious simply because the sale of one's home often touches a raw nerve. I have seen my fair share of meetings turning ugly due to differing opinions amongst neighbours. Some have even manifested in verbal and physical abuse (blood may have been shed, but thankfully none of it was mine)! I recall seeing the collective sale frenzy reach a fever pitch in the first half of 2007, with an unprecedented number of deals closed. Amid the exuberance fuelled by sky-rocketing prices, high-profile legal tussles between owners and purchasers became a common feature. Hostility was often created between consenting owners and non-consenting owners or owners who had consented but sought ways to rescind their consent to their sale agreement. To date, it is still common to hear dissenting voices complaining that rights of minorities are often railroaded in a transaction where 'tyranny of the majority' rules.

Besides putting in extra care from the outset to comply strictly with all legislative requirements to avoid accusations of unfairness, the collective sale lawyer should ensure that he knows how to control such difficult situations firmly yet fairly and even how to dispel tension at the slightest hint that things may get sour. It is a challenge to do this well as you may sometimes find yourself inundated with questions and/ or complaints from hundreds of owners, each wanting to make a point and each wanting a portion of your time. Some of these people may hurl abuse at you or fail to appreciate your work but one has to always remain professional. These soft skills cannot be learnt in law school, and can only be acquired over time by experience and keen observation of your more senior colleagues.

5. Conclusion

I hope this chapter has given you at least a glimpse of what real estate practice is like. Hopefully, you can see that the future of conveyancing is bright and that the demand for experienced conveyancing lawyers with sound expertise and skills relating to real estate practice far exceeds supply. In land scarce Singapore with a rapidly growing and upwardly mobile population, property transactions are definitely here to stay. After 30 years in this profession, I have found real estate practice to be ever-changing, exciting and challenging and I hope you will find the same satisfaction that I have experienced. In the words of business mogul Donald Trump, 'It's tangible, it's solid, it's beautiful. It's artistic, from my standpoint, and I just love real estate'.

CHAPTER 7

CRIMINAL LAW – LIFE AND LIBERTY

Anand Nalachandran

Anand graduated from the National University of Singapore and is an Advocate and Solicitor of the Supreme Court of the Republic of Singapore and Lead Counsel under the Legal Assistance Scheme for Capital Offences ('LASCO'). He is a Fellow of the Singapore Institute of Arbitrators ('FSIArb') and an Associate Mediator with the Singapore Mediation Centre – Subordinate Courts (Primary Dispute Resolution Centre and Small Claims Tribunal). He is a member of the Council of the Law Society of Singapore as well as committees of the Singapore Academy of Law and the ASEAN Law Association. He is a Teaching Fellow of the Singapore Institute of Legal Education ('SILE') and supports the pro bono initiatives of the Law Society of Singapore, such as the Criminal Legal Aid Scheme ('CLAS'), and provides legal aid through the profession and community. He is a founding member of the Association of Criminal Lawyers Singapore ('ACLS').

1. The Beginning

I believe that fate (and local university administrators) decided that I should become a lawyer. I began to embrace this prospect even before entering law school and developed an immediate interest in criminal law – although that interest did not necessarily translate into sterling academic results.

I found the factual scenarios of criminal cases more interesting but, salacious facts aside, I was particularly intrigued by the human element in each case. The analysis of crimes that were *malum in se* (wrong in itself) as opposed to offences that were *malum prohibitum* (wrong by law) disclosed that criminal law was neither black nor white but within the ubiquitous-grey of nature, nurture and culture.

I remember the criminal law textbook being a compendium of riveting stories and bizarre tales – but these were all real cases which proved that oftentimes, fact was stranger than fiction. Cases which occurred in other jurisdictions (and centuries) remained relevant by virtue of the common thread – human nature. Morality and criminality were the universal themes.

I did an undergraduate internship and observed a murder trial where the accused was convicted, primarily on circumstantial evidence, and condemned to suffer the death penalty. I queried the practical application of principles like the presumption of innocence and proof beyond a reasonable doubt. On appeal, this man was acquitted and I recall thinking that criminal law had saved him from the gallows. Looking back, perhaps this was the spark.

2. The Cases

I have credited good fortune (fate, yet again) for being drawn to a particular area of practice – and the opportunity to pursue that specialised field. I completed pupillage and began practice with Mr Subhas Anandan, handling cases running the gamut from commercial crimes to capital offences. Initially, I handled pre-trial work and drafting and in some sense, I was spared the heavier professional (and emotional) burden. Soon, I was handling cases and conducting hearings independently.

After six years in practice, I was assigned to serve as Lead Counsel in a capital case. This was significant because the mantle of responsibility was now squarely on my shoulders and the stakes could not be higher. During that trial, I lost sleep but gained invaluable experience. The murder charge was eventually reduced to an offence of culpable homicide – the accused person had avoided the death penalty and words cannot describe the satisfaction and motivation that was derived from that outcome.

Over the years, there have been peculiar scenarios and novel issues and I was fortunate to be involved in some notable cases involving a range of offences which are broadly described below:

- Capital offences include murder, drug trafficking and kidnapping. These offences usually carry the mandatory death penalty and the objective is often to reduce the charge to a lesser offence for which a custodial sentence can be imposed. The use of forensic evidence is substantial in such cases and defence counsel will require a level of technical proficiency.

- Sexual offences include rape, molest and 'unnatural' acts. These cases can involve racy details and sensational allegations but there may be vulnerable witnesses and defence counsel may have to vigorously pursue the defence in cross-examination without traumatising such a witness – and thereby aggravating the situation. This is not always easy.

- Specialised offences include corruption, computer misuse, corporate fraud and drug offences. These cases are challenging because of the technical nature of the offences and the frequent use of forensic and scientific tools during the proceedings. I have relished the opportunity to digest forensic evidence and the challenges of cross-examining an expert witness.

- General offences include crimes relating to property loss and personal injury as well as traffic offences and regulatory breaches. These would include offences in the Penal Code as well as prosecutions by the Ministries and Statutory bodies under other statutes – and can occur in a multitude of permutations with varying levels of complexity.

A criminal lawyer will encounter a wide variety of offences during the course of practice and while some cases have similarities, no two cases are identical. Occasionally, defence counsel will come across a rarely-invoked provision and will have to ascertain the legislative history and parliamentary intent behind the provisions. In law school, I thought that some issues were too far-fetched to ever present themselves in reality – and was categorically disavowed of that notion during practice whilst encountering unusual cases with uncommon defences.

In particular, I recall a case where somnambulism (ie sleepwalking) was put forth in defence as a form of non-insane automatism. I rummaged through boxes to locate that first year criminal law textbook for research – and felt some measure of satisfaction when the charges were ultimately withdrawn. This was a valuable lesson – that a criminal lawyer should not approach any case with preconceived notions and should maintain an open mind and consider all available defences – however obscure. This lesson has been reinforced in the course of practice and may explain the tenacity with which criminal lawyers doggedly pursue any viable defence.

3. The Advocate

Defence counsel have described their work as fighting an uphill battle with one arm tied behind their back – and blindfolded. Although recent legislative amendments, particularly to the Criminal Procedure Code, have moved towards levelling the playing field (or battlefield), there are still ample challenges for the criminal defence lawyer due to the limitation and inequalitiy of information and resources. However, despite the frustrations of criminal litigation practice, there will be small triumphs that can reinvigorate even the most weary crusader.

After over a decade, I still try to resist cynicism and maintain idealism. Not an easy task. Very few peers have pursued this area of practice and I have been asked the reason for remaining on this path. I sometimes reply (in jest) that I have no choice because I have no transferrable skills. In truth, I pursue criminal litigation practice because I have found this career path rewarding (in every sense) and have derived genuine satisfaction and fulfilment. And I am not a sucker for punishment – no pun intended.

That being the case, I suppose the question would be – what is satisfying and fulfilling about criminal practice? I have struggled to produce an answer that does not come across as clichéd. Unfortunately, I have been unable to avoid the reality so I shall just bite the bullet and state the reason plainly and unashamedly: Criminal practice gives you the opportunity to help someone in their darkest hour – and each case is an opportunity to make a positive life-altering difference.

Before going any further, we should disavow anyone of the notion that criminal lawyers constantly seek out damsels in distress – figuratively or literally. Our signature black-white court attire is not a superhero's uniform – although the lawyer's robe can resemble a cape. That said, the criminal lawyer can be the instrument for preserving life and protecting liberty because the accused person would struggle to navigate the criminal justice system unassisted.

There have been many urgent interviews with desperate clients to prepare defences, to prepare appeals, to prepare petitions for clemency and sometimes, to prepare for execution. When dealing with the client or the client's family, there must be a balance between being committed without becoming overly-committed. The client may want a counsellor, but the client needs counsel. Criminal lawyers should have empathy but I think defence counsel would not be optimally serving his client's cause if his professional judgment is compromised. As you would expect, this is not always easy.

An accused person may be guilty or innocent but regardless of what that person is accused of doing, the role of the criminal lawyer is to ensure that he or she is afforded due legal process and that the Court is in a position to assess the evidence to determine culpability and impose punishment (if appropriate). Even the perpetrator of the most heinous crime deserves fair treatment under the law. As such, the criminal lawyer needs to understand his or her role in the administration of justice – and should not judge the accused person. Fortunately, that is someone else's job.

4. The Practice

Criminal litigation involves regular attendance in Court and initially, I was there almost daily to attend Mentions or Pre-Trial Conferences or Hearings. During this time, I gained experience and became comfortable and confident with advocacy – although some people still make me nervous. Over the years, I have enjoyed interacting with the Judges, Prosecutors and staff in the Courts which have become, to some extent, an extended part of the work/office environment.

I quickly realised that criminal litigation was quite different from civil litigation. For example, the level of discovery was different and the bargaining strengths were disparate. There were no witness statements or affidavits in summary criminal trials and so, a criminal lawyer would cross-examine a witness just after hearing the oral evidence. There were applications made and disputed orally – often without prior notification – instead of through a summons or supporting affidavit and this made criminal litigation less document-intensive but required criminal lawyers to respond quickly and be immediately familiar with the rules of evidence and criminal procedure.

The first impressions of criminal litigation come from books, television or movies and this creates visions of dramatic scenes and twists. Interestingly, there is some truth in this. Criminal litigation attracts media coverage and, being an adversarial process, there will be contentious moments and unexpected developments which will be newsworthy Nonetheless, we should maintain proper decorum inside court and remain professional colleagues outside court. In fact, a lawyer may have better relationships with some prosecutors in criminal cases than with some lawyers in civil matters.

There are stereotypes about criminal practice and criminal lawyers – and I have endured jibes about the meeting the stereotypical requirements of race and girth. But jokes aside, I hope all budding criminal lawyers will pursue their aspirations to forge a career in their chosen field without feeling discouraged by misconceptions or being deterred by misperceptions.. Criminal law can be an intellectually stimulating and financially rewarding area of practice, and can provide a level of job-satisfaction and fulfilment that will maintain the inspiration through the perspiration. I truly believe this.

5.   The Qualities

In any form of litigation, proficiency in the law, advocacy and procedure is essential - together with qualities such as tenacity, resilience and perseverance. In criminal practice, I believe the added virtues of passion and compassion are necessary. At the presentation of the inaugural LASCO Award 2010, the Honourable the Chief Justice noted that :

> But, of course, we know that the criminal lawyer has something – some personal quality – which the civil lawyer may not have the opportunity to manifest in his day to day work. That something is a "passion" for justice and the underdog – and his sense of fairness and justice that any person who is charged with a capital offence is entitled to be accorded the benefit of the judicial process.

I believe that the combination of passion and compassion brings pro bono work close to the heart of all criminal lawyers who support the various initiatives to provide pro bono criminal defence to accused persons who are impecunious, with special needs, of young age or otherwise deserving. Many criminal lawyers practise in smaller firms which provide core legal services to the majority of the population and which may be the first opportunity for access to justice. These lawyers pursue their passions and at the Opening of the Legal Year 2011, the Honourable the Attorney-General noted that:

> It is here that we find many of the lawyers who are still sustained by the romance in the notion of helping a person overcome a potentially devastating problem, even though it may never translate into a glitzy headline or a large fee. And it is from among this group of lawyers that we find so many of those who, in addition to their daily business, selflessly carry out pro bono work under the auspices of the Criminal Legal Aid Scheme (CLAS), the Supreme Court's Legal Assistance Scheme for Capital Offences (LASCO) and the ACLS Pro Bono scheme.

These lawyers give so generously of their time and energy without expectation of reward and I think this speaks volumes about the personality and character of the criminal lawyer. It is said that a community can be measured by how it treats its weakest members. The desire to help someone in need is the basis of pro bono work – and this has received strong support from criminal lawyers.

6.   The Mission

Criminal law deals with human nature – and human failings. Perhaps a philosophical perspective would be to accept that anyone can make a mistake and a criminal lawyer can help someone get a second chance or prevent someone from being unjustly punished. To conclude, I can do no better than to quote the observations of the Honourable the Chief Justice at the Opening of the Legal Year 2011:

> The Criminal Bar plays a crucial role in keeping an eye on the proper administration of criminal justice through their steadfast defence of their clients and their legal rights. They have a crucial responsibility when defending their clients against the forensic might of the Attorney-General's team of DPPs, supported by the investigative muscle of the Home Team. Their work is essential to the stability of the criminal justice system, but unfortunately, the nature of their work and the economic profile of their clients dictate the level of remuneration that they can get, no matter how onerous their responsibility to their clients may be. Criminal law practice needs lawyers with certain social and philosophical values that give them personal satisfaction in acting as defence counsel in criminal trials.

'Fiat justitia ruat caelum' is a Latin phrase meaning *'Let justice be done though the heavens fall'* – and is the motto of the Association of Criminal Lawyers Singapore. I would like to think this encapsulates the spirit of the Criminal Bar.

CHAPTER 8

SHIPPING – PIRATES AND PHANTOM SHIPS

Chan Leng Sun, SC

Leng Sun is Co-Head of the Disputes Practice Group in Baker & McKenzie.Wong & Leow. Qualified in Malaysia, Singapore and England, he was appointed a Senior Counsel of Singapore in 2011.

Before joining Baker & McKenzie.Wong & Leow, he was a partner in Ang & Partners. He has taught Shipping Law at the National University of Singapore and was Adjunct Faculty for International Commercial Arbitration at SMU. Leng Sun has also served as a Legal Officer of the United Nations Compensation Commission in Geneva. In addition to chairing the Law Society ADR Committee, Leng Sun is also Vice-President of the Singapore Institute of Arbitrators. He sits as an arbitrator and adjudicator on the panel of various institutions. He was an Honorary Shell Scholar, a Pegasus Cambridge Scholar and a Kuok Foundation Scholar.

This is a true story. Only the facts have been changed.

Zack was very excited about his new hotel in Serangoon. He wanted to furnish it with the best materials available. Naturally, that meant going to Johor. For the marble that he wanted for his hotel lobby, however, his contractor introduced him to an Italian marble supplier named Giorgio, from Carrara. Zack ordered 100 polished marble slabs from Giorgio. Giorgio contacted a freight forwarder who booked space on a ship MV Bella to carry the marble from Italy to Singapore.

Unfortunately, MV Bella collided with MV Buta en route and ten marble slabs fell into the sea. After a detour to Port Klang for temporary repairs, MV Bella continued her voyage through the Straits of Malacca. In the dark of the night, a band of pirates boarded her, put the Master and crew into a lifeboat and took off with MV Bella and the remaining cargo of 90 marble slabs. The owner of MV Bella is an English company called Freight & Carriage United ('FCU'). FCU reported the piracy to the Regional Cooperation Agreement on Combating Piracy and Armed Robbery Against Ships in Asia ('ReCAAP') Information Sharing Centre who immediately sent out a regional alert. ReCAAP is an international organisation based in Singapore. It was set up pursuant to a multilateral agreement between 17 countries to share information and coordinate efforts in, well, combating piracy and armed robbery against ships in Asia. It has enjoyed a degree of success even if piracy is far from eradicated. In this instance, neither MV Bella nor her cargo was found.

For seven days after his cargo was lost with the ship, Zack stared at the white plaster on his bare hotel walls, where the beautiful marble slabs were supposed to be. Finally, like all heartbroken people, he sought solace from a law firm.

Zack arrived just after newly minted law associate, Nadia, walked through the door of her office. She was called to the bar just the day before. The phrase has its origin in England in the Middle Ages when barristers who were granted the right to address the Courts sat behind a wooden barrier in the courtroom. In England, the legal profession is divided between barristers, those who argue cases in Court, and solicitors, those who perform all legal services short of conducting cases in Court. These are two different professions, with very different routes for qualification and business models. In Singapore, the legal profession is fused into one, so a qualified lawyer is known as an advocate and solicitor. While admission to the Singapore bar entitles a lawyer to practise as both, there are many who focus on just transaction and advisory work, much like what solicitors do in England. Shipping work can be transactional, such as sale and purchase or financing transactions, or disputes work where advocates are needed.

Nadia does disputes. On the day of her call, the dry daytime ritual had comprised of her standing before a High Court Judge who granted the Order admitting her to the profession as a fully-qualified advocate and solicitor. Her colleagues had preferred the literal application of the phrase 'call to the bar', so she had to buy quite a few drinks in Boat Quay. As she stepped into the shipping law firm where she worked, still groggy from the Boat Quay proceedings the evening before, she thought to herself, 'Yes, today, I can finally speak directly to the clients, help them through their troubles, and send out letters bearing *my* name.'

She had barely sat down when the receptionist called. Her boss, Mr Ashiq, was out for a meeting and there was a frantic client wanting consultation urgently. Nadia walked into the meeting room. Zack told her the story. Nadia thought this was her chance to apply what she had learnt.

Nadia: Mr Zack, what you told me is sad. What do you want to do?

Zack: I have paid for the marble. Can I get my money back from Giorgio?

Nadia: It depends.

Zack: It depends on what?

Nadia: It depends on your contract with Giorgio.

Zack: I will look for the contract in my office. What about the owner of MV Bella? He carried my cargo, lost some overboard and lost the rest to pirates. Can I make him pay for my loss?

Nadia: It depends.

Zack: On what?

Nadia: It depends on the document of carriage, the bill of lading.

Zack: Oh, I don't have that document. What about that other ship, that MV Buta who collided into MV Bella and started all the trouble? Can I make that ship pay for my loss?

Nadia: It depends. It depends on how much MV Buta is to be blamed for the collision.

Zack: I bought insurance for my cargo. Maybe I can claim under the policy.

Nadia: That depends on the terms of the policy.

Zack: I will have to search for the policy. If I need to sue somebody, does that mean I should go to the Singapore courts?

Nadia: It depends.

Zack: What?

Nadia: It depends on what clause you have in your contract with that person or failing that, which court is the most appropriate forum.

Zack: Okay, I better go look for my documents.

Nadia   (checking her diary): So, do you want to make an appointment to discuss this further tomorrow?

Zack: That depends.

Nadia: Depends on what?

Zack: That depends on whether your boss will be here.

Meanwhile, halfway across town (which, in Singapore, means two blocks away), Nadia's boyfriend, Jerome, was also hard at work. He was also a shipping lawyer. Both of them had heard that lawyers were married to their work and figured that this way, they could have their cake and eat it too. Jerome was slightly more experienced, about 4 years PQE + ('PQE' means 'Pay Quantum Escalating', although it is officially and innocuously expressed as 'Post-Qualification Experience').

FCU had just contacted Jerome's boss. There was news that MV Buta would be calling at Singapore to take bunkers (fuel). FCU blamed MV Buta for the collision, but the owner of MV Buta had brushed off all demands. Jerome prepared the arrest papers and rushed off to Court to get a Warrant of Arrest. Jerome's clerk who was authorised by the Sheriff to effect service of the papers on MV Buta hired a launch which took him and a professional guard to where MV Buta was anchored. A trainee at the office, Navin, was eager to observe his first ship arrest and tagged along.

In shipping, there is a Sheriff and there are arrests, but there is usually no gunfight or showdown at high noon. The Sheriff of the Supreme Court speaks mildly even if he wields a big stick. The arrest is not effected on any dodgy individual fleeing on a gunboat, but on the ship. No handcuffs are required. Instead, arrest legally takes place when the Warrant of Arrest is affixed for a short time on the ship's mast or on the outside of any part of the ship's superstructure, followed by leaving a copy on a sheltered, conspicuous part of the ship. This usually means sticking a copy on the glass window at the bridge, as a symbol that creditors have made a claim on the ship (a bit like ah longs splashing red paint on front doors to declare that the occupants owe them money).

The ship, on the full legitimate authority of the Courts, is prohibited from leaving the jurisdiction unless the Court orders her release. This is done only if the Court sets aside the order for arrest. This can happen if the conditions for arrest are shown to be unfulfilled on further arguments or security is provided for the claim.

Navin and the clerk had obtained the location of the ship at anchorage and did not have much trouble finding her. The launch went alongside. The more sturdy, aluminium gangway ladder was not in place so Navin and the clerk had to time their hop onto the rope ladder from the bobbing launch. The seasoned clerk and guard clambered up in no time. Halfway up the rope ladder, Navin suddenly remembered why he did not like the sea when the ship and its ladder started to do the fandango on the choppy waters. From the safety of the deck, the clerk shouted meaningless words of encouragement, like 'Don't worry, it's alright' which translated into 'I am not worried, I am up here and if you fall, it's alright with me'. Navin finally made it to the deck. The clerk waved the court papers at the curious but taciturn Chief Mate, who brought them to see the disinterested and taciturn Master.

The clerk explained their presence. The Master was bothered. While the crew were still employed and earned wages during an arrest, sometimes an impecunious owner would abandon both crew and ship. At the very least, their schedule was disrupted and their home leave delayed. For a moment, the Master fantasised about throwing all three overboard, but on learning that Navin was a trainee lawyer, decided not to poison the fish. The clerk was allowed to complete the ritual of arrest without incident, and they left after posting the Warrant of Arrest on the bridge.

The guard stayed on board, as a deterrent to the ship breaking arrest. Usually, shipowners would obey the order of the Court as they would be in contempt of Court if their arrested ship leaves without permission. In this case, however, the owner of MV Buta did not care. Before dawn the next day, on receiving a clandestine order from her owner, MV Buta heaved anchor and sailed at full steam out of anchorage and away from Singapore waters. Thankfully, the guard was allowed off at one of the islets of Indonesia from where he eventually made his way home to Bedok.

The Sheriff and the Maritime and Port Authority of Singapore ('MPA') were informed that MV Buta had bolted. Enquiries with the Indonesian authorities drew a blank. It seemed that the Master and crew had received orders to sign off the same time that the guard disembarked at the Indonesian islet. They were replaced by a suspicious looking crew. One could tell they were up to no good because they wore sunglasses indoors.

FCU reported the incident to the International Maritime Bureau, an organisation set up in 1981 to combat maritime fraud and malpractices, which also has a Piracy Reporting Centre in Kuala Lumpur. MV Buta seemed to have vanished to World's End. By this time, FCU had companions in misery for many creditors such as suppliers of fuel and provisions to the ship were left unpaid, not to mention the Master and crew who did not get their wages. The shipowner was a company registered in Panama but creditors who knocked on the door found nothing but a bored office manager who multi-tasked as the receptionist, clerk and janitor. She knew not the individuals behind the company, who could not be traced.

Two months later, Zack had come to terms with the loss of his marble and decided to come to his senses. A friend of his gave him inspiration for an even more striking façade – volcanic rock-hardened magma instead of marble slabs. A few phone calls and faxes, and he had placed orders for magma slabs to be shipped from Java. The supplier arranged with a logistics company to have the magma slabs loaded onto a ship named MV Phoenix.

With mounting excitement, Zack received news that MV Phoenix had arrived in Singapore and was waiting for her berth at Jurong Port for discharge. With mounting incredulity, he received further news that MV Phoenix had been arrested and cargo operations were suspended.

It transpired that MV Phoenix was in fact MV Buta in a new guise. The rogues who owned and controlled MV Buta had her repainted, renamed and equipped with a set of false papers. Due to the persistent efforts of FCU and IMB, the phantom ship had been found. FCU alerted the Court, MPA and the Sheriff.

Zack went to his lawyer again. With a few more months of experience in her, Nadia was a more confident lawyer this time.

Zack: Please, can I speak to your boss, please?

Nadia: Certainly, Mr Zack. Mr Ashiq will be back in town next week. Meanwhile, I am pleased to answer all your questions.

Zack: I have a new cargo, of magma, that is now on a ship that has been arrested in Singapore. Can I have my cargo discharged?

Nadia: That depends.

Zack: Sigh! Okay, here are the facts [gives background].

Nadia: Oh, seems like my friend is acting for the party who arrested the ship. I will give him a call.

Nadia called Jerome. Jerome spoke to his boss, but disclosed his conflict of interest. That is, he disclosed that he was interested in Nadia but often had conflicts with her. The boss said he was not interested in Jerome's love life but there was no problem with the cargo being discharged while the ship was under arrest. Jerome returned Nadia's call with the good news. FCU had no objection to the arrested ship discharging her cargo, as there was no claim on the cargo. However, there must be sufficient insurance in place to cover the ship against damage and claims for the operation. The Sheriff gave his permission for discharge on these terms.

And that was how Nadia finally helped Zack to collect his magma slabs from the ship. They are now mounted on the walls of his hotel lobby, where their unusual texture draws admiring attention from guests.

Nadia in turn has started writing her memoirs, starting with the following chart:

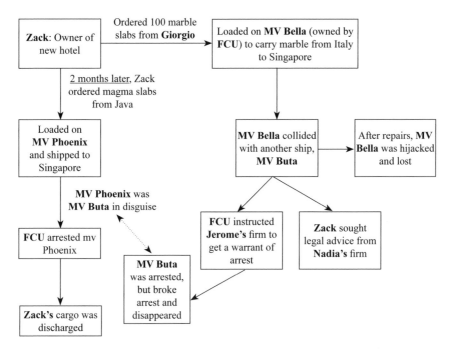

Shipping lawyers are embedded in the transport infrastructure. Their expertise is sought after by merchants, freight forwarders, shipowners, charterers and insurers. People who pray for fair winds and kind seas, but also believe in a little extra secular protection in the form of good legal advice and representation. While the episode above was rather dramatic, shipping practitioners do commonly grapple with cross-boundary problems that straddle the areas of contract law, sales law, tort law, conflicts of law and procedure on short notice. Many principles of contract law and conflict of laws, for instance, were developed in shipping cases. Research and constant updates on the law are an indispensable aspect of a shipping lawyer's practice. Legal knowledge by itself, however, may not solve every problem and lawyers can sometimes serve their clients well by offering practical and commercial solutions.

CHAPTER 9

FAMILY – MAKE IT OR BREAK IT

Alfred Dodwell

Alfred Dodwell studied law at the University of Warwick and theology at Regent College. He practices at Dodwell & Co where he specialises in family law.

'I love your tattoo', I said to my fellow traveller, Alexandre. He was from Brazil and on a tour with me in Lucerne, Switzerland.

The tattoo read 'Valentina'.

Who was Valentina? I was almost too afraid to ask. He was travelling alone. I feared he was going to tell me it was his ex-wife or ex-girlfriend. Many tattoos have been done in a love stupor only to end up in a life-time of regret. He beamed as he told me 'It's my daughter's name, I am going home to see my family tomorrow.' That was a relief. He was on a business trip, having worked out of China for some time. He went on to share with me about his lovely family.

I love family, and have a tattoo of my family name in Thai. But I grew up in a conservative Christian family where tattoos were taboo. 'It is evil', my mother said. She was a no-nonsense homemaker. My dad had lashed out at my brother over his minute butterfly tattoo. I knew that tattoos were frowned upon by my parents. So I had mine done only recently, during a family holiday in Thailand.

We are all part of a family, either literally or metaphorically. We refer to close friends as 'bro' or say that they are 'like family to me'. Family signifies a bond, a closeness that is unsurpassed by any other relationship.

Man meets woman. They fall in love. They marry. They go on honeymoon. Nine months or so later, they have a child. This is the typical portrayal of a family nucleus. It is all beautiful, save that we do not live in a perfect world.

Man sees another woman. He falls in lust for her. He has an affair. The wife is innocently browsing through the family computer, missing her husband who is away on a business trip. She stumbles across his MSN chat history and she reads on to find that her Romeo has another Juliet. All hell breaks loose. What he told her was late night work on the computer has actually been late night e-thrill rides. He has not penned one love letter since they got married but has written words of affection in poetry to his mistress and had described their planned tryst during the trip.

The wronged wife picks up the phone, wondering 'Romeo wherefore art thou?' He was panting as he answers the phone and she harangues him with expletives which on film would have attracted an RA (Restricted) rating. His game is up.

Her next call is to her mother. She cries to her. Her mother calls her elder sister. Her elder sister calls her. She puts her mother-in-law on call-waiting to talk to her elder sister. Her mother-in-law calls her husband and sighs louder than the last train that pulled out of Tanjong Pagar.

She talks to her elder sister, a savvy banker, who tells her clinically, 'Not to worry, I have a friend who is a matrimonial lawyer. He did a fine job for one of my friends and he will give your husband hell for this. I will make the appointment.'

My phone then rings. It is a Friday afternoon. I had just put my phone down after making reservations for a nice dinner date with my wife. We also had plans to take the children to the zoo on Saturday. This was before the advent of Universal Studios when most parents became 'friends of the zoo' in order to make repeated visits more economical. Being the typical Singaporean, I sought to use it 'to the max'. My banker friend tells me about her sister's woes. I listen. I asked that her sister meet me with her marriage certificate and a print-out of the relevant MSN chat history. Her sister was also advised to look for other tell-tale signs of the husband's affair. Interestingly, many men who have affairs tend to be sloppy and leave evidence of them.

She tells me her sister is distraught. She is only 25 and her husband is 32 turning 33 the following week. I suppose he wanted his cake earlier than the wife had planned. She married young. She was in love and met him during her internship at an advertising firm. Young love is nice and explosive. It is always nice to fall in love, but explosive because the young tend not to do the relevant background checks about the person they are so in love with.

I agreed to meet her at 8am on Saturday morning. I wanted to get this meeting out of the way so that it did not burn too much of my weekend, and perhaps could still make it for the 11.30am 'Elephants at Play' show.

Come Saturday morning, my phone rings. 'We are right outside your office'.

I usher them into our meeting room. My experience in matrimonial practice told me that I had to bring along a box of tissue. She was all red-eyed even as I sat down to talk to her. She came along with her mother and elder sister. The mother was holding her. I knew this was going to be a long meeting. The elephants would just have to wait. I begin with the usual introductory words explaining to her about the sacrosanct rule of solicitor-client communication privilege. This encourages the client to speak candidly to the solicitor as the solicitor cannot be compelled to divulge the communication against her will. I also informed her that she has the power to decide who she wants to bring into meetings, as I have to ask her some hard and personal questions, ranging from vivid details of the marriage to their finances.

My new client begins and sobs throughout the session. I scribble down notes. She is comforted by her mother with calming words but injected with venom by her sister. I could tell that her mother preferred forgiveness, healing and reconciliation, whereas my friend, her sister, was hissing at the adulterous husband. I surmised that she never liked her brother-in-law. The aggrieved wife says she had called to confront him. He said he would return and explain, put down the phone and turned it off. He has since been incommunicado but is due back on Monday.

'What should I do?' she asks.

Inevitably, a matrimonial lawyer becomes a counsellor, the confidante, and in some cases, even a friend. As clients come to us, be they men or women, going through the throes of matrimonial woes, we connect and feel for them. They are often down and depressed. Some are distraught and lost. Bitterness, frustration and many other emotions are on display. It is not easy being a matrimonial lawyer, for unlike most other areas of practice, we see the deepest wounds and the trauma of betrayal by the one that they loved. Matrimonial lawyers have to help a client pick up the pieces of shattered dreams and a shipwrecked marriage. It is not easy. Why did I venture into matrimonial law practice in the first place?

This brings me back to the days I first started practice. I was in a medium-sized firm. I actually had better paying job offers but had heard many good things about this firm. My bosses were known as true gentlemen and I learnt much from them. I chose wisely. I learnt that whilst we ought to fight hard for our client and never cease to act in our client's best interest, it is also crucial to maintain decorum and respect at the bar, and to resist the mindset that the opposing counsel is always the enemy.

I started off practice with much passion and lived by the motto 'I shall ask no favours and I shall give none'. So I met every deadline and would not entertain any request for an extension of time from opposing counsel. But one of my bosses, a senior practitioner, told me that whilst he was impressed by my passion and hard work, I would make many enemies. He said, 'We do not have to win every battle, but we must win the war'. Senior lawyers have much good advice. This is the very reason we all go through a period as a practice trainee (in my day it was called 'pupillage') and I was fortunate to have two pupil-masters, both of whom became Senior Counsel. One was tough and difficult, but he wanted me to learn that there is no easy ride in the profession – it is hard work, research and dedication that will prevail. I did not appreciate his hard methods then, but I certainly learnt. My other pupil-master (I had the honour of being his first pupil) was a really focused, organised and methodological person. He would always be teaching me when I assisted him at trials. He would take me out for lunch and share with me his strategies and reasons for certain questions asked during the trial.

So I was an infant lawyer in a firm which had a reputation for matrimonial lawyering. I learnt to meet clients, take down meticulous notes, gather relevant evidence from documents that clients gave us, and draft various legal documents such as Deeds of Separation and the divorce papers to be filed in court.

Like many young lawyers, I had grand visions of lawyering in court rooms, but I learnt that lawyering is more about painstaking hours of preparation, studying the case, understanding the client, researching the law, preparing written submissions and presenting them at the hearing.

One day, I was told that we had a new client and I was to meet her with one of my senior associates, two years my senior at the bar. She was very personable and helpful towards new lawyers in the firm. We sat down to meet the client.

'I almost killed my husband last night', the client blurted out.

The friendly banter we had prior to entering the room came to a halt. We asked her to explain.

She set out her tale. Coming from Kampar, Perak, West Malaysia to Singapore, she soon fell in love with the man she eventually married. He was a business man, but his business failed and he started to drive a taxi for a living. He drowned his sorrows in liquor. She was the subservient homemaker, running the house without a maid. She cooked, cleaned, mopped, washed and ironed. She took care of the three children, ensuring that they got to school promptly, finished their homework and were in bed on time. She was normally exhausted when she went to bed.

He would return home from work in the early hours of the morning, wake her up and demand intimacy with her. His sexual appetite was such that he wanted to also have anal sex against her will. He would hit her when she protested and then had his way with her. It was clearly not a marriage but a prison.

We wondered why she tolerated this for so long.

Her husband was the one who brought the money home as her children were still growing up – so she tolerated the abuse for many years. Now that her elder daughter and son were in the university, and the younger boy was in a polytechnic, she did not have to take it anymore. She came from a conservative Chinese family and she was too embarrassed to tell them about her ordeal.

I was stunned. I had come from a happy family background – my mother was strict but bags of fun and we had a happy home. My dad was the regimented civil servant, dedicated to his work. We had much fun on family holidays visiting my mother's siblings in Kuala Lumpur or Penang. I grew up in a housing estate populated by civil servants. I grew up with children of civil servants and teachers, and we all had similar experiences with responsible parents.

The client told us she held a knife over her husband as he slept on the sofa. She had just endured another brutal session with him. She said she almost stabbed him.

My senior looked as stunned as I was. We excused ourselves from the room, came out and wondered what hit us. I was too junior to know what to do. We went with this story to our boss. He was calm. He said, 'Alright, I will see her now'. We followed him back to the meeting room. I was excited as I was wondering how he was going to advise the client. He walked in and soon he was advising her that it was not safe for her to remain in her home, that she should move out and thereafter claim maintenance from him. He outlined for her a plan of action that was clearly what she needed to hear.

Oftentimes, clients come to matrimonial lawyers and they are at a loss. They would have been speaking to family or friends and would have been given advice on what to do. Whilst there might be some good advice, it is sometimes drowned in a symphony of bad advice because the client had spoken to too many people who have not been trained to deal with such situations. A classic case of 'the blind leading the blind' ensures.

Coming back to my earlier client whose husband is away in Bangkok with his lover, she is seated in front of me with her mother and elder sister early this Saturday morning. She told me she was 25 years old and works as a clerical staff in a small business. The boss whom she calls 'Uncle Sam' had learnt about her marital problems and offered to pay her legal costs. He just wanted her to get her divorce and be freed from her 'cheating, lying husband'.

So here I was, taking down her detailed statement as she relays to me the story. From the time she first met her husband, to their courtship, wedding, marriage and now the sudden discovery of infidelity.

I notice a bump in her belly. She appears expectant. She was four months pregnant. The baby was due in November. 'My son was born in November too', I said. Sometimes a human touch helps. I thought I needed to let her know that I may be a lawyer, but I have a family too – a wife and two children. It helps to be married. I know the highs and lows of marriage life.

There is no guide book for lawyers that tells us what advice to give at which stage and this is where a lawyer must make a judgment call. Whilst we always encourage parties to try counselling, in most cases, the client has spent many agonising months thinking things through before he or she graces the lawyer's office. As such, divorce is inevitable. In some cases, divorce is the best remedy, especially where there has been abuse or infidelity, or a fundamental breach of the sanctity of all marriages – the lack of respect for one another

I think Justice Judith Prakash describes the practice of family law best when she said, 'The practice of family law is one of the most challenging areas that a lawyer can engage in. This is because the job demands far more than knowledge of legal principles. Family lawyers must be skilled negotiators, competent litigators and compassionate counsellors. They also need to have a great deal of emotional maturity in order to deal with the distress most clients experience while using the legal process to resolve domestic problems'.

I have done some pre-marital counselling and much post-marital counselling. I think marriage counselling comes naturally to matrimonial lawyers as they have encountered so many marriages over the years that they know what the critical signs and pitfalls are, and also what it takes to make a marriage work.

So, as matrimonial lawyers, we have to make a judgment call as to whether there is an irretrievable breakdown of a marriage, established by adultery, unreasonable behavior, desertion or separation. If there is evidence to substantiate any of these, we can confidently proceed to file the divorce papers in court.

Divorce proceedings are a two-stage process. There is the divorce itself, and then the ancillary proceedings which deal with custody of the children, maintenance of the wife and children and the division of matrimonial assets.

In Singapore, there are approximately 24,000 marriages and 7,000 divorces a year. Muslim marriages have their own regime administered by the Syariah courts. All other divorces are dealt with by the Family Courts. Many couples spend a lot of money getting married. It is after all a significant occasion. However, a divorce also costs money and it often costs more than the wedding.

The Family Court performs a herculean task trying to deal with the many divorces and matrimonial issues that come its way. I suppose the best analogy is that which Newman, a character in the sit-com '*Seinfeld*', said about working in the post office — 'The mail never stops'. This is also true for cases being filed in the Family Court.

This brings me to an interesting case where I appeared before a very senior District Judge, known for her wit and intellect. I had to mention two cases before her. In one I was acting for the husband who was in arrears in his maintenance obligations. In the other I was acting for the wife who was claiming maintenance. I persuaded the judge to give an extension of time for the husband-client to pay. Immediately after that, I mentioned the next case for my wife-client and I sought to counter every argument the husband made in seeking an extension of time to pay his maintenance arrears. She looked at me. She smiled. I knew she had caught on. I smiled and told her, 'Your Honour, I am just doing my job'.

This is the job of a matrimonial lawyer. We act for the husband. We act for the wife. We take instructions from client. We act in their best interest and we put forward their case.

A solicitor does not make up stories for the client but must be a good story-teller as we translate the client's story through statements tendered in court. If the client is the 'cheating, lying adulterer', the lawyer must seek to settle the case for the client especially if the marriage has broken down irretrievably; there is no reason to litigate on a lost cause. However, the court does take into account all circumstance that are relevant as it adjudicates on matters. So, for instance, if the adultery takes place in the context where the wife has refused the husband sexual intimacy for many years, it would be wholly unfair to restrict the husband to the same monastic lifestyle.

My young client with her mother and elder sister gave me a tear-jerker of a story of being courted at her workplace when she was young and innocent. She was a very attractive lady, big eyed, fair and very feminine. She showed me some photographs of her husband who was not a very attractive man, but who was quite the smooth-talker, as evidenced from his flowery language in MSN chat records. She also had photographs of the husband's girlfriend who looked quite plain but who knew how to apply sufficient make-up to give the illusion of beauty — she was clearly not in the same league as my client. I told my client so

73

and this cheered her up. It is important for a lawyer to be personable, approachable, friendly and understanding. We filed for divorce. The husband tried to give the excuse that he was on a business trip with a colleague, but he conceded when we showed him the evidence, which included an erotic love note he had penned to his mistress that my client found in the house. The divorce was not contested. Many divorces in Singapore are uncontested for usually the death of the marriage is a foregone conclusion, and the funeral is the uncontested divorce hearing.

Then came the ancillary proceedings. He did not want to provide maintenance for my client and offered a pittance for the child. The court decided that he should give her a $15,000 lump sum maintenance and pay for the infant's maintenance based on a table of estimated expenses provided to court. The parties were given joint custody with care and control to my client and supervised access to the father.

He wanted the HDB flat to be wholly transferred to him on condition that he will repay her CPF with interest. The court ordered the flat to be sold in the open market and gave her 35% share of the sale proceeds, based predominantly on her indirect contributions over a short marriage. He was also ordered to pay the cost of the divorce proceedings, fixed at $5,500.00, and cost of the ancillary proceedings, fixed at $4,500.00.

She was happy with the result. He was not. He appealed. He lost. My client has since remarried a Swede and relocated to Sweden. Her ex-husband objected to the move, so we obtained a court order sanctioning the move, with reasonable access terms for the father to visit the child in Sweden, and to also bring the child back to Singapore when the child was older. As long as divorcing couples have children, they inevitably have to interact — so it is always good to encourage the client to get over the bitterness of the divorce and to deal with the other parent with civility for the sake of the child. In fact, the Family Court encourages joint parenting to recognise the importance of both parents' involvement in the children's lives. But sadly the children of the failed marriage are often the victims – being forced to take sides, deprived of access to the other parent and the subject matter of pride-driven custody battles that are not about who is the better parent to provide care and control.

Some matrimonial battles in Singapore are fought out through appeals from the Family Court to the High Court and to the Court of Appeal. Needless to say, the media is also interested in celebrity divorces — Tiger Woods', Arnold Schwarzenegger's, and closer to home, radio disc jockey Glenn Ong's second marriage to Jamie Yeo. It is most interesting to note that the Huffington Post, an internet newspaper-blogsite, has a whole section devoted to monitoring celebrity divorces. This is the reality of the world we live in, where marriages and divorces are a part of our society. But a person can remarry and have a new lease of married life, albeit a little smarter from the experience.

My client has since added me to her Facebook account and I keep track of her happy life in Sweden. I have seen the child grow up, celebrating many happy birthdays. I even saw a recent photograph of the father visiting in Sweden and they all posed together for a photograph. It was evident from the smile that the wounds of the past had healed and they are working together for the sake of the child. I suppose that is the job satisfaction for a matrimonial lawyer — to help a client through a bitter divorce and ancillary battles and then see the parties heal, pick up the pieces of their life and go on to lead a happy life.

So this is the practice of a matrimonial lawyer. We handle many cases simultaneously. I have come to realise that marriage can be pure bliss or pure hell. It is up to the parties to determine this, but divorces are a reality. We, matrimonial lawyers meet many people and we always trust that we are all doing our part as a lawyer to ensure that the divorce and ancillaries are dealt with in the best interest of our respective clients and in the hope that eventually they will heal from the wounds of their broken marriages recover and move on to a better life.

As one case closes another one begins. I get another late night call, 'I think the child is not mine, I was tricked into marrying her'. I sigh and say, 'Okay, let's meet, and if you have any evidence or witnesses, please bring them along. We shall get to the bottom of this.'

Next stop, paternity test…

CHAPTER 10

ADR AND MEDIATION – THE FUTURE OF LEGAL PRACTICE

Joel Lee

The author has been teaching at the Faculty of Law, National University of Singapore ('NUS') since 1993. He specialises in teaching law students to resolve disputes amicably through negotiation and mediation as a first resort. He has played a pivotal role in the development of mediation in Singapore and has trained many mediators in the Singapore Mediation Centre. He has most recently been responsible for designing a module in Amicable Dispute Resolution for the qualifying bar course run by the Singapore Institute of Legal Education. Joel was a recent recipient of NUS' Outstanding Educator Award which is the highest teaching award in the university.

1.   Prologue

It is one of the functions of a legal system to resolve disputes between parties. As a result of a healthy diet of Hollywood movies, we often see this resolution in the form of a fever-pitched court litigation where two lawyers; hired gladiators armed with law and wit as their weapons, battle it out with clever arguments that outmanoeuvre both the witnesses and the other lawyer. At the end, amidst rousing music in the background, one side emerges triumphant!

As with most movies, life is usually not this glamorous. The outcome of litigation is often not clear, subject to the uncertainties of evidence and vagaries of the law. Even when one party 'wins', they will have legal and court fees to pay (it is a myth that the losing party pays for everything). Sometimes, the winning party may be faced with a 'paper judgment' but is unable to enforce it as the other party may have no money or cannot be located. There are also intangible costs. Litigation is a process that is time-consuming and places both parties and lawyers under tremendous stress. It is common for one to fall ill during and after trial. One does not live happily ever after. Reality bites.

It was an increasing dissatisfaction with litigation as a dispute resolution process that the ADR movement was born in the 1970s.

2. ADR 1.0 – Alternative Dispute Resolution

ADR stands for 'Alternative Dispute Resolution'. It represented a search by judges, lawyers and parties to find processes of dispute resolution that were alternative to litigation. The common forms of ADR 1.0 are arbitration, negotiation and mediation.

Arbitration

Arbitration is a dispute resolution process where parties appoint an arbitrator who will listen to the matter and make an award. An award is similar to a court judgment and parties have to comply with the terms of the award. A key similarity between litigation and arbitration is that the method of resolving the dispute is via adjudication and the arbitrator essentially decides who wins, based on the law. As there is a separate chapter on arbitration, we will not look into this any further. It suffices to note that arbitration was a favoured alternative to litigation as its proceedings were confidential (unlike court hearings which were largely open to the public) and, during that time, was cheaper and faster than litigation.

Negotiation

Negotiation is a process that is engaged by lawyers to structure agreements and deals for their clients. It is also commonly used as a dispute resolution process under the ADR rubric. In fact, it is a misnomer to say that negotiation is an ADR process as more cases are resolved through negotiation than by litigation. This is referred to as the '11th Hour Settlement' where lawyers decide to settle just before trial. However, from an ADR perspective, there is far more value for lawyers and parties to attempt to negotiate even before the matter is escalated to the courts as this will result in savings of time and money. When done well, negotiation can also result in an outcome that is beneficial to both parties without resorting to their strict legal rights. This is sometimes referred to as a 'win-win' outcome.

To illustrate, consider this situation: Beng has borrowed $5,000 from his friend Huat and has promised to repay it in three months. Three months pass, Huat has not received payment and consults a lawyer. The lawyer can advise Huat to proceed in a number of possible ways.

The first is to sue Beng. While a legally correct way to proceed, it may not be a practical solution for Huat as the cost of suing Beng is more than the amount owed. If Beng is unable to pay the full amount because of tight financial circumstances, then obtaining a judgment may still yield very little and in some case, nothing. In addition, this course of action may irreparably damage Beng and Huat's friendship.

The second option is for Huat to do nothing. This has no benefit to Huat and there will certainly be some damage to Beng and Huat's friendship.

The third option is for Huat to negotiate with Beng. Since Beng is unable to pay the full amount, one negotiated settlement might be for Beng to pay a lesser amount now and the rest in installments over time. If Huat is not in a hurry to get this money, this option will allow Huat to get his money and preserve the friendship.

In many situations, it is important to acknowledge that resorting to one's legal rights may not necessarily result in a practical and sustainable solution for the parties.

Mediation

Mediation is the final ADR process. It is sometimes referred to as 'assisted negotiation' where a neutral third-party, the mediator, helps the parties resolve their dispute. While this assistance can take many forms, unlike litigation or arbitration, the mediator does not have the power to impose an outcome on the parties. At the end of the day parties must agree to the outcome that results from the mediation. Once they have agreed, the agreement is binding.

How then is mediation different from negotiation? At one level, it is not that different. Parties essentially engage in confidential negotiations and have to come to a binding agreement that can be a win for both parties. However, negotiations can break down. What a mediator does is to guide parties through the mediation process (designed to foster agreement), facilitate effective communication and provide a neutral perspective. This is often enough for parties to see through their negotiating impasse, explore possible agreements and agree in 75% of cases referred to mediation worldwide.

Mediation formally became part of the Singapore legal system in the mid-90s with the establishment of the Primary Dispute Resolution Centre (in the Subordinate Courts), the Community Mediation Centre and the Singapore Mediation Centre.

Mediation has the advantage of being a process that is fast, cheap and confidential. It is also conducive to preserving and strengthening relationships between the parties and helping them achieve closure. These advantages are largely not obtainable via litigation or arbitration.

By way of illustration, in a medical negligence case where the children of a deceased patient sued a hospital for negligence, many lawyers might think that this is a typical case that belongs in court. If it did go to court, there would be a long involved trial where expert medical evidence would have to be heard to determine whether medical negligence had occurred. If it did, the court would then order the hospital to pay damages or in lay terms, money.

The problem is that money is a poor substitute for what the children may actually want. Even if they win and feel vindicated, money may not help them achieve closure. At mediation, it may turn out that they sued the hospital because they were feeling guilty about being unable to do anything for their parent. They may not understand how the death occurred and feel that the hospital, the doctor and the staff were being unsympathetic. Above all, they may want to ensure that this does not happen to other families in future. These are all concerns that could not be addressed at trial. The role of the court is to determine liability according to the law.

It would likely take a maximum of two days at mediation to resolve the matter. In a case in similar circumstances, the matter was resolved at mediation with no money being paid and an apology given. The apology did not mean the hospital was at fault but gave the children understanding and closure. While rarely this dramatic, this is a prime example of how mediation can achieve what the courts cannot.

Although mediation has become an undeniable part of the legal landscape, many lawyers are still resistant to the idea of mediation for two main reasons. First, the nature of classic legal education is fundamentally opposed to mediation. Law school teaches us to think in terms of rights and liabilities. In the eyes of the law, there is a winner and a loser and this is determined by an adversarial process in the courts. Put simply, lawyers are trained to fight and think in terms of a win-lose paradigm. To their minds, 'real lawyers' do not engage in mediation because being willing to seek out a cooperative solution must mean that one is not confident of winning in court.

This win-lose mindset is exacerbated because many lawyers in practice today are unfamiliar with the process of mediation and have misconceptions about mediation such as 'mediation is not binding' and 'you only mediate if you can't win in court'. In fairness, many senior lawyers have not had the opportunity to study mediation in law school. Even when they do engage in mediation, because they are unfamiliar with the process, it is natural for them to approach it with the adversarial mindset that they have been trained in and excel at. This impedes the mediation process and hurts the clients' interests.

It is said that to change the culture of legal practice, education is the answer. The Faculty of Law at the National University of Singapore began mediation workshops in 1996 and law students have since had the opportunity to learn mediation. These opportunities are also available at the Faculty of Law at the Singapore Management University. Unfortunately, the numbers that are reached are small and when these younger lawyers go out into practice, they will encounter the biases and misconceptions of their seniors. As a matter of survival, they will often fall into pace with their seniors thereby perpetuating the adversarial paradigm.

The second main reason is a financially practical one. Lawyers often bemoan that mediation takes money away from them. As a dispute resolution process, mediation is faster and cheaper than litigation or arbitration. This means that the amount of time a lawyer spends on a case that is resolved by mediation is far less and consequently can only charge a significantly lesser amount for it.

I have experienced firsthand a senior lawyer's ire who, when he found out that I taught mediation, lost his temper and accused me of 'undermining the legal system' and 'breaking his rice bowl'.

While his reaction was understandable, this attitude misses two key points. First, clearing appropriate cases through mediation will free time up. This time can then be used to take on new cases, some of which may be appropriate for litigation. While a lawyer will earn less from any case that goes to mediation, it may not be correct to say that their overall earnings will drop. Secondly, lawyers are expected to act in the best interests of the client. Litigation may not always be in the best interests of the client. Often, it is not. Choosing a certain course of action simply because it is financially more advantageous to the lawyer is simply not ethical.

2. ADR 2.0 – Appropriate Dispute Resolution

It bears repeating: We, as lawyers, must act in the best interests of the client. This realisation is key. And just as it is absurd to say that litigation is *always* in the best interests of the client, it is similarly absurd to suggest the same for mediation.

The focus on the best interests of the client has seen a shift in thinking about what the acronym ADR stands for. ADR 1.0 viewed arbitration, negotiation and mediation as *alternative* dispute resolution processes.

At that time, this was correct. These processes were indeed alternatives to litigation.

However, at this point of the ADR movement's development, the word 'alternative' is no longer accurate. Arbitration has become so firmly a part of legal practice that it cannot properly be called 'alternative'. It is now a mainstream dispute resolution process that can sometimes take as long as court trials and cost more. Interestingly, lawyers took to arbitration far more easily than mediation because arbitration shares the same 'win-lose' paradigm as litigation. Cynically speaking, it probably didn't hurt that lawyers can charge quite a fair bit for acting in an arbitration.

The word 'alternative' also connotes a sense of being second-class; not being as good as the main form. There has been a call to re-label ADR as '*Appropriate* Dispute Resolution'.

This reflects the reality that there are many ways to deal with a client's problem and the lawyer needs to gather information from and explore with the client the various avenues available before deciding on the appropriate method for resolving the client's problem. It may well be that in one case, the *appropriate* method is litigation; in another mediation, etc.

This search for the appropriate dispute resolution process in every case helps the lawyer keep an open mind to all the possibilities that are available. More importantly, what is 'appropriate' is referenced to the client's needs and means. That way, the best interests of the client are served.

The legal system has supported the move to thinking about appropriate dispute resolution in three ways. First, the highest court in Singapore, the Court of Appeal, has made pronouncements that it is the duty of a lawyer to provide enough information to the client so that he/ she can make an informed decision about the course of action to take. This includes taking the client through a consideration of the costs involved with each option and the likely benefits associated with each option. Failure to do so would be a breach of the professional conduct rules by which all lawyers are bound.

Secondly, the Subordinate Courts now require lawyers to complete and submit an ADR Form indicating whether their case is appropriate for ADR and whether they are willing to consider ADR. The court can then use the information in this form to recommend the most appropriate form of dispute resolution to the parties.

Thirdly, the High Court can exercise its discretion to award the costs (of court proceedings) by taking into account the parties' conduct in attempting to resolve their dispute by mediation.

These developments will make lawyers more aware of and sensitive to the need to consider appropriate forms of dispute resolution for their clients. While legal education will still primarily revolve around the win-lose paradigm, with courses in law school introducing ADR to all students at an early stage of their education, this is a clear step towards changing the culture of legal practice.

It is an exciting time for lawyers engaged in ADR. While change will not be immediate and it will be some time before lawyers still schooled in the old ways of thinking are persuaded, there is tremendous potential for lawyers to carve out a practice in mediation. They can do this by becoming either a mediator or more likely, a mediation advocate.

The latter is a much newer concept in Singapore and envisions the lawyer playing the role of helping their clients select an appropriate form of resolution for their dispute, as well as helping their clients prepare for mediation and in some cases representing or assisting them in mediation.

At this nascent stage, there is a great deal of uncertainty moving forward. Lawyers sympathetic to ADR will still need to develop ways of deciding which form of dispute resolution is suitable for their client's case. As it is clear that going into mediation with an adversarial mindset will impede the process, lawyers will also have to define and refine their mindset and role when representing or assisting their client in mediation.

While guidance can be drawn from countries where the practice of mediation advocacy is more developed, lawyers in Singapore must ultimately choose their own path, taking into account the, sometimes unique, characteristics of legal practice here.

Looking on the bright side, the uncertain challenges facing the legal profession are also its exciting possibilities. First, it is not often that a lawyer gets to write his or her own job description in a field of practice. By taking an active role, the legal profession can and will affect how law will be practiced. Secondly, lawyers often bemoan that legal practice is infested with sharks. This in part stems from the adversarial mindset. Sadly, those who are not inclined to be sharks may sometimes have to behave that way simply to protect themselves and their clients. Making mediation and mediation advocacy a real part of legal practice may see lawyers who are more comfortable with non-adversarial means of lawyering being able to act in the best interests of the client and live with themselves.

3. Looking to the Future: ADR 3.0 – Amicable Dispute Resolution?

It is impossible to predict the future. We cannot know if Appropriate Dispute Resolution ('ADR 2.0') will flourish in Singapore or if lawyers will carve out a legal practice area of mediation and mediation advocacy. If the experience of common law countries like the USA, UK and Australia are concerned, ADR 2.0 has a bright future. The choice is in our hands.

By looking at present developments in those countries, it is also possible to get a glimpse of the future. While it is ideal to say that a lawyer must consider the entire range of dispute resolution processes in order to select the most appropriate one for their client, some lawyers engaged in ADR found it difficult to consider litigation, arbitration, mediation and negotiation in the same breath. It is almost as if litigation and arbitration on the one hand are so paradigmatically different from mediation and negotiation on the other hand that one would have to figuratively be in two minds.

Some lawyers have overcome this 'schizophrenia' by taking the view that it is always in the best interests of the client to avoid adversarial proceedings (where possible) and to commit to resolving their differences collaboratively. These lawyers limit their practice to ADR 3.0 – *Amicable* Dispute Resolution. In every case, they will attempt negotiation and mediation first to resolve their client's matter. If these do not succeed and it becomes clear that more adversarial methods of dispute resolution have to be engaged in, they will then refer those clients on to other lawyers who have as their expertise arbitration and litigation.

While this may seem utopian, this may well be a realistic adaptation to legal practice in an increasingly complex world. Stated simply, it is not satisfactory to be a jack-of-all-trades and no longer possible to be a master of everything. Specialising in this way allows lawyers to cleanly define the scope of their practice and congruently act in accordance with that definition. This can only benefit the clients.

4. Epilogue

I was recently asked why I chose teaching over a potentially lucrative legal practice. Apart from the fact that I like to teach, the truth is that in my chosen areas of specialisation, the only way to meaningfully affect the development of legal practice was to educate. And while it has taken more than a decade amidst sacrifice and occasionally derision, these efforts have begun to bear fruit. ADR is now part of the practice of law and many of those I have taught or trained are finding fulfillment and satisfaction in helping their clients resolve disputes amicably. If this has increased the sum total of good in the world, then it has been worth it.

CHAPTER 11

PRO BONO WORK – THE POIGNANCY AND POWER OF PRO BONO PRACTICE

Gregory Vijayendran

Gregory Vijayendran is passionate about pro bono practice. He is privileged to know and serve with many unsung heroes and heroines of the legal profession who selflessly and sacrificially serve Singapore society.

1. The Challenge

In law school, we study law (black letter and other chromatic variations) and become super-skilled in various subject areas. Aspiring masters and maestros of some of the most technically complicated areas of the law. Our legal education puts us in good stead as we prime for practice, whatever our chosen specialisation as a budding lawyer and future career aspirations may be. But it is not just the 'paper chase' that we pursue in halcyonic university days. It is also the ideas about, and ideals of, justice. The fight against tyranny or abuse of power. Of helping the man and woman in the street with rights wronged and wrongs to be righted. These ideas and ideals are not necessarily congruent with the glamourised images of lawyers that are hurled at us by television shows or cinematic productions although sometimes, there are exceptional exemplars. Gregory Peck's dramatic portrayal of Atticus Finch in the 1962 film adaptation of Harper Lee's *'To Kill a Mockingbird'*, whom the American Film Institute named in 2003 as the greatest movie hero of the 20th century (ahead of Indiana Jones and James Bond), comes to mind.

Often time though, all the ideals imbued in us in law school come crashing down or even stripped away, little by little, when we face the gritty realities of the practice of law. A practice that, in early years, is characterised by demands (from senior lawyers and clients), deadlines, turnaround time for research and drafting, billable hours, training, training and more training. In those early years, it is indeed about learning, learning and more learning even after the initial apprenticeship. And indeed, the education will be ongoing and continuous. What more could one expect from a profession where you are expected to be a life-long learner? And where, at every stage of the journey and even during the best of times, you know you have never really arrived. In those early years of practice, one of the greatest challenges apart from teething issues and the (oft-time, steep) learning curve is that it is so easy to lose your ideals in the way described (suddenly or gradually). It is an open secret that the legal profession generally pays well. Juniors today in large law firms start off earning approximately 2.5 times what their seniors earned when starting practice close to two decades ago. The lucrative compensation and lifestyle trappings have a seductive allure. And it could cost you your soul if you are not vigilant.

There must be more to the practice of law than this.

2. The Calling

A significant number of lawyers have found that the sacrosanct ideals forged in law school and sense of purpose and meaning in the profession become actualised when they learn to use what we have been blessed with – our legal skills – to give back to the community. The specific community I have in mind are the indigent (not the indignant, although sometimes, the indigent can be indignant too!). It is the man and woman in the street who cannot get access to justice. No other profession can provide legal counsel necessary to solve the law-related issues that the ordinary Singaporean man and woman face. It is a unique privilege that those of us who are in practice have. There are times that it may feel a chore or an additional burden to the myriads of other legal deadlines crying out for attention from our work desk. But the honest truth is that lawyers gain. With every consultation, every advice rendered, every opinion furnished, every client we meet, we gain. We gain new and rich insights into human nature, psychology, sociology and most of all, life. I know that I certainly gained so much with every pro bono assignment that I undertook.

Pro bono (shortened form of *pro bono publico* – Latin phrase meaning 'for the public good') comes in different forms of course. There are legal aid cases assigned by the State that we undertake as counsel. There are legal clinics where we volunteer. There are walk-in clients or matters undertaken pro bono based on an assessment of a number of circumstances. Let me share about legal clinics first.

3. The Clinics and Counsellors

One of the clinics I volunteer at is a unique community-based legal clinic. It is not one-dimensional (ie only purveying legal advice) but offers holistic counselling solutions. One of the dangers that lawyers (young and old) must avoid is in assuming that the law holds all the answers for a client's problem. We will have a blinkered view if we espouse such a perspective. Many times, especially for individual clients, a multidisciplinary approach could hold the key to a more impactful, more nuanced, more multifaceted and ultimately more enduring solution to the legal needs presented. In one example, at a community-based legal clinic, the presenting problem was legal but the deeper issue discerned by the counsellor present was depression. After five minutes, the lawyer stopped talking (a little hard to believe I know!) and the counsellor started counselling for depression. In another example where I was personally involved, a lady whose eyes were red when she walked into the clinic with a mournful expression on her face came to seek legal advice on probate and administration. Her face was etched with grief. The penny dropped minutes into the session. Her husband had passed away very recently. About 45 minutes into the session (after I had fielded a number of practical questions relating to estate matters), she broke down and wept. I stopped. The counsellor in attendance went around the table, hugged the lady and spoke words of comfort and encouragement. These two examples in the clinic setting highlighted to me why the law is not always a magic bullet. Of course, lawyers are essential. Without the legal advice, there would have been no practical legal solutions prescribed for the presenting issue. And so, the lawyers are necessary (even if this lawyer is attempting to rationalise the *raison d'être* for their value!). But by practising humbly as a team, together with other professionals, we can make a more meaningful difference and leave a lasting impact in the lives of hurting and needy individuals.

Just last week before completing this chapter, I attended a community legal clinic again as a volunteer lawyer. The final counsellee of the night was a lady who had been physically abused in the course of marriage and whose husband had divorced her. The matrimonial home had been sold by the husband. She had nowhere to stay – living an almost vagabond-like existence. She was depressed and suicidal. The team of counsellors and lawyers present worked with amazing compassion and teamwork. Helping her at her point of need, they were able to give much needed practical legal counsel and psychosocial counselling. Beyond the words spoken though, I think the lady heard two messages loudly and clearly: that Singaporeans care and that she is not alone.

The clinics are, often time, a first port-of-call. It is no substitute for legal advice. But those who have helped know that (in some small way) we play our part to improve the lot of the attendees by using the legal knowledge we had. This is a setting where the clock is not ticking for billing purposes and where (as patience-stretching as it can be at times), we help simplify and demystify the law for lay people. We then apply the same to solve bread and butter issues involving personal law matters touching on matrimonial, children, estate, employment, personal injury and immigration issues. The 'clients' are not often cut from the same cloth as the well-heeled, well-dressed clients we see in our day-to-day sophisticated legal practice, Instead, it shows you another side of life in Singapore – an underbelly that we do not often get to view. People that we do not often interact with in our lives and sometimes are cocooned from. But these are the men and women who often time need the most practical legal help. Access to justice is a key concern for them. Volunteer lawyers are uniquely placed to do our part to touch their world.

4.   The Confidence and Client Care Skills

There is another type of pro bono case. These are assigned cases or pro bono cases that are undertaken from 'cradle to grave' of a legal matter. At a young stage of your career, you need to build a huge corpus of expertise and experience. Yet, the landscape today (certainly, in the bigger firms) is that you may not get to do a trial or very many contested cases in your first few years of practice. There is a lot of assisting work (as the old name for Legal Associate, which was in vogue when I was a junior, Legal Assistant, connotes). However, through assigned cases or pro bono cases, you cut your teeth early and make the judgment calls on a case. As you take ownership of a matter and see it through to a logical conclusion whether at trial or by brokering a dispute settlement, you will have gained invaluable experience and confidence. Confidence begets more confidence. I have seen young lawyers bloom with incredible self-belief when they make judgment calls, build valuable client-care skills and are able to achieve the client's objective (of either litigation success or a satisfactory outcome). That is not to say that clients are guinea pigs for greenhorns to experiment on. There are always seniors to learn from and who could provide guidance on difficult, tricky and complicated aspects of a case. And a prudent, wise and sensible young lawyer will still go to his seniors for advice and guidance. Ultimately though, the young lawyer still makes the judgment calls about the steps going forward [in his or her own right].

A word or two about client care skills. There are all kinds of clients. The good, bad and ugly. And there are some who could be rambling and incoherent in a supreme test of patience (it may even feel more like long suffering rather than patience!). You will learn good communication skills: the ability to relate to various types of client from different backgrounds (eg nationality, ethnicity and culture-wise). In one state-assigned case that I undertook, I had to field call after call from the client long after the case was over. At times, I felt harangued and harassed. However I had discerned that there was a past trauma in the client's past (arising out of a previous criminal conviction) that he had experienced. While I could not do anything to heal his pain, I felt that I certainly need not aggravate it by being curt or brusque to him.

The gratification you get when you do pro bono work is more than any pay cheque can bring. These are often the intangible internal rewards including an intrinsic sense of satisfaction about practising law. In one unforgettable pro bono case for me, a foreign lady's daughter had been abducted during an access visit. Months later, the girl was finally returned from overseas through international police cooperation to her relieved mother in Singapore. The husband, who had 'kidnapped' the daughter, was eventually subjected to committal proceedings for disobeying the court order on the parameters of access or visitation rights granted to him. When the brief was over, she thanked me with tears in her eyes. I will never forget that scene for as long as I live. It was worth more than winning a multi-million dollar litigation or negotiating a fantastic settlement of a civil dispute. Her tears of gratitude were priceless. Despite the language barrier (she was more Mandarin-conversant); there was a quiet, palpable sense of satisfaction I felt at that moment in helping someone through one of the darkest periods of her life.

The duties owed to such clients are no less than that owed to a fee-paying client. You must still do your best even if it is for the least in society. Not just because of ethical duties undergirding the lawyer's relationship with his or her client but because the indigent have dignity too. Doing pro bono work is therefore not so much about doing charity but about respecting the dignity of the indigent in facilitating their access to justice.

5. The Charities

There are times when a charity needs charity! Even if you may not choose a litigation career and nothing in what I shared earlier about clinics and assigned cases resonate, there is definitely a place (and need) for corporate lawyers as well. One area of help is incorporating charities that are on start-up mode or troubleshooting issues they face. I have had the joy and privilege of seeing a few such charities born. The genesis was often time very simple: a conversation over coffee or an informal get-together. Sometimes, it even developed into a full-blown retainer for which our firm waived professional fees and only billed disbursements. Many charity leaders want to do good. The challenge is how to do good well. There is a dearth of volunteer lawyers who lend their time and talent to advise charities, non-profits and voluntary welfare organisations on legal governance. And so, across the charity sector, volunteer lawyers have contributed their expertise not just during the charity's birth but also as it grows after the infancy stage. When issues of charity governance need to be addressed. You will gain the fulfilment of being an architect of the legal infrastructure of the charity concerned so that charity managers and leaders can provide community service in ways that foster confidence among external stakeholders.

6. The Clarion Call

As I put the finishing touches to this chapter, my attention was drawn to the Singapore Law Gazette June 2011 edition where Senior Counsel Lok Vi Ming, the Vice President of the Law Society in his message entitled *'It Is All Worthwhile'* issued a clarion call for Law Society members to become pro bono volunteers. As part of his passionate and informative plea (reproduced with his kind permission), he shared about the Law Society's commitment to the same:

> The Law Society does offer an extensive suite of pro bono services, mainly through its Pro Bono Services Office ('PBS Office'), launched officially on 10 September 2007 to manage and administer all of the Law Society's pro bono objectives. The idea that led to the establishment of the PBS Office was the challenge to each member to donate 25 hours per year towards pro bono work. With a membership of about 3,800 members, the pro bono challenge of 25 hours per member will translate into a potential bank of almost 100,000 pro bono hours which can be invested for the good of the community. This is a considerable arsenal that can be deployed for community outreach in a variety of ways:
>
> - *Criminal Legal Aid Scheme ('CLAS')* which offers legal representation for accused persons regardless of nationality, who claim trial for certain criminal offences and who do not have the means to pay for a lawyer. Means testing applies.
>
> - *Community Legal Clinic ('CLC')* which offers free basis legal advice to Singaporeans/Permanent Residents who are facing a legal issue on personal matters and do not have access to legal advice or representation. The CLC operates four nights a week (Monday to Thursday) every week of the year.

- *Ad Hoc Pro Bono Referral Scheme ('APR')* which offers legal representation for persons who do not meet the criteria for existing legal aid schemes but nonetheless are in urgent need.

- *Community Organisation Legal Clinic* which offers free basis legal advice by a volunteer lawyer on operational issues for charities, voluntary welfare organisations and non-profit organisations.

- *Project Law Help Scheme* which assists charities, voluntary welfare organisations, non-profit organisations and social enterprises in Singapore by matching eligible organisations with a volunteer law practice to provide pro bono non-litigation commercial legal assistance.

- *Law Awareness* is a public education initiative to raise public awareness of the law via public education seminars and exhibitions and through the publication of educational information.

Reader, we badly *need* you. I mean that: we *badly* need you. The practice of pro bono needs champions, crusaders and comrades. There is much to do as the snapshot of different pro bono services outlined in this chapter would have hopefully informed you. And for those contemplating a career in the law, always preserve the law school ideals and carefully consider whether you too will be one of the champions, crusaders and comrades of pro bono. A quote featured on the web page of the National Federation of Paralegal Associations Pro Bono Web Page (at http://law. lexisnexis.com/communityportal/articles) sums up the heart of pro bono work well: *'To the world you may be one person, but to one person you may be the world.' (Anonymous)*. You can change the world – someone's world – one person at a time. That is the greatest power of pro bono.

CHAPTER 12

WORK-LIFE BALANCE IN PRACTICE – FACT OR FICTION?

Thio Ying Ying

Ying Ying has been a litigation lawyer since 1985. She is a founder partner of M/s Kelvin Chia Partnership and heads the litigation department. Ying Ying is an active trial advocate who has argued cases in the Court of Appeal. She has also represented clients in arbitration cases and in mediations. She is a member of the Marriage Central Advisory Committee and is a Board member of the Catholic Junior College Board and the Family Life Society of the Catholic Church. She is a mother of six children aged between 13 years and 23 years. Ying Ying has also been an active community volunteer for the past 30 years.

1. Introduction

A young lawyer rushed in just as we were about to execute an *Anton Pillar* Order ('APO'), which is a private law search order. He explained that he had to leave his expectant wife at the Accident and Emergency ('A & E') Department to represent the Defendant Company at the APO. I was immediately reminded of how, earlier that same morning, I had to tell my mother that I was unable to accompany her for her medical consultation for a condition which had concerned her. It struck me that the one thing I had in common with the opponent lawyer was that we had to choose between work and our loved ones that day.

We spent the next few days together at his clients' premises and in between tense discussions and involved negotiation, we managed to have some casual chat in between. When he learnt that I had six children aged between 13 years to 23 years, he kept asking me; 'How do you manage?', 'How did you cope when the kids were young?', 'How do you balance an active practice with your family's needs?'.

These are the same questions which I have been repeatedly asked by many people but which I have difficulty in providing an adequate answer to in one sitting. These questions reflect the deep concern that many people have about maintaining a balanced lifestyle.

I have often wondered how much I was prepared to sacrifice for work. In June 1995, one of my matters was fixed for trial at short notice when I was in the advanced stage of pregnancy. I was reluctant to leave my colleague to take over the conduct of the trial as I had been handling the matter from the beginning. I found myself having the conduct of a three-day trial just days before my daughter Michelle was due when my application to have the trial postponed until after my maternity leave (which would have been only one month later as I had to rely on my annual leave for my fifth child) was rejected. The District Judge was sympathetic and offered to adjourn the trial as soon as my labour pains started. I cross-examined the Plaintiff from my seat and the trial ended uneventfully. In fact, we succeeded when new evidence surfaced after the second day. I will always remember with amusement that the policeman who was on duty approached me as I rushed out of Court to review the evidence. He said 'Madam, can you slow down please? We do not want you to give birth now!' His earnest request was obviously prompted by his reluctance to have to attend to me. What surprised me was the level of commitment I had to my client's case and how disastrous it could have been.

'Work-life balance' is a term that first appeared in the late 1970s to describe the balance between an individual's work and personal life. In Singapore, a survey conducted from 1989 to 1990 on professionals (including lawyers) revealed that performance pressure and work-family conflicts have been identified as the main cause of work stress.

Most people know the dangers of having a high-stress career and a lifestyle imbalance. Yet, work-life balance remains elusive to many. The consequences of lifestyle imbalance range from 'burnout' and medical issues (mental and physical) to family/social issues in the long term.

With the increased pace of litigation over the years, there are unending challenges. I recall that when I started practice in 1985, the expected response time for correspondence was between three to seven days and there was more flexibility in the fixing of Court dates. With the changes to the Court's policy on fixing hearing dates, court schedules can be stressful especially when one needs to factor holidays and other family commitments or when trial/hearing dates are fixed 'back-back'. Whilst changes have been made to our work organisation and working styles to accommodate the increased pace of litigation practice, it remains a difficult challenge for women.

Today, more than ever before, we women grapple with how to be wife, mother, daughter, daughter in-law, homemaker and worker. We have to deal with guilt and frustration as we juggle the physical and emotional needs of young children as well as the demands of our profession, with the dissatisfied feeling that we have not performed the respective tasks as well as we would like to.

As a working wife and mother, time is the most precious commodity and from experience, the proper allocation of time requires planning, good relational skills and sacrifice. Despite planning and sacrifice, there will often be times that things do not work out as planned.

My husband and I celebrate our 24th wedding anniversary today on 1 May 2011. These 24 years have been the happiest years of my life and yet the most trying in having to balance work and family. My husband often reminds me, half in jest, that it was *my* idea to have six children and how that has caused us spend at least 5,000 nights (about 13 years) waking up to attend to crying kids. I worked full time but made it a point to break off from work at 6:30pm each day especially when the kids were young. My husband and I fed, played with and bathed the kids before putting them to bed. After the kids were asleep, I would put in a couple more hours of work before going to bed. It was a real challenge to appear in court to argue contentious applications/cases after a night of broken sleep. I realised only much later that all that 'stretching' helped me to build up a resilience and doggedness that helped me to handle the difficulties and uncertainties of litigation.

In a nutshell, my life for the past 24 years has been one of learning, through trial and error, to balance the multiple demands on me as wife, mother, daughter, partner/lawyer. I will say at the outset that I could not have made it without the support my husband and my family members.

I have had to learn to accept in humility that whilst I aim to be a good mother and a competent lawyer, I cannot be the perfect mum who attends to the kids' every need, who is present at every rugby/badminton game/concert and who attends every parent-teacher's meeting. But I have made it a point to be involved in their lives and in helping to nurture each of our six kids who are so different in their personality traits, areas of interest and dreams.

There is no set formula for work-life balance that would fit all. Each person has to work out his/her own set of priorities and to make time for work/ambition and family/personal and community needs. It would be over simplistic to think of work-life balance as a case of setting out equal time for work, family, personal and community needs and activities. One needs to have goals and to work towards those goals. The truth is that one does not always cope but, if after 20 to 30 years, the passion to practice law is still there and some of that passion and work ethic have been passed on to the kids, then you may start to think that you have done something right. I will share my own story which can be best described as a life-long quest for a balanced lifestyle. I hope that it will provide a few useful insights and pointers.

2. Work-life Balance – Expectations Set by Our Family of Origin

My mother was a school teacher for 30 years. Although my parents both worked, my mum remained responsible for the home and for the needs and education of children. My dad was not involved in the household chores or the care of children. Like most traditional men, he saw his role as that of the worker.

As a primary school teacher, my mum worked half a day which left her with time to attend to the household chores with the help of my grandmother and a maid, as well as the needs of the children. She made time for my father by going on their regular holiday trips, playing mahjong and going to the movies. I remember being very proud of my elegant mother who spoke with such ease and confidence. I would be so thrilled whenever she turned up in school to meet my teachers on the odd occasions and admired her ability to multi-task the demands of work and family, which included attending to the needs of an intellectually challenged son.

My parents' marriage retained the hallmarks of a traditional marriage as my mother took charge of the needs of the home and the children even though she worked. She managed only because she worked half the day and had long school holidays which were not broken by remedial classes or co-curricular activities. I always knew that I would be a working mother but I never figured out how we were going to manage as law was a significantly more demanding career.

My husband and I have a modern day marriage where both partners work and share responsibilities jointly. We have, what American sociologists and authors, Judith Wallerstein and Sandra Blakesee in *The Good Marriage: How and Why Love Lasts* (Warner Books, 1995), describes as a companionate marriage. They write that the companionate marriage has at its core, *equality, shared roles and mutual respect* in the husband wife relationship which arise from a re-definition of roles of the liberated women and their men. Companionate marriages are typically younger marriages which are reflective of the social changes of the last two decades. The major challenge for the spouses is to balance the emotional investment in the work place with their emotional attachment to their children. It takes no less than heroic efforts to make a companionate marriage work especially when the couple has no role model.

3. Work-life Balance – Start With A Goal

Our work experience, no matter how interesting or rewarding, is checkered by tiredness, disappointment and stress. The toil of work is something which I had to grapple with right from the start of legal practice. I was employed as a legal assistant to take over the conduct of contentious shipping litigation files left behind by lawyers who were already five years in practice. I recall living in fear of overlooking the one year time bar that was applicable to cargo claims while trying to cope with contentious applications. The steep learning curve and long hours made the first year almost unbearable. I had to face eminent shipping litigation lawyers in contentious applications and learned quickly that the only chance I had of winning was hard work. I also learned that I was not in control and that the harder one worked, the more painful the defeat. I went on a roller coaster of 'highs' when I won and 'lows' when I lost.

The toil of work became more bearable when we were able to discern the objective of our endeavors and efforts. Therefore, we need to work out our mission/objective in life before setting our priorities. In my case, I worked out that objective/mission with my life partner when we married two years after I started work. We wanted to build a loving home and to raise kids who are well-balanced and responsible individuals, and to help other families to do the same. Bernard and I are very passionate about our respective professions but the only title that we care to boast about is that we are the parents of six children. God has blessed us richly in our lives but especially with six kids who are very much a part of our primary goal in life.

We have a family set-up that is very different from the typical 'nuclear family' because our home is shared with our six kids, my elder brother who is intellectually challenged, two sets of in-laws and two maids. The extended family of uncles and aunties (including those we have encountered in our ministries) drop by very often as well to lend their support and provide the range of role models that the kids may choose to model their lives on. As they say, it takes a village to raise kids.

My parents-in–law have since passed on but for many years, our kids had the benefit of two sets of grandparents to care for them in our home while Bernard and I were both building our respective careers. Our parents have contributed much by helping with the care of the kids and the home even though there were the inevitable issues with disciplining styles. They have experienced great joy in sharing our home and our kids, but their greatest contribution are the lessons in humanity that they offer. As we believe in caring for our aged parents and in holding their hands to the end, my in-laws were nursed in our home when they contracted cancer within eight years of each other. They passed on with the family gathered around them. Our kids watched as their paternal grandparents grew old and died as part of the natural cycle of life. Our children have been enriched by the involvement of their grandparents in their lives.

The spousal relationship, which is the foundation of the family, is the key to a loving family environment which supports a healthy work-life balance. It demands understanding/patience on the part of the spouses and it requires them to make constant effort, including making the necessary adjustments in order to effect changes.

Work-life Balance Is About Making Choices To Be Supportive At All Costs

Men have to come to terms with the social changes to the woman's role in the family. Childcare is no longer a woman's sole responsibility. Women have re-defined their status in the family and identity, and a man might have come from a home where the wife did everything for her husband and her children.

Roles are interchangeable in a companionate marriage; shopping, vacuuming, laundry, cooking, child care. Both parties are called to work beyond convention and convenience.

The excitement of companionate marriages lies in the freedom and control both spouses have over their life and marriage. However, there is a need to resolve contemporary issues such as when to have children, whether to have a joint account, whose career will be given priority, and how will the couple take turns and decide on their career paths and make financial decisions together.

My husband and I were already going steady when I started law school. He knew that I would be a working wife and had to adjust his expectations as his own mother was a homemaker and he enjoyed her presence in the home.

When I experienced difficulties with coping with work, he chose to encourage and to support me to carry on as he knew that I would be happier working. He continued to be supportive when I started a new law firm with a few others in 1997 and took on even more responsibilities. He understood that to me, work had become more than a livelihood; it was a fulfillment of my talents and an extension of my self-worth.

Work-Life Balance May Sometimes Involve A Review Of Career Options In Order To Accommodate The Needs Of A Family

My husband pursued a specialty in A & E medicine for five years after his graduation. He had to work shifts, spend his nights in the hospital and worked through weekends. He would be at home when I was at work and working when the kids and I were at home. Our church ministries had to take a back seat as we were not able to commit to any social functions. I never voiced my unhappiness as I felt that that decision was his to make.

Five years into our marriage, we made a joint decision that he would discontinue his specialty in A & E medicine to make room for our growing family, our involvement with church ministries and my own career demands. He joined a GP practice but never gave up his dreams to pursue a Master's degree. He pursued a Diploma in Occupational Medicine and in the 15th year of our marriage, he pursued a Master's Degree in Occupational Medicine.

Work-Life Balance Requires An Adjustment Of Our Expectations To Accommodate The Dreams Of The Other

My husband had to make adjustments to his expectations and to work through his concerns that I am not a 'stay-home' mother. We have on-going discussions on my work schedules and how I should make adjustments to accommodate the needs of the growing family. He needs me not only to be physically present but also to have enough energy to address the emotional needs of the family. I have made efforts to be there for the kids such as the night feeds that went on for the first 13 years of our marriage and caring for sick kids during the nights. As they grow and their physical needs evolve to more emotional ones, I have to watch for moments to catch them for chats about their own lives, concerns and challenges, whether it be school work, friendships, heartbreaks, enlistment into National Service or pursuing studies overseas.

There are times when trials and urgent assignments take me away for long hours for days and weeks. There are many moments when my husband has felt 'robbed' of my presence. He has had to put up with the frustration of my taking calls from the office after he has taken the trouble to organise holidays.

We are constantly negotiating and reviewing strategies that would accommodate the family's needs and to limit the incursions of work. It could be as simple as limiting calls to a certain time slot or making time for holidays and family time.

101

Work- Life Balance Involves Making Changes To The Way One Works

My strong sense of responsibility towards work affects my ability to be fully present when I am with my family. I recall how difficult it was to take the kids out for a walk in the park on a Sunday evening and to concentrate on their discovery of the insects and plants along the trail without being distracted by thoughts of the start of a trial the next day. My kids often tease me and exclaim in jest, 'Mummy is in twilight zone, mummy is in twilight zone!'.

Through the years, I have made efforts to change my working style. I delegate my work and compartmentalise my moments in order to achieve a balance between my sense of commitment and responsibility for my clients, and my loyalty to my husband and kids.

Yet, Inevitably, Work Pressure And Long Hours Cause Misunderstanding And Hurt; Relationships Are Restored Through Reconciliation And Negotiation

One day, I rushed home on a Saturday evening. I had been preparing for a trial and was rushing to file papers to meet an urgent deadline. We had an agreement to meet back home and to proceed to a wedding dinner at 7pm. I was half an hour late only to discover that my husband had been so frustrated about having to wait for me again that he left for the wedding dinner on his own.

I felt so misunderstood and even as our kids gathered around me to console me, I felt that I was at the end of my strength. After a while, I decided to stop dwelling in self pity as I realised that what our marriage needed was for me to stop holding on to my hurt and anger, and for me to empathise with my husband's frustration of having to be a single parent during that weekend.

When the kids and I met up with him later on that evening, I approached him and sought his forgiveness. After we were reconciled, I told him that he is the reason why I have managed to remain an active litigation lawyer for 20 years and I would stop being one if he insisted. I also told him he needed to trust that my schedule would be more manageable after the trial. Friends again, he told me he would not dream of asking me to stop doing what I loved.

Work-Life Balance Requires The Couple To Make Time For Each Other

One of the key ways of keeping a work-life balance is to make time to spend time with each other. At the heart of a successful marriage is an intimate friendship between the spouses. A marriage where couples do not make time for each other is like a plant deprived of water. We tend to put our spouse and our family on hold. I was particularly impressed by this quote from Rob Parsons, an international speaker on business and family life:

> You can run several agendas in life, but you cannot run them all at a hundred per cent without somebody paying a price... We have so many excuses. The main one is that we convince ourselves a slower day is coming. We say to ourselves, 'When the house is decorated, when I get my promotion, when I pass those exams – then I'll have more time.' Every time we have to say, 'Not now, darling...' we tell ourselves it's okay because that slower day is getting nearer. It's as well that we realise, here and now, that the slower day is an illusion – it never comes. Whatever our situation, we all have the potential to fill our time. That's why we need to make time for the things that we believe are important – and we need to make it now.

This couple time does not simply happen but has to be planned. It takes effort to create the time and space for each other and to keep the romance in the relationship. For the past 24 years, we have been going on dates every Friday night after work. This gives us time to talk about the week's events and to make time for building our intimacy and friendship. We have taken up new games and hobbies together. I was persuaded by my husband to take up golf. As my caddy and my coach, he has been extremely encouraging throughout the proficiency certificate and handicap tests, and had patiently endured my occasional tantrums about the hot sun and tiring walks. I have learnt to enjoy the exercise, the refreshing greens as well as the time shared with my husband. I have grown to appreciate the benefits of playing golf. I have discovered that playing and having fun together cuts down the seriousness of life and helps us to be in a better position to deal with challenges. We also take short holidays together every three to six months as these present us with the much needed time and space to recreate and rediscover the romance in our relationship. We spend time talking about the kids and the family, and make plans for them in a constructive and life-giving manner.

4. Work-life Balance – Personal time

We all need the time and personal space to restore our sanity. Apart from hobbies and other mindless distractions, I visit my elderly and widowed friends who are sickly as this gives me a sense of peace and a perspective of life which I lose sight of when I get too engrossed in work.

I have found the practice of law to be an extremely enriching and rewarding experience despite the inevitable toil and disappointments in the past 26 years. I have seen changes in myself that would never have been possible if I had not been stretched and tested with difficult situations and moments of uncertainty. Most of all, I see the practice of law as a journey where each person I encounter is a human being whom I am called to deal with in a fair manner and with dignity.

I was pleasantly surprised when our first two sons announced to the family in turn that they had decided to pursue a law degree. Jonathan is a second year law student at the University of Southampton while Justin is a first year law student at National University of Singapore. In a blink of an eye, we will see the fruits of the life we have chosen to live. Will these young men become loving husbands and devoted fathers? Will they be conscientious and fair in their dealings and become professionals who are respected by their peers? Will they be competent lawyers who are serious about their responsibilities but never too serious about themselves? Like all parents, I pray and hope that these young men will someday surpass their mother.

LEGAL SERVICE

CHAPTER 13

INTERNATIONAL AFFAIRS DIVISION – THE PRACTICE OF INTERNATIONAL LAW AT IAD

Davinia Aziz

Davinia Aziz is Deputy Senior State Counsel at the International Affairs Division of the Attorney-General's Chambers. She read law at the National University of Singapore and has a Bachelor of Civil Law from the University of Oxford where she matriculated at Magdalen College. She later graduated with a Master of Laws in International Legal Studies from the New York University School of Law where she was a Hauser Global Scholar and Mamdouha Bobst Global Scholar. Davinia has held previous Singapore Legal Service appointments in the Supreme Court and in the Family and Juvenile Justice Division of the Subordinate Courts. She is also an Adjunct Assistant Professor at the National University of Singapore Faculty of Law where she teaches public law.

1. Introduction

Since 2007, I have practised international law as a government lawyer in the International Affairs Division of the Attorney-General's Chambers (or 'IAD', as the Division is known in government circles). The Chambers support the Attorney-General, whose constitutional role is to act as the legal adviser to the Singapore government. Like the lawyers in Chambers' other Divisions, the lawyers at IAD are officers of the Singapore Legal Service.

2. International Law

When people ask me what it is that I do, they often follow up with the question (sometimes with a politely quizzical look): 'What is international law?'

There are many ways to explain what international law is. People far wiser than I have spilled untold quantities of ink in order to compose a satisfactory answer to this question. And at the other end of the spectrum, there are those who would have us believe that international law is just a fancy name for nothing more than the thrust and parry of international politics. I cannot say that I have a definitive response to any of this. But I generally find that it works best for me to explain what kinds of things international law regulates, rather than what it is.

So I say that international law regulates relationships between and among states. Put this way, the whole enterprise still sounds rather abstract. The issues of high politics that occupy world news headlines seem far removed from our tiny island-state. What do United Nations Security Council debates on military intervention in North Africa, quarrels about voting shares in the International Monetary Fund or a declaration of independence in the Balkans have to do with Singapore? These events seem to have no direct relevance to us, safely ensconced as we are on this relatively quiet little island.

But all states, including Singapore, need to ensure that the world functions on the basis of a set of equitable, determinable and predictable rules. Imagine what the world would look like if there were no such rules. States with the economic and military power to do so would be in a position to make other states act as they wished. This is not something that any state can afford to countenance, but small states like Singapore have a particularly vital systemic interest in preserving networks of interaction based on the rule of law. Just as the law regulates and restrains opportunistic behaviour among individuals who must live together in one society within the state, so too does international law regulate and restrain opportunistic behaviour among states in international society.

The Singapore government invests in this system of rules by participating constructively in international organisations such as the United Nations and, closer to home, regional organisations such as the Association of Southeast Asian Nations ('ASEAN'). In addition to the regular work of these organisations, Singapore has been a member of the United Nations Security Council (from 2001 to 2002), and participated actively in the work that led to the conclusion of the landmark ASEAN Charter in 2007. The Singapore government has also used peaceful dispute settlement mechanisms available under international law to resolve outstanding issues with other states. For example, Singapore and Malaysia have referred disputes to the International Tribunal for the Law of the Sea (in the Land Reclamation case) and the International Court of Justice (in the Pedra Branca case). IAD lawyers are invariably part of Singapore delegations to the United Nations and ASEAN, and were part of the Singapore teams in both the Land Reclamation case as well as the Pedra Branca case.

These are the matters that tend to make the news headlines, but international law deals with a plethora of other substantive issues that we do not always traditionally associate with foreign affairs. Apart from the United Nations and ASEAN, Singapore is a member of other regional and international organisations, each with its own mandate. For example, the International Maritime Organisation, headquartered in London, is charged with overseeing the safety and security of shipping, and the prevention of marine pollution by ships. The World Intellectual Property Organisation, headquartered in Geneva, was established to promote the protection of intellectual property through cooperation amongst its Member States. And the International Civil Aviation Organisation, headquartered in Montreal, develops the principles and techniques of international air navigation, and fosters the planning and development of international air transport. To all of this, we must add Singapore's considerable list of commitments in the area of international economic law. These are undertaken under the auspices of the World Trade Organisation, of which Singapore was a founding member, and in the context of Singapore's network of free trade agreements ('FTAs') and bilateral investment treaties ('BITs').

In each of these issue-areas — maritime safety and security, international intellectual property, international aviation, trade and investment — Singapore undertakes certain commitments under international law. These commitments are sometimes supplemented or reinforced by smaller, more specific agreements to which Singapore is party. In the field of international aviation, for example, the exchange of air traffic rights has to be specifically negotiated between states. So a solid network of air services agreements is what undergirds Changi Airport's status as an international air transportation hub. These air services agreements also allow Singapore-based airlines to fly over, into and beyond the territories of other states, with the necessary arrangements for taking up and dropping off passengers and cargo.

This laundry list of issue-areas is illustrative, not exhaustive. I have not mentioned many others that are just as important, including diplomatic privileges and immunities, climate change and other aspects of the environment, extradition and mutual legal assistance, financial services and human rights. International law has something to say about all of these things. And the impact of international law translates downstream, in the most quotidian way, to the kinds of products we see on our supermarket shelves (through our trade commitments), the different options we can choose from when planning air travel out of Changi Airport (through our air services agreements) and our ability to send a simple e-mail or a text message (through arrangements that protect critical infrastructure, such as underwater fibre optic cables or satellite communications).

3. The Practice

The sheer breadth of the issues I have just described manifests itself in the variety of work that crosses the desk of an IAD lawyer each day. IAD functions much like a clearinghouse for all of the international legal obligations taken on by the Singapore Government. This means that we work closely with the professional diplomats at the Ministry of Foreign Affairs and our overseas Missions, as well as with policymakers across the full range of government agencies tasked to lead inter-agency decision-making processes on each of the issue-areas under their purview.

A key difference between the practice of law at IAD and most kinds of domestic legal practice is that the work does not segment neatly into transactional (or advisory) work and litigation (or dispute settlement) work. An IAD lawyer has to be able to perform both functions. In other words, the IAD lawyer is usually asked to advise government agencies on compliance with international law while policy is being developed, and before a decision is taken. When the Singapore government negotiates with other states, whether at bilateral or multilateral meetings in Singapore or abroad, an IAD lawyer typically joins the Singapore delegation as legal adviser. Dispute settlement is a costly affair for any government, in both financial and political terms, and so the IAD lawyer spends a lot of time on advisory work so as to avert the possibility of the Singapore government being inadvertently hauled into international litigation! On a serious note, however, dispute settlement is sometimes unavoidable — and in certain cases, may even be the optimal way forward. In those situations, IAD lawyers will assist the relevant government agencies with building the legal case, drafting written arguments and preparing the oral submissions in much the same way as a domestic lawyer might prepare for litigation in court.

The nature of IAD work is such that you very rapidly learn how to think on your feet. While we do work in teams, there are also many occasions when the IAD lawyer is the sole lawyer on the delegation. This is a heavy responsibility because when policy colleagues look to you for legal advice in the midst of negotiations, there is no time to refer the matter to a more senior lawyer for approval — though there is, of course, allowance for such referrals if the issue is truly critical. And IAD lawyers take on such responsibilities very quickly. I learned this when I received my first overseas assignment days after I arrived at the Division. I remember the occasion distinctly. I was called in to see the Head of the Division. At the time, the Head of the Division was the late Mr Sivakant Tiwari. Mr Tiwari handed me a file and told me to get up to speed because I would be advising on some air law issues in November (I arrived at IAD in October). He explained that the Civil Aviation Authority of Singapore wanted to constitute a delegation to Ottawa for air services negotiations. When I asked who else from IAD would be going to Ottawa, he looked at me with raised eyebrows and said: 'You!'. I was suitably panicked. Not only would I be advising an overseas delegation alone, I would be advising them in a timezone that made it nearly impossible to telephone any IAD colleague at a civil hour for immediate consultations! In the end, the negotiations went smoothly and I need not have panicked. I had also managed to complete a good deal of preparatory work before the Ottawa meeting with help from more experienced IAD lawyers. But to me at least, the episode demonstrates the level of responsibility that an IAD lawyer is expected to assume at an early stage in his or her career.

As will be evident from all that you have read thus far, the work does involve a significant amount of time spent abroad, though this will vary according to the different kinds of assignments that one receives. For example, I spent most of 2010 advising on international human rights law from 'capital' (to use the diplomatic lingo for the home base), and chunks of 2011 in Geneva and New York when it was time for Singapore to comply with her human rights reporting obligations to the UN Human Rights Council (for the Universal Periodic Review) and the UN Committee on the Elimination of Discrimination Against Women (for the UN Convention on the Elimination of All Forms of Discrimination Against Women). Typically, an IAD lawyer also joins the Singapore delegation to the UN General Assembly each year to participate in meetings of the Sixth (Legal) Committee. This is an assignment that can involve up to two or three months in New York, depending on the schedule of meetings for that year. In 2011, it will be my turn to take up this assignment. There is also now one IAD lawyer attached to the Singapore Permanent Mission in Geneva, to assist on the legal issues arising in connection with the work of the international organisations headquartered there, such as the World Trade Organisation.

In addition to the daily practice of international law, IAD lawyers who are interested in scholarly work are encouraged to contribute to the international legal enterprise by writing and, where possible, teaching. This is because practice and the academy are not, in the field of international law, perceived as distinct pursuits. Several members of the International Court of Justice, for example, are recognised as both noted practitioners and professors of international law. IAD promotes Singapore scholarship in international law by allowing IAD lawyers to set aside a little time each year to write and publish articles, and to attend international research conferences and workshops to share their work. IAD is also very supportive of collaborative work with our universities. For example, IAD recently started a joint project with the Centre for International Law at the National University of Singapore ('NUS') for students to conduct research and work directly with IAD lawyers on selected topics in international law.

4. My Path to IAD

I keep an adjunct teaching position in public law at the NUS Faculty of Law, and sometimes my students ask me about the path that led me to IAD. So I thought it might be helpful to close with this — not because everyone is bound to take the same path, but because someone contemplating IAD work might find this information useful.

I first became interested in the different ways in which states co-operate and co-exist in junior college. At the time, our 'A' Level history syllabus included the study of something called 'World Affairs', which was essentially a very basic version of International Relations 101. So I decided that I wanted to study international relations at university. I ended up instead on the LLB programme at the NUS Faculty of Law, for a variety of reasons that are now neither relevant nor important. At NUS, I discovered international law. I found that law and the legal method brought welcome depth and clarity to the way that I was thinking about how states behave. So I decided that I wanted to be an international lawyer. I was, however, much less clear about how I could make this happen!

After I graduated, I interviewed for a post in the Singapore Legal Service because I had the opportunity to join the Service as a Justices' Law Clerk in the Supreme Court. I got the post and spent the next couple of years assisting the Court of Appeal and the Chief Justice on various civil and criminal appeals. Then I was rotated to the Subordinate Courts where I was a judicial officer assigned to the Family and Juvenile Justice Division. Finally, in 2007, I received the long-awaited posting letter for IAD.

The path I took was a circuitous one. But in retrospect, I think that my time at the Supreme and Subordinate Courts was good preparation for the work that I do at IAD. To be an effective government legal adviser in the field of international law, you have to know what the domestic legal landscape looks like, and how the domestic institutions in your government are organised. Otherwise, you will not be in a position to advise your policy colleagues on what international obligations Singapore is realistically able to take on, and what kinds of changes to domestic law are likely to be needed to ensure that Singapore is in compliance with those obligations.

These days, it is true that IAD is no longer the only option for young Singaporeans who seek a career in international law. They might, for example, turn their sights on a job in the legal adviser's office of a large international organisation, such as the United Nations or the World Bank Group. Alternatively, they might choose to join a private law firm with a practice in international investment arbitration (involving disputes between private investors and governments of states that host the investments). Yet a third option might be to teach and write on some aspect of international law at one of our universities.

These are all excellent possibilities. But for the young person who wants to learn the practice of international law in the most robust, varied and exhilarating way, the best place to do this is still the government office responsible for giving advice on issues of international law. And that office, for the Singapore Government, is IAD.

Further Reading

- Vaughan Lowe, *International Law* (Oxford University Press, 2007).

- S Jayakumar, *Diplomacy: A Singapore Experience* (Straits Times Press, 2011).

- Michael Wood, 'Legal Advisers' in Rüdiger Wolfrum (ed), *Max Planck Encyclopedia of International Law* (Oxford University Press, 2008) online edition.

CHAPTER 14

THE DEPUTY PUBLIC PROSECUTOR AND THE HIGH COURT REGISTRY – PRACTISING IN THE PUBLIC SECTOR – PERSPECTIVES

Jeyendran Jeyapal

Jeyendran graduated from the National University of Singapore's Law Faculty with first class honours, and holds a LLM from Harvard Law School. He joined the Singapore Legal Service in 2003 and worked as a Justices' Law Clerk and a Deputy Public Prosecutor before joining the Supreme Court in 2009 as an Assistant Registrar.

I would have to admit. The practice of law and me – it was never love at first sight. I was a Junior College student the first time the thought of reading the law crossed my mind. Even so, it was not because I knew anything about what legal practice entailed, but more because gaining entry into the NUS Law Faculty was tough, and the pure challenge of getting a place in that faculty made poring through Shakespeare and cracking the Economics code worth the effort. At that age, it really felt as if the 'A' Levels was the mother of all exams. So what was an unenlightened seventeen-year old to think?

But as all stories go, there was a twist of fate that led me to where I am now – practising the law, and in the public service at that! It came, unexpectedly, in the form of National Service. I got a notice one day that said I was posted to the Police Force, much to the envy of all my friends who thought it was a way better option than the Army. You can call it fate or pure luck, but there is no denying that this posting started it all.

Apart from long runs, defence tactics training and taekwondo, police training also involved intellectual pursuits such as learning about the offences that make up the Penal Code and the powers of the police under the Criminal Procedure Code. I found the classes very interesting, but as the lessons progressed, niggling little questions rose at the back of my mind. Yes, I now knew when and how to make a lawful arrest. I also understood the concept of 'reasonable suspicion'. But I was itching to find out how these theories played out in real life.

The opportunity came quickly. I was posted to a team at one of the police divisional headquarters after graduating from police training school. I started off in the patrol team, scanning neighbourhoods for suspicious characters, making arrests and so on. I learnt a lot about observing people, sieving out the suspicious from the ordinary, and most importantly, how serious the power of arrest is. Each arrest fortified my conviction that it is not enough to just believe or suspect, but to be very sure in your belief or suspicion before you arrest someone.

But at the back of my mind, I always wondered what happened to those people I had arrested. Did they all get charged? Did they all end up in prison? I was mulling through questions like these when I met her, an investigator in my division (whom, for the purposes of this piece, I will call 'Big Sister'). Big Sister offered to co-opt me into the team she was heading so I could see for myself what investigations were all about. I was, of course, more than happy to accept.

I started the very next day. It began with learning the ropes about interviewing accused persons and potential witnesses, and later moving on to visiting crime scenes and picking up clues. But to be frank, I was none the wiser. I still wondered where all of this led to.

I think Big Sister must have sensed my concern, because one day, she took me to the Attorney-General's Chambers to meet the Deputy Public Prosecutor ('DPP'). On our way there, Big Sister explained that we were now embarking on a stage beyond police investigations, when the Prosecution decides whether someone ought to be charged. Big Sister and the DPP spoke at length about the case while I watched. The DPP told Big Sister to charge someone and wrote something in the file that Big Sister had brought along with her.

Back at headquarters, I asked Big Sister how the DPP could decide in just a few minutes whether someone should be charged, especially since it took several days for investigations to be conducted. What if the DPP decides not to charge someone – all the investigation would have been wasted. Big Sister replied that nothing done in investigation is a waste of time. She explained that investigations are a necessary part of the criminal justice process. It is the investigator's job to look into every allegation made against the accused person to determine if there is sufficient evidence to merit charging that person. Based on this assessment, the investigator makes her recommendation to the Prosecution. Should the evidence be lacking, the investigator must make this fact known to the Prosecution.

Big Sister said – and this rings in my mind till today – that the worst thing that can happen to a person is to be charged in error. You should always put yourself in the position of an innocent man facing a charge for a crime he never committed; imagine the frustration and outrage he must feel. An investigation is meant to uncover the circumstances and the truth behind an allegation. Allegations are easily made, but not every allegation may be true. Every investigation is a success, even if the result is that an allegation is disproved.

But if investigations do reveal that an allegation is true, why do the Courts let some people off? According to Big Sister, that is where the Prosecution comes into the picture, to lay the evidence gathered in the course of the investigations before the Court. While the police and the Prosecution take pains to ensure that only the strongest cases are proceeded on, the Courts may view the evidence as insufficient or unreliable. In such cases, an acquittal may follow.

How then does the Prosecution go about laying the evidence before the Court, I asked. Big Sister said that was something even she was curious about – the work of the Prosecution. Someday we will know, she said. She was right – Big Sister became my colleague in my time with the Prosecution; she is still there today, as an Assistant Public Prosecutor.

This conversation with Big Sister was a defining moment for me. I was itching to find out how the Prosecution worked. How did the DPP arrive at a decision on the charge in such a short time? How would the prosecution bring the case to the Court and lay the evidence before it to prove that the charge was brought properly? I had to wait a little while more to find out.

I completed my National Service stint and went on to law school. It was bit of a challenge to pick up the books again after two and half years. But I eased in fast, quickly realising that the law was not about memorising obscure concepts, but about understanding the principles behind it and why we had these principles in the first place. Once that realisation hit, I had a lot of fun in thinking about interesting legal conundrums and making arguments about them. Naturally, I had a soft spot for Criminal Law, but I discovered how the other areas of the law were also equally intriguing. It was mind-boggling how many separate branches of the law there were. Four years of study just did not seem enough.

Before I knew it, final year was over and I was ready to start with my new life in the Prosecution. It was at this point that I got the invitation I could not refuse – to start off as a Justices' Law Clerk ('JLC') with the then-Chief Justice Yong Pung How. It was an odd moment, really, as I was longing to start prosecuting but had to put it on the backburner to try my hand at something completely different. I did however, while waiting to enter the JLC pool, work a month and a half as a DPP. On the very first day, I met the head of the criminal justice division, a veteran prosecutor himself. In the short meeting with him, I took away with me a big reminder of why I had chosen the public service over the private sector.

Public service means just that – service to the public. It does not discriminate, it does not seek favours and above all, it is impartial. It bestows powers on its servants which have a direct impact on people. But these powers are not granted for one to sit around and gloat about, but are necessary to the functions that need to be carried out in the interest of the public. Every file is important. It does not matter who the personalities involved are, or what the offence is. Behind every file, there is someone whose life and liberty is at stake; to that person, it does not matter whether he has been accused of a big crime or a small one. Whether he wishes to be exonerated or intends to plead guilty, it is imperative that his case is dealt with fairly and expeditiously. He should never be made to wait by reason of inefficiencies on the part of the Prosecution.

It was a pity though that my stint with the Prosecution, a place I had been longing to try out for such a long time, was such a short one. But I knew I would be back someday. So, after that brief time, I went over to the Supreme Court to start my work as a JLC. To be frank, I had no clue as to what exactly I was supposed to do, but I was eager to find out. A lot of the work revolved around appeal matters – both criminal appeals from the Subordinate Courts and civil and criminal appeals to the Court of Appeal. It was heavy-going in terms of research into legal issues, and writing opinions on them. But it was certainly not routine. Every case was different and I found myself researching into and writing on a variety of legal issues. I actually derived a whole deal of joy in writing legal opinions.

True, I was looking forward to litigation work. But I also learnt that good oral arguments are only successful up to a point. You may be the best debater or mooter in your year, but if your legal arguments are not well researched into and thought out, even an average litigator can trump you.

How did I know that? As a JLC, I had one of the best seats in the court house. Sitting quiet as a mouse at a table just below the Judges' bench, I got to watch some of the best litigators in the country throwing up complex arguments to the Judges, the Judges grilling them with questions, and opposing counsel fighting back with vigorous comebacks.

Of course, real litigation did not happen at the frenetic pace you see in TV courtroom dramas. But it was still a sight to behold. As a fresh graduate with zero experience in litigation, it was fantastic learning. Not just because of the pointers I picked up watching some good litigators in action (manners and respect being the most important of them all), but also in realising that some of the best arguments are those that pay heed to the practical way of things. As a student, my approach was largely academic. This was naturally so because I had little to no experience on industry practices and customs. I was surprised how crucial some of these unwritten practices were, especially in specialised industries such as shipping. It frightened me to think how silly and unschooled I would seem if I had appeared before the Court of Appeal as a fresh graduate, arguing about beautiful intricacies of the law – and nothing else.

During lunch with the Judges, I asked, casting aside the fear of appearing ignorant, on certain customs within an industry and how they came about. Not a single judge gave me a 'what a stupid boy' look. They were as happy to explain as I was to learn. Saying I was grateful would be an understatement.

After a fulfilling two years in the JLC pool, I moved back to the Prosecution. My first stop was the Financial and Securities Offences department. My first hearing was opposite senior counsel. Great! Was it not a little early in the day to be pitted against a senior counsel?

I decided to speak to one of the most senior officers in the department about this (she is now a senior counsel herself). She told me that she believed in me, and added, 'One of the reasons why they became senior counsel is because they are always professional in the way they conduct themselves. I don't see why they will not be the same with a newcomer. Know your work, know your case, know your law and speak like how you are capable of.'

These were encouraging words, but it was still difficult to keep the jitters away. I had to psych myself up and at the same time, focus on the case. This included understanding finance terminology, how derivatives and other financial instruments worked, how the complex product in this case was created and so on. This was my first foray into the arcane world of finance.

D-day arrived sooner than I would have liked. A few minutes after I arrived in the courtroom, the senior counsel walked in with his entourage. At first, he gave me a quizzical look. Clearly I was a new face to him. Then he strode over, beaming, and we exchanged courtesies. It was a good start I thought. It got better. We started talking about our respective cases, putting forward our differing positions in a matter-of-fact manner and trying to interpret a judgment common to both our cases. I was completely at ease by now and felt that I was speaking as an equal. This was a man with years of litigation experience, but he never once made me feel like the greenhorn that I actually was.

Now, whenever I think about my first day in Court, I do not recall much of the oral arguments I actually made that day. What really stood out to me was the professional manner with which senior counsel conducted himself and his case, and the respect he accorded to me. Most memorable were his words to me just before he left the courtroom: 'Well done. Thanks for a fair fight.' 'A fair fight'. Somehow that phrase stuck in my mind a lot more than 'well done'. It really made me think about the type of reputation I wanted to build for myself as a litigator. Eloquent, but underhanded? Or adequate, but fair? I will be frank. I wanted a hybrid: Eloquence and fairness.

Eloquence is a matter of *how* one delivers an argument. But fairness refers to *what* was delivered – a fair argument. I told myself that at the end of the court day, I just wanted to be known as having conducted a case fairly.

Yes, as a DPP, you are given a mandate and you appear in Court as the Attorney-General's representative. This is not to say that the DPP has no hand in determining the outcome that the Prosecution desires to achieve. In fact, as a DPP, you are an integral part of the decision-making process. A case, post-investigation, starts at the desk of a DPP. The DPP looks at the evidence in totality, makes necessary enquiries with the police and interviews witnesses prior to recommending a mandate to the Attorney-General. It is then for the Attorney-General to determine if the Prosecution should proceed with the recommended mandate. Viewed in this light, DPPs have a personal say in every case that passes from their desks. Their names are attached to these decisions and no responsible DPP would want his name to be associated with a poorly rationalised decision. Of course, with effective management, poor decisions are sifted out at a very early stage, so only well-considered decisions come before the Courts.

In my time as a DPP, I literally saw thousands of files and made just as many decisions. Not every DPP would see eye to eye with me on some decisions, but that really is where the beauty of the job lies. When I was there, the Attorney-General's Chambers had an open door policy. Any DPP could walk into another DPP's office and trash out a case. I did not see a problem with another DPP taking an opposing view, testing my decision and most importantly, assessing the fairness of the outcome. I still remember very fondly how I could sit with another DPP in the Head of Crime's office, and all three of us could have a purely intellectual debate. There were no ego battles between us or a competition for who has made the better decision. Everything hinged on the evidence and how reliable it was.

I guess it was this work culture which really made me love coming to work every day. The bandying about of ideas, the freedom to discuss, disagree and take an independent view. Ultimately, whatever the differences in opinion, at the core, the decisions were always founded on principles of fairness and the public interest. The Public Prosecutor is the *public's* prosecutor, acting on behalf of the public and its interest. The interest is served both in prosecuting a legitimate case, and in ensuring that an offender has a fair trial. This must be the case, as the public has as much an interest in ensuring that crime is met with justice as it does in ensuring that a trial is conducted fairly. Otherwise, the public will lose faith in a Prosecution which rides roughshod. Whether an accused person is to be convicted or acquitted is a matter left for the Courts to decide. Whatever the outcome, the Prosecution has to ensure that the decision to prosecute was well thought out and was made on legitimate bases.

It was with these beliefs in mind that I continued my adventure in the Prosecution, prosecuting about seventy trials in a very short time. Some of them were highly technical, document-intensive ones, some were more straightforward cases with an abundance of evidence, yet others relied on circumstantial evidence. But the ones which I found to be the most challenging were those involving sexual offences committed against children. When doing those cases, I sometimes wonder if I am a prosecutor or a counsellor. A large part of such cases requires you to step out of your role as a prosecutor in order to gain the trust of the child victim. The child has been violated; she may not even understand that what had been done to her is wrong. Some know that the acts they have been subjected to are wrong and are offences under the law. However, shame and fear of embarrassment prevents them from speaking about them, especially not to a complete stranger like a prosecutor.

I remember this 8 year old girl who had been repeatedly violated by her relative over a one-year period. My experience with child victims taught me to build a rapport with them first. I did so and she appeared to warm up to me. However, at the slightest mention of what had happened to her, her face went pale. She just would not talk. I found out later that it was not that she did not want to talk about the incidents, she could not. She had been so badly affected by the incidents that any reminder of them caused her to clam up immediately. I knew it was going to be a very long road with this child. I told myself that even if I was not going to be able to prosecute this case, considering that the victim herself was unable to talk about what had happened to her, I was at the very least going to try to help her in whatever way I could. I met her regularly after work over the next few weeks. We spoke about anything but the incident; she would even ask me about her homework.

One day, on one of our usual meetings, she spoke about her family. She said she liked everybody in her family, with the exception of one person. I knew I had her trust now. But I had to take it slow, and simply waited for her to continue. That opened the floodgates. She started talking. I just played the part of the listener. When she was done with her story, she frowned and asked me what we could do to him. I turned the question around and asked her what *she* wanted to do to him. She told me she wanted to beat him; she wanted retribution, she wanted a result. I had won half the battle with her. We met up a few more times before I was finally able to assure myself that I could put her on the stand as a witness. It was going to be a big risk though. Thus far, she had the comfort of speaking in my office. Now, the setting was going to be different. Still, on her version of events, I felt there was a case to prosecute.

The trial went along fine, until the cross-examination started. It was hard to pin down why she responded the way she did. It could be a general distrust of adults or perhaps shame and embarrassment. She started to crumble. She became unsure of her version of events, appeared confused and eventually, clammed up at crucial points. I tried to jog her memory when I got my chance to re-examine her, but it was really pointless. She had lost her confidence and was on the brink of tears. I made the call to end her contribution to the trial at this stage. Yes, my case was in shreds, but I did not think I could have, in all good conscience, pressed her to answer my questions. It was simply not humane. I did not think a vigorous examination on the stand would have done her any good; it would have been a further negative memory to her.

So, the rosy ending I had hoped for was not to be. The accused person was acquitted. The Judge had reasoned that it was not about whether the accused person or his accuser was lying. It was about whether the accuser's version of events, inconsistencies and all, could be relied upon to convict the man and pack him off to prison.

The result hurt. I felt I had let the poor girl down. To make matters worse, the papers reported the case the next day, with the girl's parents talking about how the result would effectively ostracise them from the rest of the extended family. I got a call from the Head of Crime to go see him about the case. I thought, oh well, here goes. I thought through on how to explain the acquittal to him. When I got to his office, I saw him sitting at his desk reading the newspaper report. He looked at me and asked, 'First acquittal?' He told me to not feel bad about it. An acquittal was not a defeat, but a testament to the fair trial process. The adversarial process reveals the weaknesses and strengths in a case that you may have never seen before. The Prosecution must first know that it has brought the best case to the Court. The rest would be for the Prosecution to convince the Court that this *is* the best case.

We spoke a little more on whether an appeal was necessary. I thought carefully. Would I have decided the case the same way the Judge did? I think the Judge was right. As a neutral party determining the case on the evidence before the Court, the Judge was correct in giving the man the benefit of doubt. Every case may have some inconsistencies. But there are some inconsistencies which go to the root of the allegation, casting doubt on the Prosecution's case itself. In such a situation, how could it be said that the Prosecution had proven its case beyond a reasonable doubt? I agreed that we would not go on to appeal the decision.

In retrospect, I must say that the case was a real turning point for me. I started approaching my trials at angles which I had not looked at before and learnt that it was never wrong to be just a tad more careful. At the same time, with each trial, I realised that every case was like a thumbprint. They had their own individual set of facts, features and evidence.

I was really enjoying myself exploring the mechanics behind trials, polishing up on my cross-examination and taking my research to different levels. I moved steadily onwards to do tougher trials involving corruption offences and High Court cases that attracted non-capital and capital punishments. I also started conducting High Court and Court of Appeal cases, a wholly different experience that took my research, writing and advocacy skills even further. The pressure intensified, but I was finding the challenge almost addictive. It was at this juncture that I got the posting letter. I was to move to the Supreme Court Registry as an Assistant Registrar ('AR'). From my time as a JLC, I knew that ARs sat as judicial officers to hear civil, pre-trial applications. However, where criminal matters were concerned, their role was largely administrative.

To be honest, I tried to resist the move as I thought it would be a little premature. I spoke to the new Head of Crime about the situation and tried to buy some time. She, however, felt that I had already learnt and grasped more than just mere basics in my time with the Prosecution, and that it would be good to expand the horizons with civil work in the Registry: 'The best time to learn is when you are younger and more receptive to new experiences. It will be a new area. Learn how the Judiciary functions. It is a rare chance to exercise your mind from a neutral perspective.'

So the time came for me to head off to the Registry. I said my goodbyes to all my wonderful friends and packed my bags for my new office in the Supreme Court. The assimilation process was simple. I knew several people here, both in my time as a JLC and when I was a prosecutor. The work, though, required far greater effort. This was a different ball game altogether. I had no clue about the technical aspects of civil cases and the last time I had touched the Rules of Court was when I was a JLC. I suddenly felt a little crippled outside of the comfort zone that the criminal law and procedure had established for me. Needless to say, the learning curve was very steep. I read the Rules of Court from cover to cover, scoured available resources for any information I could get, and soon enough, the famous White Book on Singapore Civil Procedure became a bedtime reading favourite. I was immersed into hearings just as quickly and had to find my feet fast.

But I had a good support network. There was always someone to turn to; someone would have encountered something similar at some point. I fed off their experience and added the learning points to my ever expanding list. It was a trying process because I had to understand the basics fast and at the same time, learn how to spot issues, concerns and strategies. The work of an AR was not a mechanical process of looking at solitary applications without understanding the background of the entire case.

While the work in the Registry was different from what I did as a prosecutor, I must say that my time with the Prosecution did help me to a certain extent. I felt that the experience of having litigated before made me understand some of the constraints that lawyers were under. Most importantly, I was able to spot issues fast and focus on the root of the matter at hand. I realised that if I was able to delineate the various issues at trial, I would be able to understand the relevance of applications better. I approached my hearings with the big picture in mind, much like how I conducted my Prosecutions. This way, I was able to engage with lawyers on the case better, and my hearings had a lot more focus to them.

The learning curve did not end at hearings though. The surprise awaiting was the administrative work. When I was with the Prosecution, administrative work was kept to a minimum. Now, I had to deal with several portfolios, including heading the Finance and Financial Policy department. I had a team and people to manage. I had never managed people before! Plus, I would never say I was a champion at maths and now I had to think about policies? My only real brush with finance matters was in my Masters programme where I did predominantly Finance and Economics based law subjects, and of course, when I worked with the White Collar Crimes Division in the AGC. But surely that cannot be enough?

Thankfully, I had some amazing colleagues to turn to, many of whom had been managing people for years. I observed their style of management and how they organised themselves. I 'spied' on the Registrar and the Deputy Registrar, and wondered why they chose to say and do things in a certain way when another approach would have sufficed. I dissected these approaches and delineated the keys to effective management – trust and leadership by example.

To gain that trust, I needed to first know my portfolios inside out. I attended courses, read literature on Government Financing, bugged Ministries with questions and ate up the Government Instruction Manual. It was turning out to be a far steeper learning curve than I imagined. But in time, I started to stabilise and things began to click in place, like a giant jigsaw puzzle finally coming together.

I depend a lot on my team to do the pure finance aspects of the department, though I do try my hand at some of the pure finance work with the people in my team at hand to guide me along. The maths is mind-boggling at times, but it does help me to understand the pressures that my team face. I came out understanding them and their work better and gained the ability to read and make sense of some accounting hieroglyphics. Most importantly, I felt that my relationship with my team got a big boost. I think the most significant moment came when some of the members in my team came to me of their own accord to discuss their problems, even personal ones. It was a sign that I had done something right.

Of course, I could not rest on my laurels and think that I had arrived. I continued to work closely with my team, meeting them virtually every day to sort some finance policy or the other out. There was always something cropping up and the team had to be on standby mode to tackle these issues. The fact that we have a close relationship made these tough moments a little easier to bear and, I daresay, fun in its own way.

It was the same story with other departments in my portfolio, with the only difference being that these other departments are legal in nature; the administrative aspects in these departments involve a heavy amount of legal research work and even being part of legislative working groups

– I worked with the Ministry of Law and hordes of other departments on major legislative changes. On the whole, it was administrative work with a twist. There was a great deal of legal and policy issues to consider, a challenge that brings with it a completely different set of pressures from those that a prosecutor faces. So I guess the head crime was correct when she said that the posting as an AR was a rare chance to look at things from a different perspective. To this extent, I must say that I am extremely glad that I made the move to the Supreme Court Registry. It was a different role which brought experiences that I never thought I would encounter.

These days, I sometimes wonder as to where my adventure with the public service will take me next. What I do know is that I will definitely be a lot more receptive to take the leap this time round. There is no end to learning and I will not deprive myself of that opportunity if it comes along. Looking back, a lot of my thoughts and beliefs, and the very reason why I chose the public service as a career option, are a product of first-hand learning experiences through the years. I am encouraged to think out of the box and articulate my views, and I see my views being adopted in ways that changed lives. At the end of the day, it is important to understand that the public service is a higher calling that requires some sacrifices to be made. Once you have reconciled yourself with this, the satisfaction you get with a vocation in the public service is unparalleled.

CHAPTER 15

DISTRICT JUDGE AND LEGAL AID LAWYER – TACKLING PERSONAL AND SOCIAL PROBLEMS USING LEGAL TOOLS

Lim Hui Min

The author is currently a state counsel with the Attorney-General's Chambers. Her first job was as an associate in a large law firm, doing mostly banking, commercial and general litigation. She then joined the Subordinate Courts as a Deputy Registrar and Magistrate, working in the Civil Registry for about a year. After this, she moved to the Family Court (later known as the Family and Juvenile Court), where she was subsequently appointed as a District Judge. She joined the Legal Aid Bureau as a Senior Assistant Director and was subsequently appointed as a Second Deputy Director. She has spent almost four years with the Bureau.

Note: The names of persons in, and certain facts of, cases discussed in this article have been omitted or modified in order to protect the confidentiality of the parties involved.

> My mother cooks better, so I would like to stay with her. But my father has more money. Anyway, I told my mother and father that I will go with whoever gives me the most money.

The teenage boy I was interviewing grinned at me as he said this. He was a charming, personable and articulate young man. I did not think that I would like to have him as my son, however.

At the time this conversation took place, I was working as one of the District Judges at the Family Court. The boy's parents were locked in a custody battle over their three children. This boy was the eldest, and I decided to speak to him to get some insight into what the family was like. I sighed at what he said. The parents may have been fighting over the child in court, but both of them had already lost his heart. I believe I eventually decided that all three children should be in the mother's care and control – she was, after all, the better cook.

I have talked to many children over the years in my role as a District Judge. Some of them have been painfully tongue-tied. Others have been chatty and curious. Once, a boy of ten asked me how old I was. 'You look much younger' he said cheekily after I told him. I remember speaking to a girl that just looked down and shrugged to every question, even an innocuous one like 'What do you like to do for fun?' She had conflicting loyalties to both parents, I believe, and did not want to say anything that might hurt either side. There was a boy that kept spinning around in his chair when I talked to him, like a human top.

There was also a teenager whom I spoke to, who disliked her father so much that she did not want to see him at all, even once a month for just two hours. 'You can make whatever orders you like.' she said coolly. 'I am not going to see him.' I remember agonising over the decision in that case. The father was, I admit, a trying individual. I had spoken to him as well and had gotten quite irritated by his continual insistence that the children were poisoned against him by their mother. He was one of those people who could not accept that others could have a different point of view from his. He had no interests and hobbies, and made tedious, patronising conversation. I did not enjoy the twenty minutes I spent in his company and the prospect of having to spend any time at all with him on a weekend was a rather dreary one. But, well, he was the children's father. He had not actively sought to harm them. In fact, he cared about them in his own way. I thought it was important for a child to know his roots, and was reluctant to cut off access completely in this case, before the children came of age. I finally ordered the girl and her brother to meet their father once a month for two hours. She was as good as her word and did not turn up a single time. Neither did her brother. Thus, a decision which I had made with the children's best interests in mind did not achieve its intended effect. The father went on to file court application after court application in fruitless attempts to see them. I do not think he ever succeeded.

From this case, and from many others that I have done, I have often thought that there are no right decisions in family law – only very difficult ones.

One thing that the practice of family law teaches you is the limitations of the law. Court orders cannot heal fractured relationships or repair broken hearts. I once helped a divorce client at a mediation session in the Legal Aid Bureau. She was willing to let her teenage children (a boy and a girl) stay with their father, but wanted to see them every weekend, and to have them stay overnight with her. The children had other ideas. They were open to going for a shopping trip with my client over the weekend, but vetoed the idea of spending the night at her flat. 'There is no Internet access.' explained the girl. Well, I suppose one could not argue with that. It is not often that a child prefers his parent's company to playing computer games and chatting with friends online.

After being told that the children did not want to spend nights at her house, my client suggested that they spend alternate public holidays with her, for the whole day. I spoke to the husband's lawyer, who said the husband had no problems with this, but that he had to check with the children. I could overhear the lawyer talking with the children, explaining the proposal. There was an immediate wail of: 'So *ma fan*! [Mandarin for 'troublesome'] No!' from the children. My client heard it too. The other lawyer came up to me and shook his head. I cleared my throat and said to my client 'Er...I don't think...' Thankfully, she anticipated what I was going to say. 'I know, I know, they don't want to.' she said. She was silent for a moment. 'All right. Whatever they want. One day they will know.' she said, her lower lip quivering. 'They are still young. One day they will understand what a mother's love is.' 'Teenagers nowadays...' I said, apologetically.

There are no legal solutions to disappointment and sorrow.

What the law can do, though, is to help people regulate their relationships and dealings with each other, and thus enable them to move on, or at least, move forward, in a practical way. If, while doing the legal work, the lawyer can, at the same time, reconcile parties or give them useful insights into themselves, that is a bonus. But this is often not possible, given the constraints of time, and the nature of the parties.

There was a case I did in the Legal Aid Bureau involving two brothers (let us call them Andrew and Ben) who were joint tenants of the same flat. They had bought the flat together and lived together in that flat ever since. However, after a quarrel one day, they did not speak to each other for over 11 years. Andrew finally decided that he had enough of this unnatural environment and applied for legal aid to get a court order to sell the flat. He wanted to purchase a flat on his own. I drafted the court papers for him. We filed them and served them on Ben. I turned up in court, wondering what Ben would be like, expecting to meet a difficult, intransigent individual – the sort of person one would not speak to for 11 years. However, Ben turned out to be both mild-mannered and soft-spoken, and even reasonable. He did not wish to hire a lawyer to act for him, even after I explained to him that he too could apply for legal aid, if he liked, to fight the case. After some discussion he said he was agreeable to selling the flat. But he wanted Andrew to share in some repair costs for the property, as the repairs had to be done before the flat could be sold. I thought that was a reasonable request and asked him to go back and talk to Andrew about it.

'I can't talk to my brother. You ask him for me.' he said. So I went back to my office and got in touch with Andrew while Ben went back to the flat in which he stayed with Andrew. Andrew agreed to share in the repair costs. However, he, of course, could not talk to Ben directly either. So the Bureau contacted Ben on behalf of Andrew, and told him that an agreement had been reached. A consent order was drafted, which both brothers signed at our office, on different days. The order was then approved by the court. Ridiculous as it felt to be playing a post-box between two brothers living in the same flat, I took comfort in the fact that but for the Bureau's intervention, they would still have been living together unhappily – and who knows, the frustration of doing this may have escalated into further quarrels or even family violence.

It never occurred to me that I would become so deeply involved in other people's personal problems when I started out in my career. My first job, as a junior lawyer in a big law firm, involved mostly commercial litigation. I did things like sift through invoices and order forms, examine company contracts, and read bank documents. I looked up the law in areas like letters of credit and corporate insolvency, and drafted lengthy court documents. Every day I filled in a time-sheet and worried about my worth. To better understand the world my clients operated in, I struggled to learn more about banking and finance and business – a challenging thing for someone who much preferred reading English literature and travel writing. For a while I conscientiously flipped to read the financial section of the newspapers each morning, but the effort petered out in time – the mind was willing, but my heart was not in it.

I found that I was more drawn to non-commercial work. Aside from all the commercial cases, on which I was usually the most junior member of a whole legal team, I had a few divorce and adoption cases, and smaller cases involving individuals, which I handled mostly on my own. Some of these cases involved less well-off clients, and I often had instructions from a kind-hearted partner not to charge them too much. I found that I liked dealing with people, rather than organisations. I liked the human interest element, finding out the individual's story. I may not always have liked the clients, but I appreciated how important their cases were to them. A squabble over $100 in wife maintenance, for instance, might seem extremely trivial beside most commercial matters. But for my client in that case it represented a third of all that she spent on food in a month. In a successful adoption case that I did, I was happy that I could play a small role in giving the child a stable future with a good family. The natural mother, a teenage girl, told me: 'I can't keep her. How can I buy her what she needs? A computer? I can't afford that. Or tuition? She will be better off without me.' The mother of the natural mother, the child's grandmother, was not so certain. She turned up in court on the day of the adoption hearing. It was she who had cared for the child since birth, and she was sad to let her go. By this time, the child was already living with the adoptive parents. 'I thought the child would come to court today.' she said in Hokkien. 'I wanted to see her one last time. I brought a present for her.' She proffered a gift wrapped in pink paper, in her wrinkled hands, and asked me if I could hand it to the child's adoptive parents to give to her.

These were the stories and events that caught my imagination. The scenes played in my mind like a film, and I empathised with the characters. I also felt that what I did made a difference to another human being, and that made the hard work worthwhile.

And there certainly was a lot of hard work being done in my law firm. Files came in hefty brown boxes. I took notes for many meetings after office hours, and rode cabs home after midnight. It was a novelty to leave the office when the sky was still light. There were good moments – a court victory, praise from a partner, a thank you note from a client. The legal points were often quite interesting. I enjoyed the office camaraderie, and made good friends. But I never stopped wondering what it would be like to find my 'true calling' – whatever that meant.

One Friday night, I was going through the work to be done in the coming weekend, in preparation for a trial starting on Monday. I felt like a wilted lettuce. My supervising partner, in contrast, still seemed to be full of energy. I asked him, out of curiosity, why he liked his job. His eyes lit up. He smiled. He said 'I love my job. I love the law. I love doing research, making submissions, appearing in court, talking to clients. One day, maybe I will be old and sick and lying in bed, and I will think to myself "Wow, I made arguments in the Court of Appeal!" And what's more, I get paid for doing all this. Yes, I love it. I can't imagine doing anything else.' He really meant it. I felt very moved by his sincerity and passion.

I decided that it was time I looked for another job.

It was through a friend's suggestion that I applied to the Singapore Legal Service, and requested for a posting to the Subordinate Courts. I felt curious about what life would be like on the 'other side' of the Bench. I was appointed as a Magistrate and Deputy Registrar, and sent to the Civil Registry. The Civil Registry does lots of things. Court hearings there take place in chambers – that is, in private, without the public being allowed to sit in. Some parts of the work were very simple and routine, and some of it could be quite difficult and time-consuming. However, almost all of what I did was civil (as opposed to criminal) work, and I was fairly familiar with it. Remembering how nervous and bewildered I used to feel as a young lawyer in court, I tried my best to be patient and courteous in hearings. I read everything as thoroughly as I could, as if I was still in my law firm, preparing to be quizzed by a partner. Not having to deal with clients and prepare the paperwork for the cases gave me a lot more time to think about the law, at a deeper level. The Civil Registry also took continuing education very seriously. We had regular sessions where judicial officers would take turns to present papers on various legal topics for discussion.

Something that changed the course of my life quite significantly was a project I was given to do: to write a paper on a new procedural rule that had just come into effect. The paper was originally just meant to be stored in the judicial officers' internal database. However, the more I researched, the more I wrote. The paper grew in both words and complexity. My Senior Deputy Registrar suggested that I write it up with a view to publishing it in the Singapore Academy of Law Journal. He provided many useful tips on how to write the article so that it would be of a standard that could be published in a journal, yet practical enough for practitioners to want to read. He helped me by vetting it several times and was unsparing in his criticism, which I was grateful for. After many months of writing and re-writing, the article finally got published, and I found myself hooked on legal writing. There were lots of opportunities to write in the Subordinate Courts, both in the Civil Registry, and later when I was sent to the Family Court. I continued to write even after leaving the Subordinate Courts.

I contributed to books on assessment of damages from personal injuries, juvenile justice and family law. I wrote lots of articles, particularly on family procedures and practices, and family law. I even edited a book on the law for teenagers, published by the Singapore Association of Women Lawyers, and authored a booklet on the effects of divorce from a child's point of view, published by the Ministry of Community Development, Youth and Sports. None of this would have been possible without having that 'break' in the Subordinate Courts.

When I went to the Family Court, my writing expanded to the writing of judgments. If the case had interesting legal issues, I would usually try to write a judgment. Often I would not make a decision first, but leave it until after I had written the judgment. In the process of writing, which forced me to set out my thoughts in a methodical way, I would often 'discover' what the right decision was. There were also certain areas of the law, particularly in the more technical areas of family procedure, where there were very few judgments, and I got a thrill when I heard of my judgments being cited (for want of better authority) by lawyers arguing matters in these areas.

Having to make thousands of decisions over a few years helped me to become a more decisive person. I used to be guilty of thinking in circles – mulling over a point for ages, worrying over it like a terrier with a bone, but not being able to actually decide what to do. Having to make many decisions within limited time-frames forced me to think in a more disciplined way, not letting go of my thread of thought and not letting it loop back until I arrived at a satisfactory answer. I also learned how not to be afraid of being wrong. Making a decision is often intimidating because of its potential impact on other people. As a judge, your decision could have a very serious impact on someone – deprive them of their liberty or livelihood, of the presence of their children, or the roof over their head. You could also be told, on appeal, in the most public manner (that is, in a written judgment), that you have been utterly wrong. I became braver about my decision-making when I learned how to stop worrying about whether I was making the *right* decision, and started to focus on making the decision in the right *way* – that is, hearing the parties out patiently, reading the case thoroughly and thinking through the issues methodically.

Of these three things, hearing the parties out patiently was probably the most challenging. The Family Court was a place full of drama – and frequently, of dramatics. I think hardly a day passed without me seeing someone break down in tears, or explode in anger. I found myself encountering a great many more litigants in person (people without lawyers) when I was there. A lot of them were very confused and had no idea of what was going on or what they had to do. They carried around plastic bags full of disorganised and crumpled documents, and often made unrealistic demands. The court process was much harder for them to navigate than for someone with a lawyer.

There were tissue boxes in all the courtrooms, as well as panic buttons. To be fair, my safety was never threatened, though my ego took a battering quite a number of times, from upset and emotional litigants, lashing out in their anger and distress at the person that they thought could determine their fate. I credit the Family Court for giving me much practice in the art and discipline of being patient.

I mediated many settlements and heard many contested cases. I sent numerous people for counselling by the court's in-house counsellors. I covered the Juvenile Court when the Juvenile Court magistrate was on leave. There were children appearing in court who had been in fights, taken drugs, stolen from shops, or worse. But those same children often had parents who themselves did all these things, or who had gone missing, or who had such tumultuous and difficult lives, that they had no time to care for their children. I remember speaking to a pair of brothers, both aged under twelve years. Their mother had passed away, and their father would give them $200 a month and then leave them to fend for themselves alone in the flat, while he lived with his girlfriend somewhere else. They were caught stealing food from shops because they were hungry. There was another father who sent his children to a children's home because he did not want to care for them himself. He also refused to contribute any money to the children's home, saying that he could not afford it. When he gave the breakdown of his monthly expenses, it turned out that he was spending at least $100 a month on cigarettes. When asked whether this money could instead be paid to the children's home, he said it could not, because he needed to smoke, due to stress. When asked what he was stressed about, he replied 'My children stress me out.' There was a single mother who brought her four children to the supermarket and got them to help her steal groceries. What chance did they ever have in life with a mother like that?

My role was to decide what was to be done with the children – whether they should be given probation, or sent to a children's home, for example. There were many difficult decisions to make. Before making any decision, I had a conference with the MCYS officers who prepared the social reports of the children, the Family Court's in-house counsellors and psychologists, and the Juvenile Court's Panel Advisers. (The latter are two persons who sit with the Juvenile Court magistrate in court, to give a community perspective on the court's cases. They are drawn from a panel which includes members of the business, social work, and educational communities.) I learned a lot from talking to these experts from different fields. I learned how to look at people in the context of their environment and family circumstances, and to look for the evidence to build up the picture of their lives – and to resist the temptation to slot them into pigeon-holes for the purposes of making a quick decision.

I come from quite a sheltered background – I have always lived in an intact, happy and economically well-off family. To make up for my lack of experience with family conflict and poverty, I read dozens of books on family dynamics, relationships, divorce, and children's issues. It interested me. I really tried hard to understand what was going on in the cases that came before me, beyond just the legal issues.

The more I read, the more I realised that the root causes of dysfunctional families lay far beyond the ability of the legal system to address. It required an army of social workers, and co-operation across different sectors, legal and non-legal. Many of the litigants I saw were from low-income families, and I used to wonder what more could be done to help them, outside the narrow confines of the courtroom. The Family and Juvenile Court had many contacts with social service and other agencies serving those with personal, family and economic problems. They helped out in the Court's programmes, such as its counselling, mediation and youth programmes. There was even a programme to refer low-income women in maintenance enforcement applications to Community Development Councils for longer-term job and financial assistance. I helped in the design and implementation of many of these programmes, and felt glad that we were trying to help the litigants in a more holistic way.

We were often asked to give talks to social work and other agencies on family and juvenile law processes and procedures, and the workings of the court. I gave many of such talks. I found that I enjoyed the process of explaining legal concepts to lay persons. The process of teaching helped me to understand the system better myself. I talked to social workers, counsellors, medical personnel, students, officers in the community development councils and many others. I also spoke at legal conferences, to both lawyers and lay persons. I was not very used to public speaking before coming to the Family and Juvenile Court, and was rather worried before I had to give my very first talk. At that talk, I treated my powerpoint slides like a security blanket and read off them word for word, in a way that I am sure my listeners found extremely boring. But I loosened up at question time, since that could not be scripted, and began recounting personal anecdotes and having a real conversation with the audience. After that experience, I read many books on public speaking to try and improve. As time went on, I became more and more comfortable with giving talks, and I continued to give them even after I left the Family and Juvenile Court. In fact, legal education for the lay person has become something of a passion with me, and I regularly give such talks, even now.

After some years at the Family and the Juvenile Court, I had the privilege of going on a non-legal secondment, to the Ministry of Community Development and Sports. I went there as a Senior Assistant Director (and was later appointed as a Deputy Director). My mission was to help design and operationalise programmes to help low-income families. It was a chance to do something for all those low-income litigants in person that I saw in the Family and Juvenile Court. This is a book on the practice of law, so I will not go into details about what I did in MCYS. Suffice to say that I thoroughly enjoyed my two years there. I grappled with budget spreadsheets, crafted social assistance programmes, visited social enterprises, and attended focus group discussions with low-wage workers. I met people from all walks of life, from academics to entrepreneurs, from social workers to bank managers. I saw how helping the less privileged is a national effort, and involves – should involve – every sector of society, including the less privileged themselves.

After those two years, however, I had a yearning to go back to the law, and practise those skills that I was trained for. So I applied to be posted to the Legal Aid Bureau, where I worked for almost four years. The case-load was heavy here. Each officer handled a few hundred files. But the atmosphere was very supportive and friendly. I could knock on anyone's door at any time to ask them a question, even the Director himself. I did not have to fill in a time sheet or worry about having to 'generate business' – ie attract new clients and cases – to justify my usefulness to my employer. I could do as much work as I liked for the client without being concerned about whether he could pay me. The variety of work was good. Although more than half of the Bureau's caseload involved family matters, there were also a lot of other civil matters, ranging from industrial accidents, contractual, employment and tenancy disputes, to probate and administration matters, and even presumption of death cases. There were also opportunities to do non-case-file related work, from operational matters such as designing pamphlets to help our applicants understand certain court procedures better, to policy-related ones such as reviewing the Legal Aid and Advice Act, with a view to making improvements to it.

The Bureau also hosts many interns every year, who are personally mentored by legal officers such as myself. One of my responsibilities was to oversee the Bureau's internship programmes and its clinical legal education programme with the National University of Singapore, under which students can do the Bureau's work for course credit, supervised by NUS lecturers or the Bureau's legal officers. I generally liked interacting with students – their enthusiasm and eagerness to learn was always refreshing. By letting them have a chance to help the less privileged now, I am hopeful that they will, when they have graduated, be inspired to do pro bono work in their spare time, or even join the Legal Aid Bureau, using their legal skills to help those who cannot afford it get access to justice.

My core work, however, was serving the people who come to us for help. They can be helped not just through the court process, but by being given practical advice, or being helped (in appropriate cases) through the writing of a letter. A 'gahment' letter can sometimes solve what appeared to be an intractable problem. In one case, after his wife died, the husband asked his own mother to help him look after his young son. After a couple of years, the husband wanted his son to come back and live with him and his other child, a daughter. The grandmother refused to let him go. I wrote a letter on the letterhead of the Legal Aid Bureau, demanding that she return the boy back to his father immediately, since, as the child's biological parent, he was the rightful person to have custody of the child. She complied a short while after receiving the letter and the boy went back to live with his father and sister. In another case, a prisoner sought our help in finding out where the monies from the sale of his flat had gone. The sale of the flat had been handled by his brother to whom he had given a power of attorney. He was afraid that the brother had taken the sale proceeds for himself. After writing letters to the brother and the relevant bank, we found out that the brother had in fact banked the money into the prisoner's bank account and informed the prisoner accordingly, which put his mind at ease. As to why the brother could not have visited or written to the prisoner with the information – well, it is probably the same situation as for the case I described earlier where I was told: 'I can't talk to my brother. You ask him for me.'

To work in the Legal Aid Bureau is to have to deal with a lot of people's personal and relationship problems, many of which stem from an inability to communicate with others and a lack of insight into how the world works, and how other people think and feel.

I once handled an adoption case where both the parents were in prison. They had given their baby to the husband's sister to take care of, ever since birth. The husband's sister agreed to care for the child on the basis that she would adopt the child. She did not wish for the child to be placed with her, and to grow close to her, only for her to be taken away. A few years later, after she and her family had bonded strongly with the child, and the child was ready to start kindergarten, she applied to adopt the child. The parents then changed their minds and refused to consent to the adoption. They had no plan on how to care for the child since they were both in prison. Their only suggestion was that the husband's sister should continue to take care of her and support her financially, and once they came out of prison in a few years' time, if they were so inclined, they would take the child back. They already had a few other children, all of whom were fostered out to different relatives. Their position seemed to me a selfish one, though strongly and sincerely held. They were brought from prison to attend a mediation session with the sister and her husband. They sat in the room, handcuffed, in their bright prison uniforms and plastic slippers.

'I have made so many mistakes in my life.' said the natural father with moist eyes, 'I just don't want this to be another mistake.' 'I want her to know who her real parents are.' The natural mother said, tears rolling down her cheeks, 'And that we wanted her. That we were not the ones who wanted to give her up.' I suggested that the adoptive parents swear a statutory declaration, to be given to the child when she came of age, stating who her biological parents were. After a long conversation with the adoptive parents (and many tears), the natural parents eventually agreed to the adoption, on this condition.

Sometimes the solution can be a very practical one indeed. One day, I was asked for advice by a sister who complained that her brother, who lived with her, kept eating the groceries she brought home but refusing to pay her for it. She had begged and pleaded with him to either not eat her groceries or to pay her for what he took, but to no avail. She and her brother were planning to sell their flat soon so she only needed to keep him away from her groceries until then. I had a brainwave. 'Buy a small fridge and put it in your room. Put all your groceries in your room. Then lock your room when you go out.' I said. The applicant nodded, surprised at the suggestion, but approving. She thanked me and said she would do as I asked. I did not see her again.

However, one must also be careful that practical solutions do not end up involving the lawyer too deeply into other people's personal problems. You should not go where even friends, relatives and social workers fear to tread. One such case involved a white-haired gentleman who pleaded with me to call his grown-up children living overseas, to tell them to talk to him. 'I am all alone.' he said. 'They never talk to me. When I call, they put down the phone. You call them for me. They will listen to you, you are a government lawyer. You tell them to talk to their father.' He said he was afraid of dying alone, in his five-room flat. I shook my head, and told him that much as I sympathised with him, I could not do that. I was not authorised to give that kind of non-legal assistance, and there was no law that compelled grownup children to talk to their parents. There was no practical solution to repair this broken relationship, since the children were thousands of miles away. I could only refer him to a family service centre, to see if a social worker there might be able to help him – at least to talk to him to soothe his loneliness and feeling of abandonment.

I have found that working in the Bureau makes me appreciate all that I have – everything which has allowed me to be the lawyer doing the legal aid case, rather than the client, applying for legal aid. I have also learned, however, not to judge clients too quickly. I once had a client who was blind and had to thumbprint all his affidavits. He did some work as a masseur, but earned very little income. To me, he fell squarely into the category of persons that needed help and who could not be expected to help anyone else. However, some time after his case with us was over, I learned that this same client was a filial son to his aged mother who was in frail health. He would soothe her aches and pains by massaging her, buy her favourite food, and even cook herbal chicken for her to eat – all this when he could not even sign his own name, or see his own face.

This made me realise that it is within the power of almost every person to help another, if he has the will to do so. Of all the lessons that I have learned in the different jobs I have had over the years, this has been the most important one for me.

CHAPTER 16

JUSTICES' LAW CLERK AND STATE COUNSEL, CIVIL DIVISION – LAW IN THE PUBLIC SERVICE

Low Siew Ling

The author is currently a Deputy Senior State Counsel in the Civil Division of the Attorney-General's Chambers. She was a pupil in a large law firm for a brief period after graduation before joining the Legal Service as a Justices' Law Clerk. After this, she was appointed an Assistant Registrar of the Supreme Court. She joined the Civil Division in 2009.

Just as I fell into the study of law quite by accident rather than design (picking university courses by a random process of elimination), I never planned on a career in the Singapore Legal Service. However, I have never regretted the path onto which my fortuitous choices have led me, and now I cannot imagine doing anything else.

1. The Legal Service

In law school, my embarrassingly limited understanding of the Legal Service was that one should sign up only if one had a passionate interest in prosecuting crimes as a Deputy Public Prosecutor. As criminal law and advocacy in general were never subjects that particularly interested me, I did not seriously consider the Legal Service as a career option at the time. It was only after I graduated and was invited to apply to become a Justices' Law Clerk that I began to realise that the practice of law as a Legal Service Officer encompasses a great deal more than just criminal prosecutorial work.

In fact, the Legal Service offers some of the most challenging and wide-ranging areas of practice for any young lawyer. There is an established Rotational Posting System which exposes officers to the broad spectrum of legal work available within the Service. The postings are generally divided into four clusters: (i) Judicial (the Supreme Court Registry and the Subordinate Courts); (ii) Criminal Justice (the criminal divisions of the Attorney-General's Chambers); (iii) Civil (the non-criminal divisions of the AGC such as the Civil Division as well as legal posts in ministries and statutory boards such as the Ministry of Health and the Economic Development Board); and (iv) Regulatory (the Ministry of Law's Legal Policy Division and other policy posts in agencies such as the Competition Commission of Singapore and the Insolvency & Public Trustee's Office) (the posting framework of the Legal Service is continually subject to review and refinement).

Unlike private practice, where you would have to specialise in a particular area after pupillage, a Legal Service Officer would not find himself doing the same thing for the rest of his career unless that was his choice. You could instead spend a number of years in different areas of practice, learning new skills and adapting to new challenges before moving on to contribute to the work of another department. For a generalist like me who came out of law school with a genuine interest in a legal career but no particular affinity for any specific area of work, the Legal Service was a perfect fit.

2.   Justices' Law Clerk

When the prospect of becoming a Justices' Law Clerk (or 'JLC', as we are more commonly referred to) was first open to me, everyone encouraged me to apply because it was a privilege that was open only to the few of us who were fortunate enough to graduate with a First Class Honours degree. Even the partners at the law firm where I was serving my pupillage told me that it would be an invaluable and richly rewarding experience, regardless of whether I would later choose to return to private practice or stay in the Legal Service.

I served as a JLC under former Chief Justice Yong Pung How from 2003–2005. In those two short years, I learnt more about the law – and about a life in the public service of the law – than I could ever have hoped for.

When I served as a JLC, our work was mainly to: (i) assist the Court of Appeal in the consideration of appeals; and (ii) assist CJ Yong (whom we all affectionately refer to as 'Chief' to this day) in the consideration of Magistrate's Appeals. Each month, we would each be assigned a number of Court of Appeal cases and Magistrate's Appeals. Our job was to study the judgments of the courts below, identify the legal issues, analyse the submissions of the parties, do whatever further research was necessary and then consolidate our inputs into the form of a Bench Memorandum (which we called 'BMs') to be submitted to the Judges for their consideration (the JLC scheme has since been expanded and further refined. Besides serving the Court of Appeal, the

JLCs are assigned to a specific High Court Judge every three months to give them exposure to trial and chambers work as well. The JLCs are also given the opportunity to sit concurrently as Assistant Registrars of the Supreme Court, presiding mainly over interlocutory hearings with all the powers of a High Court Judge in chambers).

We were not given a choice about the kind of cases we would like to do – the appeals were assigned to each of us, and what I loved most about being a JLC was the variety of the legal work. While foundational subjects such as contract, tort, property and trust were familiar to me, I had to also grapple with other areas outside my comfort zone such as criminal law (something I never thought I would have to do!), shipping and navigation rules, financial procedure and basically any other principle of law that could possibly be raised by the parties.

Even if the appeals dealt with familiar subjects, they frequently raised new propositions and principles that had never been decided by a Singapore court. The absence of precedents and the freedom which we were given to write our BMs – though somewhat daunting at the beginning – also freed me to think more deeply about the form that the law should take as a matter of principle. As a young lawyer, there is no greater luxury than to be able to spend your working hours playing a part in shaping the growing jurisprudence of Singapore law.

There is a popular myth among local lawyers that JLCs 'decide' cases by their BMs, which subsequently become judgments. This is a misrepresentation of the JLC scheme and how JLCs and Judges work together. The Judges are appointed to the Supreme Court Bench because they are the very best legal minds in the country. Indeed, it would be difficult to imagine that the Judges would be content to place their decision-making powers in the hands of fresh graduates with little or no practical experience in the law (whatever their perceived intellectual capabilities may be). JLCs are there to assist the Judges – to raise questions; to discuss issues; to offer their views – and no more. Judges have frequently disagreed with the position I took in my BMs, and I was humbled by their greater wisdom and learnt from their judgments. Indeed, it is this constant intellectual exchange between the Judges and the JLCs that forms the core of the JLC experience.

The close working relationship that you develop with the Judges during your time as a JLC is also a significant part of that experience. Besides formal discussions over BMs, Chief also frequently arranged for us to lunch with the Judges. During student internships, I had the opportunity to attend a few hearings in the Supreme Court, and the Judges – presiding grimly over their hearings – were always the subject of deep reverence and awe (and no small amount of fear as well!). Seeing the Judges cast aside their stern judicial demeanour to engage in laughter and banter over the lunch table helped me to see them not as forbidding men and women who inhabited the rarefied air of a higher realm, but as intellectually generous and kind mentors who were never too busy to lend a listening ear or share a good story over the lunch table.

For good stories and pithy wisdoms about law and life in general, there was no greater personality than Chief himself. When people (lawyers and non-lawyers alike) first found out that I was working for him, they all inevitably asked: 'Is he very scary?' The press loved to portray Chief as a harsh and unforgiving Judge who thought nothing of doubling an appellant's sentence simply because he had the temerity to appeal. Nothing could be further from the truth. Chief was kind and compassionate to a fault when such sentiments were deserved – not just in his decisions but also in his interactions with us and in his dealings with others.

Chief was the man who had initiated the JLC scheme when he first became CJ, and has always been its greatest champion. He saw the introduction of the JLC scheme as a way to inject young talent into the Legal Service, and he made it his personal mission to ensure that each of us got the most rewarding experience out of it.

For example, while I enjoyed the intellectual challenge of legal work in general, I was no academic and my interest in the law was focused more on how I could apply legal principles to solve the very real problems which were presented to me by the cases before the court. Nevertheless, Chief encouraged me to write articles for publication, and tried to persuade me that academic articles could also solve practical problems.

Over lunch one day, Chief pointed out that some lawyers in Singapore appeared to have forgotten the most basic principles of citing legal authorities, choosing instead to rely on voluminous and often irrelevant and untested material such as, in one extreme case, a private legal opinion issued by a local lawyer! The craft of advocacy, he pointed out, was being lost to the almost competitive deluge of 'authorities'. He suddenly turned to me and said: 'Did you know that in the old days, you could only cite dead authors in court? I think you should write an article about this.'

I tried to ignore the comment since I had no interest in writing anything other than BMs at that point, but he persisted, dropping gentle hints that became progressively more overt over the next few lunches. His resolve ultimately wore down my indolence and a draft article was duly produced. To my surprise, that draft quickly became the subject of a Registrar's Circular that was issued by the court – proof positive that articles could sometimes have a very direct impact on the law in practice.

I must also admit that I had more fun than I thought I would researching that article, and I learnt a lot about the historical practice of law along the way. For example, before Chief told me about it, I had absolutely no clue that at one time, the English courts refused to allow counsel to cite the works of living authors. There were a number of justifications for this rather morbid rule, but my favourite one was this from Sir Robert Megarry, a famous English jurist: 'It must be admitted that there are a number of living authors whose appearance and demeanour do something to sap any confidence in their omniscience which the printed page may have instilled; the dead, on the other hand, so often leave little clue to what manner of men they were save the majestic skill with which they have arrayed the learning of centuries and exposed the failings of the bench.'

Being a JLC gave me the opportunity, time and luxury to steep myself in the study of the law without any distractions as I did not have to worry about billings, clients or partners' demands. Stepping into my office in the old Supreme Court was akin to stepping into another world (and not just because of the rumoured ghosts that haunted the historic building or the bats that flew noisily through the corridor every day). My entire surrounding was infused with the law. Hearings were constantly taking place in the courtrooms; lawyers would pace up and down the corridors in their robes; and legal submissions, judgments and texts littered the shelves and floors of our offices. Even our conversations with each other as JLCs were frequently about the law, whether we were bouncing ideas off each other while writing our BMs or discussing the latest judgments that were being released.

In retrospect, those times seem almost surreal to me now. That is not to say that I did not pick up some practical tips along the way. One invaluable thing that I learnt as a JLC was that while good writing is a gift, disciplined writing can be trained. Although we were given a great deal of freedom in how we wrote our BMs, Chief had one golden rule: our BMs could not exceed twenty pages (I understand that the rule has since been abolished). It did not matter if the appeal was extremely complex and the appellant's and respondent's cases ran into hundreds of pages. Chief was a great believer in the virtue of brevity and he expected us to practice what he preached. One of the first few notes we received from him was a minute emphasising the importance of good legal writing. As an example of a fine work that we could hope to emulate, Chief enclosed a copy of a judgment written by current Chief Justice Chan Sek Keong while he was a Judicial Commissioner.

I must confess that the twenty-page limit used to cause my fellow JLCs and I no small amount of hardship, and we probably spent more time ruthlessly 'cutting' our BMs rather than actually writing them. Surprisingly, this was never impossible, even if our first drafts were fifty pages long and all hope appeared to be lost at that early stage. The golden rule forced us to exercise discretion and judgment, stripping away the red herrings and minor technical arguments to focus on the most critical issues in the case. This is a skill that any lawyer will find useful in practice – no Judge wants to read an academic treatise disguised as a submission, just as no client wants to sieve through a rambling advice in an attempt to discern the answer to his queries. The experience also taught me to appreciate good legal writing as a matter of technique, and I now read judgments with a critical eye for their mastery of the language as much as for their legal content.

3.   State Counsel, Civil Division

After two years as a JLC, I was appointed an Assistant Registrar of the Supreme Court, where I remained for another two years before leaving to do my Masters at Harvard on a Legal Service Commission Scholarship. Shortly after my return, I was posted to the Civil Division of the Attorney-General's Chambers ('AGC') as a State Counsel.

Everyone knows about the criminal work of the Deputy Public Prosecutors in the AGC, but very few know that there is also a Civil Division within Chambers that functions independently as the equivalent of the Government's 'law firm'. Put simply, the Government comes to us for legal advice on all civil matters (whether public or private) and looks to us to defend its interests in court proceedings and other disputes which do not involve criminal prosecutions.

I recall that shortly after I was posted to the Civil Division, I ran into a lawyer I recognised while waiting for one of my cases (involving an alleged breach of contract by the Government) to be called for a Pre-Trial Conference in the Supreme Court. He came up to me and asked, 'What are you doing here outside your chambers?' I told him I had left the Supreme Court and was now a State Counsel in the Civil Division of the AGC. He looked genuinely perplexed. 'You mean there is such a thing?'

Yes, there is, and like any other large law firm in Singapore, the Civil Division has a broad practice in various areas of law. Unlike most major firms, however, we are not split into individual departments. There are currently seventeen Legal Service Officers in the Civil Division serving the legal needs of the entire Government (including fifteen Ministries, the Cabinet and other Organs of State), and every State Counsel is expected to manage and deal with all types of cases independently.

Our work can broadly be categorised under three main headings: (i) Advisory; (ii) Contract; and (iii) Litigation.

In terms of Advisory work, our job is to advise the Government in all its legal queries. These include issues ranging from more obvious public law matters such as constitutional and administrative law (for example, the constitutionality of certain policy proposals, or the limits of the Government's power to compulsorily acquire land) to private law areas such as contract, tort, equity, finance, insolvency, trusts, charities, company law and intellectual property (just a few examples of the issues that I have dealt with in my two and a half years in the Division). Many people may be surprised that a public lawyer also has to field queries on such a wide range of presumably private law matters, but this is simply a function of the fact that the Government is also a legal entity with its own private law dealings. Besides formulating and implementing public policies to govern the nation, the Government is also, amongst other things, an employer, a landlord, a tenant, a customer, a trustee, a beneficiary, a shareholder, a bond-issuer, etc.

As for Contract work, the Civil Division advises the Government on its contractual negotiations and obligations and also vets all contracts and agreements which the Government is a party to. Besides relatively simple contracts like scholarship agreements, we also deal with more complex documents such as procurement tenders, construction contracts and financial guarantees. The general public would be well-acquainted with high-profile events such as the F1 race and the Youth Olympic Games. What they would not be aware of are the reams of contracts, MOUs (Memoranda of Understanding) and other agreements behind these major events that must be vetted by our Division.

Finally, in terms of Litigation work, the Civil Division represents the Government in court proceedings and other disputes which do not involve criminal prosecutions. We defend the constitutionality and legality of the Government's decisions and decision-making processes when these are challenged in court (for example, the clemency process recently came under attack in a death penalty case), and also protect the Government's interests in other legal proceedings (such as filing claims in court when monies are owed to the Government or defending private law cases that are brought against the Government, such as the breach of contract case I mentioned earlier). In addition to such general litigation, our dispute resolution work also covers more uniquely specialised areas such as compulsory land acquisition appeals and internal disciplinary hearings involving public officers.

To say that the work of a State Counsel in the Civil Division is challenging would be an understatement. Translated into private practice terms, imagine yourself as an associate serving all the departments of a large law firm concurrently. One day you could be asked to handle a personal injury trial or a judicial review hearing, whilst the next day (or even on the same day!) you could also be asked to vet a construction tender and also advise on the legal merits of a complex securities transaction. The learning curve for any new officer is very steep, but therein lies the challenge. I enjoy my work immensely and find great satisfaction in learning new law with every case that I am assigned. Indeed, I can honestly say that I have never been bored or found my work dull or routine because it never has been.

Every piece of work we do is cleared through a circulation process all the way up to the Chief Counsel, the Solicitor-General and even the Attorney-General. The circulation process itself has also been a transformative experience. Each senior officer who clears my work offers a new perspective on the issues. Besides educating me on the law, I have also had the privilege of being schooled in the unique considerations of public policy by some of the most brilliant lawyers in Singapore who have dedicated themselves to the public service of the law. I would like to believe that I have developed and matured as an officer under their guidance.

There is also a great emphasis placed on training and development within the Division. In October 2009, I was given the opportunity to attend a six-week attachment in London as part of the then-Attorney-General's plans to strengthen our litigation practice. I spent two weeks in a major international law firm studying the organisation of its litigation department and its knowledge management and dispute resolution framework. I also had the opportunity to spend four weeks in one of the leading inns of court, where I got to witness first-hand how the English barristers (and in particular, their Queen's Counsel) hone their court craft. What struck me the most about that experience was the barristers' passion for advocacy and the importance that the English courts placed on oral arguments. During my time as a JLC, I found that many lawyers in Singapore were content to let their written submissions do the bulk of their work for them, often relegating oral arguments to a short exercise in formality. The emphasis is markedly different in England. For the English Bar, oral arguments define the case in a way that written submissions – formulated without any interaction with the court – never could, and that is why their counsel can take three full days to present oral arguments for an appeal in which extensive written submissions have already been filed. Whether such a practice is practically workable in Singapore is another question entirely, but I certainly remember the passion with which the barristers spoke (long after my memory of what they wrote has faded away).

People sometimes ask me how my experience as a State Counsel in the Civil Division compares to the work of a JLC. In terms of intellectual rigour, I would say that the work is comparable, but the pressures are far greater as State Counsel also have to manage practical concerns such as urgent timelines, multiple caseloads and client expectations. As a JLC and a judicial officer, my sole priority was to assist the court in arriving at a sound decision as a matter of law. As a lawyer serving the Government, however, I have a responsibility to ensure that the position the Government takes is defensible not only as a matter of law but also as a matter of public policy (in the sense of being practically workable), and I have far less time to research the law and formulate my decision because there will always be other urgent files sitting on my desk with clients clamouring for an answer. The pace of law in day-to-day practice is frenetic because the Government, perhaps even more so than any other private client, does not have the luxury of keeping public policies in suspension indefinitely whilst waiting for legal advice.

Let me also stress that while the Civil Division acts for the Government, our ultimate responsibility – indeed, the ultimate responsibility of any lawyer – is to uphold the Rule of Law, the core principle being that the law applies to all individuals and entities within the state, whether public or private. Indeed, as public lawyers freed from the commercial pressures of keeping clients and generating billings, we have no incentive to defend anything other than the public interest. It is this independence of purpose that I value the most as a Legal Service Officer.

4.   Some Concluding Remarks

The public service aspect of Legal Service work is sometimes ignored by the wider community. I remember speaking about my job at a forum for Junior College students who were interested in studying law in 2009. During Q&As, one of them asked me very bluntly: 'Why did you choose the Legal Service? Won't you be able to make a lot more money if you join a private law firm?'

My answer may sound trite, but the truth is that although I did not seriously consider a career in the public service when I first graduated, I have, in time, come to appreciate the truly remarkable nature of the work that Legal Service performs. There is sometimes a tendency to regard the law as a mere body of arid rules to be applied like mathematical formulae to the facts of a particular case, but the very public impact of what I do on a daily basis reminds me that the spirit of the law animates every aspect of the society in which we live. It is in the work of the Legal Service that the Rule of Law has been made most real to me. While money is certainly important (and let me say that the pay in the Legal Service – though not equivalent to that of a high-flying lawyer in private practice – is not half bad), there is a far greater satisfaction in knowing that you are devoting your intellectual efforts to doing what is right.

I will conclude with an enduring memory of one of my first Contract law classes with Professor Andrew Phang, now a Judge of Appeal in the Supreme Court. The class was discussing when a binding contract is formed – this happens by what lawyers call 'offer and acceptance'. Although an offeror (A) is entitled to withdraw his offer to the offeree (B) any time before B accepts the offer, A must also prove that B had knowledge of the withdrawal before B purported to accept the offer, failing which A might still be bound to perform the contract (and liable to pay damages to B if he failed to do so). Say, for example, A had offered to sell his house to B for $1 million and the offer was conditional on B accepting the offer by 1pm on Friday, but A managed to sell his house to C for the same price on Thursday morning. A forgot to inform B of this, but B found out about the sale from someone else (D) on Thursday evening. Could B still try to accept A's offer on Friday morning despite knowing that A was no longer capable of performing the contract, and sue A for failing to do so? The answer is no, because B already knew, before attempting to accept A's offer, that A no longer had any intention to sell his house to him.

Prof Phang then polled the class: What if we were in B's position and we had found out about the sale, but there was absolutely no way that anyone would know that we knew about it (let us say D died of a heart attack shortly after telling us about the sale, and nobody else knew what he had told us)? Would we hide our knowledge, accept A's offer and then sue A for breach of contract? To Prof Phang's horror, the majority of the class said 'Yes'. It was raining heavily at the time, and there was (somewhat poetically) a lone plastic cup sitting on the ledge outside the window of the classroom. Prof Phang told us all to look outside. 'As future lawyers, you cannot be like that cup – just mere receptacles of legal principles with no soul. You must process what you learn and use it to do what is right by your own conscience.' While many in the class may have long forgotten the intricacies of contract law principles, I think few of us could ever forget Prof Phang's impassioned plea for us to apply the law to the best of purposes.

I am very grateful for the opportunity to try to live up to that goal in my work. Indeed, I deeply admire the young officers who join the Legal Service because they truly believe that it is their calling to use the law to help the people and the nation. I will be the first to admit that I was not quite so noble all those years ago. What I hope is that the young officers who come with such fine ideals will find fulfillment in their work, and those who join for other reasons will, like me, come to appreciate the intangible rewards of a life devoted to the public service of the law.

CHAPTER 17

LAW WITHIN GOVERNMENT – LAW AS A PURVEYOR OF JUSTICE, VALUES AND CULTURE

Valerie Thean

Valerie Thean is Director, Legal Policy and Legal Industry Divisions, Ministry of Law. All views and comments expressed here are personal, and do not reflect the views of the Ministry. Valerie has a MA from Downing College, Cambridge University and a LLM from Harvard Law School.

1. Introduction

Policy-making and law can at first appear a mismatch of concepts. To readers who have grown up on a staple of television shows *The Practice*, *Damages*, or even books like *Bleak House*, the law appears worlds away from discussing a country's safety and continued prosperity.

Yet, in a modern economy, the law is the framework that underpins a citizen's compact with the State, and the State's interaction with the wider world. Government, in implementing its policies, uses the force of law. At the same time, the rule of law is such that no government is above the law: its officers and policies are subject to the supervision of the courts and the law. The law is thus the muscular system that binds policies into coherent governance in a fully functioning body.

2. Law As An Instrument of Governance

The citizen sees the law in its most obvious form as an instrument of governance. At its lowest level, we see this in the specifics of legislation. When the executive branch of government must impose tax or dispense benefits, it does this through legislation. Where the government seeks to regulate behaviour, it does this through laws which penalise, either administratively or through the criminal law. The law sets up our key institutions, including Parliament and the Courts, and informs as to how they relate and interact with one another.

3. Law As A Construct of Society

Law, in its more comprehensive sense, is also a construct of society. As a society, we have our own unique social mores and characteristics. This we can see when we look at our laws in the round. An example is our multi-racial, multi-ethnic and multi-religious history. This issue is not a novel one within the current international eco-system. Singapore's specific resolution of the various problems, however, is a product of our history. We have a web of different laws, grown up through the years, and an approach that is extremely local.

Our legacy of communal tension has ingrained within us a deep concern for racial and religious fault lines. The Constitution specifically provides that the Government is to care for the interests of the racial and religious minorities, and to recognise the special position of the Malays. This is supported by the possibility of prosecution. The Penal Code has offences against deliberately wounding the religious and racial feelings of a person, the Sedition Act has an offence for speech tending to promote feelings of ill will and hostility against specific races. Religious leaders are also held accountable for their actions. Thus the Maintenance of Religious Harmony Act ('MRHA') provides that a restraining order may be imposed against religious leaders who mix politics and religion.

Our approach is a distinct and unusual one. While many countries, such as Germany, United Kingdom, Ireland, Sweden and Finland have hate speech offences within their legislation, we have a framework that protects these interests at a deeper level, through the Constitution, and at a religious leadership level, via the MRHA.

At the other end of the spectrum, there are also countries where the right to free speech could be considered more important than the multi-ethnic harmony which we prize. In the United States, the First Amendment gives citizens an unfettered right to free expression. Thus, Florida pastor Terry Jones put the Quran on trial and burned it. As an event, it was attended only by a few. Subsequently, a video was put on Youtube, and two days' of violent unrest in Afghanistan was attributed to the video.

4. Society As A Construct Of Law?

What about the converse? Could the law ever be used to mould society? This would be an idea that may seem quite intuitive to those who would like to describe our government as patriarchal. At a certain level, perhaps it is possible, as law is often used to modify behaviour. We have littering laws, for example, and that has enabled us to keep our streets clean.

But law cannot be used to change society's deeper held beliefs and mores. One example was discussed at Singapore's recent Universal Periodic Review of Human Rights at the United Nations Human Rights Council. At the last revision of the Penal Code in 2007, there was active debate about whether section 377A, which criminalises homosexual acts, should be deleted. Reactions on both sides were vehement, with a Nominated Member of Parliament characterising homosexuality as 'an abomination'. The government concluded that our society, being essentially conservative, was not yet ready for an amendment, and that the *status quo* should remain until the time was appropriate. The Prime Minister framed the issue thus:

> If you try and force the issue and settle the matter definitively, one way or the other, we are never going to reach an agreement within Singapore society. People on both sides hold strong views. People who are presently willing to live and let live will get polarised and no views will change, because many of the people who oppose it do so on very deeply held religious convictions, particularly the Christians and the Muslims and those who propose it on the other side, they also want this as a matter of deeply felt fundamental principles. So, discussion and debate is not going to bring them closer together. And instead of forging a consensus, we will divide and polarise our society.

Nor can the law be used to reshape reality. A fairly technical example of this is the evidential presumption of no access. This presumption dated from Victorian times, where, given the stigma attached to illegitimate children, children were presumed to be the offspring of their married parents save for a clear exception where it could be proved that the offspring's parents had no access to each other. When colonial drafters of our early legislation worked this into our Evidence Act, they made this an irrebuttable presumption. Section 114 of the Evidence Act states: 'The fact that any person was born during the continuance of a valid marriage between his mother and any man, or within 280 days after its dissolution, the mother remaining unmarried, shall be conclusive proof that he is the legitimate son of that man, unless it can be shown that the parties to the marriage had no access to each other at any time when he could have been begotten.' Therefore, the law now said that it could not be proved otherwise. It did not create a rule of substantive law, which was derived from legitimacy law, but provided an evidential aid which excludes other methods of proving paternity, creating thereby, a legal fiction used to shape reality. But technology is relentless, and with DNA evidence, parentage may be proved now with extremely high levels of accuracy. Courts have tried, with varying levels of success, to make sense of a legal device that is no longer in accord with reality (The High Court in *WX v WW* [2009] 3 SLR(R) 573 refused to apply the presumption, and at [6] commented that its application in the face of DNA evidence 'offends both justice and common sense'. See, further, for a discussion of the case and its difficulties, (2009) 10 SAL Ann Rev, *Family Law* (Ong & Thean), 15.35–15.46).

A more colourful, fictional example would be if we were to suggest a new law to impose the death penalty on all persons who wear red on Tuesdays. This would be met with odium, and no government could propose this without losing the mandate of its electorate. In a democracy, the law cannot construct what society cannot accept. Thus, in an indirect way, the law reflects society's sense of where justice and fairness lies. As the means to the ends which society intends, the law gives an insight into a country's soul.

5.   Rule of Law As The Fulcrum

How does it happen that the law must be a construct of society, but society, in some cases, but not always, might be a construct of law? Our institutions and democratic processes limit executive action. Each bill must be passed by Parliament. The rule of law is such that no government is above the law. The courts have the power of judicial review. Within the common law system, the courts also apply and extend the law in keeping with prior cases, ensuring consistency of approach in the context of the justice of each case.

6.   Law and Society in Tandem

We see from the examples given above, that the relationship between society and the law is largely an iterative one. Policy informs the law: the law, in its turn, informs policy.

We see this in our historical choices. At independence, Singapore was fortunate to inherit a strong legal infrastructure, grounded in the common law. This stood us in good stead. Throughout our young history, however, we have seen an intelligent search for forms, to retain that which works, and to eschew that which does not. As then-Prime Minister, Lee Kuan Yew, said in 1962: 'Justice and fair play according to predetermined rules of law can be achieved within our situation if there is integrity of purpose and an intelligent search for forms which will work and which will meet the needs of our society' (The Prime Minister, University of Singapore Law Society, 18 January 1962).

Good illustrations are provided by controversial examples. Corporal punishment has been and will remain topical. In Singapore, vandalism is punishable with caning. The context is a historical one, seen as a necessary tool of the colonial government to contain certain kinds of unrest. In the modern context, many other countries see it is a minor offence, common amongst juveniles. At the height of the *Michael Fay* incident, where an American was to be sentenced under our vandalism laws, our Ambassador was interviewed by Larry King on CNN. Ambassador Nathan explained that we would not shy away from retaining mechanisms where such were useful for meeting society's collective aspirations:

> Larry King: Okay, why not, Mr Ambassador? Britain doesn't do it anymore and the international courts say don't do it, and Britain was the one that gave it to you when you were a colony. Why not wipe it out?

> Ambassador Nathan: No, why should we? I mean, this is deterrence against people who perpetuate that sort of crime and we see as justified as keeping it in our books, and this is as far as we are concerned, for the welfare of our people.

An example of eschewing what does not work would be our abolition of jury trials.

While jury trials had been a part of our laws from the colonial period, the post-independence Government abolished them, on the footing that judges, rather than juries were more competent to deal with issues which arose during trial. At the Second Reading of a bill to abolish jury trials for capital cases, the Prime Minister referenced continental civil systems of law, and his own experience as a criminal lawyer. When the Minister for Law read, for the third time after Select Committee hearings, the same Bill, he explained thus at the Third Reading of the Criminal Procedure Code (Amendment) Bill on 22 December 1969:

> Sir, when this Bill was introduced in this House, I emphasised the fact that the proposed abolition of the jury had not been conceived impulsively but that Government had given considerable thought to this Bill and could not ignore experiences in recent trials by jury. I would not hesitate to reiterate that rather than allow justice to be thwarted, through either squeamishness or ignorance, Government is prepared whenever necessary for the well-being of the community to amend the procedural methods of administering the law.

7. Law and Society in Progress

Society does not stand still, however. And so, neither does the law. As society progresses, we see an increasing sophistication in our approach to the law. The recent Criminal Procedure Code revision provides an example. Within the common law world, sentencing an offender involves the four main principles of deterrence, retribution, protection of the public and rehabilitation. Capital and corporal punishment, preventive detention, corrective training, longer imprisonment terms emphasise the first three. Probation orders, where offenders are allowed to stay within a home environment subject to strict conditions, are an illustration of the last principle.

Community-Based Sentences were introduced in 2010. Four sentencing options place a greater weight on rehabilitation in the context of offenders and offences which are, in the larger scheme, less serious. Community Service Orders, previously only available tied with probation orders, are now available for offenders of minor offences, who would do a stipulated number of hours of work with charity, volunteer and civil society organisations. Mental treatment orders emphasise a targeted programme for those with mental disorders. Short Detention Orders serve to give a short, sharp insight into prison life for younger offenders. Agencies may propose new Community Work Orders, which thus far have been used for littering offences, where offenders are ordered to clean streets. For minor offences and novice offenders, these options give those convicted a better chance to change and reintegrate into society. The more comprehensive sentencing framework is a reflection of our holistic approach to sentencing.

8. The Impact of The Global World

Singapore is a small country, and as such, respect for international legal norms, as opposed to power, is important for us. In delimiting our boundaries, we have sought recourse to institutions such as the International Tribunal for the Law of the Sea, n a land reclamation dispute with Malaysia, (an ad hoc tribunal established pursuant to the UN Convention on the Law of the Sea) and the International Court of Justice in a dispute with Malaysia over Pedra Branca.

The international platform is one that is changing rapidly. Since the Second World War, the burgeoning volume of global trade has made international norms on trade more important. Attempts by international institutions to make laws across countries consistent to ease international commerce have grown. As a trading nation, we have also sought bilateral and multilateral free trade agreements. The Universal Declaration of Human Rights, too, has brought into the conversation not simply aspects of war, survival and commerce, but normative ideals and ethical propositions which underpin societies. As more and more States come to joint consensus on issues, it becomes advantageous for Singapore to align with various norms. Our International Arbitration Act, for example, is based on UNCITRAL Model Law. Singapore has ratified the Hague Convention on the Civil Aspects of Child Abduction, to assist residents who have cross-jurisdictional child custody disputes. Amongst the UDHR's core international human rights treaties, Singapore has ratified the Convention on the Rights of the Child and the Convention on the Elimination of All Forms of Discrimination against Women.

Not all of our engagement may be entirely voluntary, in time to come. Customary international law may also be invoked in domestic courts of common law countries. Such a challenge was made in *Nguyen Tuong Van v Public Prosecutor* [2001] 1 SLR (R)103. Discussion in this case centred on the reception of customary international law into Singapore law. There were two points of interest: (1), the position taken by international law on the punishment of death by hanging. It was argued that the death penalty fell within the customary international law prohibition of torture and cruel, inhuman or degrading treatment or punishment. The Court of Appeal found that there was no general customary rule as such which prohibits the punishment of death by hanging. On (2), the reception into Singapore law of certain consular rights under customary international law, the Court of Appeal held that although consular rights of the accused were applicable under customary international law, they did not assist the accused on the facts of the case.

Worldwide legal norms are but one aspect. Technology is the more powerful other. Many attribute the ease and speed of the widespread Middle East unrest seen in early 2011 to social networks and new media, which reinforce the power of traditional media. With the reach of mass media and the internet, no state may be an island unto itself.

9. The Future of Law Within Policy

Whither the future? At the start of the article, I likened the law to the muscular system. This is one that requires development over the years. As a country, we have been a youth in an arena populated by those with much longer histories. Increasingly, as the world stage includes newer states and infant countries, Singapore is seen as an older, rather than younger, sibling. *Its value at the table can grow if its proposition remains strong.*

A second development is the increasing complexity of the world stage, where international norms are strengthening, and domestic law reform is constantly referenced against such norms. As Singapore seeks to advance its interests in the world, it would need to position as a savvy world citizen. Singapore is a small country, and cannot afford to ignore norms and standards. *Its best course is to seek to influence the conversation by intellectual leadership.*

A third is the globalised citizen. Singapore is now one of the most connected countries in the world. How the world looks at us has become important to those who look at the world. As society matures, its sense of social justice becomes more important. Normative ideals come to the forefront in the context of law reform. The values that drive the laws we amend and those we do not will become increasingly contentious. *Governance requires an ever more intelligent and discerning search for forms and concepts that work within the local context.*

In finding answers, good governance will also require good explanation. The increase in our literacy rates and the success of our education system has created an increasingly sophisticated citizen, one which expects discourse within an increased public space. *Policymakers will have to make sense of, and communicate, the architecture of our laws in an accessible way.*

These new challenges will become stronger, but the old ones of creating economic value out of scarce resource and forging a nation from divergent aspirations remain. As the Prime Minister said recently in April 2011: 'We will always be vulnerable, always a small country with an open economy, having to hold our own against larger countries, having to live by our hard work and our wits.'

In pulling together the various strands, the call to embrace an autochthonous legal system is apposite (most notably by Andrew Phang, 'An Autochthonous Legal System' (1989) 1SAcLJ 68). While many details of our specific pieces of legislation take reference from legislation from other common law countries or international standards, this article has sought to show that much of the design of our legal framework has been inventive. Going forward, this imperative for pragmatic creativity is more compelling, not less.

10. 'If justice perishes, then it is no longer worthwhile for men to live upon the earth' – Immanuel Kant, Rechtslehre

At its lowest level of contribution, the law has always been an instrument of governance that cannot be ignored. In modern society, it has potential for much more: it may be part of a process to inform and educate; it may be used as a purveyor of justice, values and culture. In an evolving dynamic where a nation seeks to grow within and without, its role and rationale is the challenge – and the promise – of law within government.

As with all nations who mature, our muscular system will require more work. In a well-functioning body, no muscle is atrophied; some gain greater prominence than others depending upon the stage of growth, usage and need. This enables the various limbs to work in tandem in a stance that is effective domestically and internationally. If that which is needed is lacking, the dictates of mind and heart, while more crucial, will be impossible to execute.

OTHER PRACTICES

CHAPTER 18

IN-HOUSE COUNSEL – STILL ENJOYING THE RIDE AFTER 18 YEARS

Ruby Lee

Ruby Lee is currently in-house legal counsel with a company listed on the Singapore Exchange Securities Trading Limited. She graduated in 1985 from the National University of Singapore and obtained an LLM from the London School of Economics in 1990. She was in private practice for approximately five years before going in-house.

1.   How I Unintentionally Became In-House Counsel

One day, nearly 18 years ago, while I was in the midst of preparing for yet another trial (I was working for a medium-sized law firm and had all sorts of trials almost every week), I received a call from a head hunter asking if I would be interested in joining an aggressive international organisation as regional legal counsel.

I had not thought of leaving legal practice at all, but the offer was tempting. The job was a regional one, as the organisation's headquarters was in Hong Kong, and it had factories in Malaysia, Thailand, Taiwan and the Peoples' Republic of China. The organisation was looking at setting up a regional office in Singapore for the Malaysian and Thai operations. I went for a very odd interview held in the suite of a hotel and before I had a chance to mull over the pros and cons of leaving practice, I was hired.

One month later, I was on my way to the headquarters in Hong Kong. It was agreed that I was to spend a couple of months in Hong Kong to familiarise myself with the operations and the culture. I was collected from the airport and taken to a delicious lunch. It was all very civilised until I was driven into an old industrial part of Hong Kong. The headquarters was an old, dirty factory building and I was ushered into a rattling goods lift to meet the board of directors. Inside the old, dirty, rattling goods lift, I thought to myself, 'Oh no!!!... What have I done!!!... I want my old job back! I want my smart office in Shenton Way back... I want to be back in Singapore... help...'.

Now, 18 years later, I know that making the move from legal practice to in-house was the best move I have ever made.

2.   What Is This 'In-House Counsel' Creature?

An in-house counsel is like a general practitioner. The in-house counsel is the first person that the company consults when it has anything remotely related to a legal issue, or when it has an issue but does not know how to deal with it. The in-house counsel would work out the problem and decide if the problem can be handled internally, or should be best referred to a specialist. This is very much like whether the general practitioner would prescribe or recommend the treatment for the complaint, or would refer the patient to a specialist.

The scope of an in-house counsel very much depends on the organisation that you decide to work for. The work can range from merely keeping the organisation's books and records, to being a key executive of the organisation so that all matters, including commercial matters would require your input. It also depends on how interested and willing you are to take on responsibilities in the non-legal aspects of the organisation.

In small organisations, the in-house counsel's roles could range from being in charge of keeping the company's books and records being named as the company secretary and being a nominee director assisting in the operations of the company. The in-house counsel will be expected to handle the day to day legal matters such as review suppliers' contracts, tenancy agreements, employment contracts and assist in drafting responses and letters to external parties. In cases when external counsel's assistance is required, such as litigation matters, (in-house counsels do not hold practicing certificates and hence do not have a right to appear in court), the in-house counsel acts as the liaison between the organisation and the external lawyers.

In larger organisations, the job scope would include managing or working with a team of in-house counsels, and managing books and records of the companies within the organisation. You may have the assistance of a qualified company secretary for the keeping of books and records. You will have, as your clients, the many companies within the organisation.

3.   What Did I Do For 18 Years?

When I got back to Singapore after the orientation in Hong Kong, I was the only employee based in Singapore. I was tasked with finding an office, setting up the office, recruiting staff and assisting in the relocation of expatriate staff in addition to the legal matters that were beginning to trickle in from the various subsidiaries of the organisation once they realised that there was legal counsel on board.

Singapore subsequently became the legal headquarters for the organisation and duplicate copies of all company records were kept in Singapore. From an in-house counsel's point of view, it was extremely exciting for me to be responsible for companies registered and governed by Malaysian, Thai, Bermudian, British Virgin Islands, Cayman Islands, Japanese, Hong Kong Special Administration, Chinese, British, Canadian and American laws. I had the opportunity to learn the listing requirements of many countries and dealt with company secretaries of such countries. In addition to attending board meetings for both listed and non-listed entities of the various companies, I also attended the meetings of the executive committees of active companies to record operational issues discussed and resolved at such meetings. It was indeed a great learning experience as all the details of operations such as that of an electronics factory, construction of a factory complex or management of a distribution chain would be discussed openly.

The organisation was manufacturing based and expanded by mergers and acquisitions on an international level. As in-house counsel, I had the opportunity to see the deals from inception all the way to completion, instructing and working with external lawyers to close deals as quickly and as efficiently as possible. As in-house counsel, I was able to participate in corporate deals and proposals and work with top lawyers and law firms in many jurisdictions.

Some of the more exciting matters that I had the opportunity to participate in included the debt restructuring of three Japanese listed companies and the subsequent restructuring of such companies, including relocation of their manufacturing bases to Asia, the acquisition of US listed entities, purchase of a Learjet, a yacht, and the purchase and development of residential properties. I also had the chance of working with the Economic Development Board for grants, building and setting up a manufacturing plant in Singapore, setting up and operating an entertainment division which dealt with restaurants, cafes and game centres, buying and selling hotels in the United States, listing companies in Malaysia and Singapore, setting up research and development as well as industrial design centres in Singapore and exhibiting in international fairs.

When an organisation grows by mergers and acquisitions, the organisation will face a myriad of claims and legal actions. It is exhilarating to experience the court systems of the different countries.

I have had the opportunity of attending hearings in Malaysia, Hong Kong, United States, and of course Singapore. In some jurisdictions like Australia and United States, mediation is widely used as an alternative means of dispute resolution and I had the opportunity of taking part in mediations in both Australia and United States. It was refreshing to see prominent retired judges working at such mediations as they are ever so professional. I had taken part in a mediation in the United States where the mediator, a retired judge, had within two hours, told everyone to go home as the parties were too far apart to reach a settlement and there was no point wasting any more time, even though he was to be paid by the hour.

4. What Makes A Good In-House Counsel?

Good Overall View of Law, Generally

An in-house counsel should have a good general knowledge of the law so that he or she is able to identify the area of law involved (if it indeed is an area that requires legal assistance) and propose solutions that are in the best interest of the company. I realise now that I was only a competent practicing lawyer (at best), with good general skills. I now know that I did not and do not have the potential to be a great lawyer in any particular field. On hindsight, going in-house gave me the best opportunity to exploit my core competency.

Common and Commercial Sense

A good in-house counsel must possess a great deal of common and commercial sense. The in-house counsel must accept that the legal portion of a commercial deal is not the important part of the deal. The legal formalities must accommodate the commercial deal as far as possible. In many cases, the in-house counsel may have to compromise on the wording of certain contracts in order to assist the company in closing a deal. Commercial and common sense will come into play as you will need to assist the management in weighing the risks of certain issues against the commercial gains. The in-house counsel should be able to assess when it is important to insist on certain legal measures to be taken and when to be more flexible.

The in-house counsel must know when to advise a settlement if a full blown trial in court will not be worth the cost even if the company has a strong case. The cost of a trial to a company may not just be the cost of the law firm handling the case. It will include the cost of management and employee time in preparing for a trial and in many cases, cost of tracking down old documents and ex-employees and the like. Again, this calls for some exercise of common and commercial sense.

The in-house counsel would have much more information about the company and should have an objective view of the means of the company, whether in monetary or manpower terms. The in-house counsel should then exercise his or her common and commercial sense in the light of such knowledge to ensure that the company does not enter into obligations that it cannot properly fulfill. The in-house counsel should also be able to advise and instruct external lawyers far more effectively as he or she would have more in-depth knowledge of the workings of the Company.

Good Communication Skills

The in-house counsel must have good communication skills. It is the in-house counsel that has to translate a corporate deal to external lawyers. Many of the deals may be structured by the board of the company, members of which may not be legally trained. In-house counsel has to be able to translate to the company's team of non-legal people, the external lawyer's advice on why a certain deal cannot be structured in the way that the commercial people want. The in-house counsel will also have to deal with different professionals with different levels of education within the company, and must be able to understand the problems as well as be understood by these people in giving out advice. In many international corporations, the board of directors will comprise of people from different countries, and it is essential that the in-house counsel is able communicate with the various directors in order to accurately record minutes of meetings as well as to assist in the concerns of the directors and shareholders. Many times, I find that I am translating Singapore-English to American-English, or Indian-English to Japanese-English at meetings!

Enjoy Interaction With All Kinds Of People

The in-house counsel must enjoy dealing with people from different cultures, different educational and social backgrounds. The in-house counsel will be consulted by the human resource department, by the administration department, by the sales department, by the factory managers, by purchasing departments, and not forgetting the board of directors. So in one day, you might be working on a disciplinary matter with your human resource department over a factory incident, while after lunch, you might be working with a team of external lawyers on the acquisition of a company listed in Tokyo. The in-house counsel is always dealing with people as the in-house counsel depends on information in order to perform his or her job efficiently. The co-operation of co-workers is key to the in-house counsel's performance and he or she will need to elicit confidence and inspire management and staff so that he or she will be able to obtain accurate and timely information in order to complete the deals or to fight a case effectively in court.

Some Practical Experience

An in-house counsel should have some practical experience. The practical experience will give the in-house counsel more confidence in dealing with external lawyers and at the same time, give him or her an understanding of how the external lawyer operates. He or she will then be able to better manage the external lawyers in terms of fees and time. One of the most important key performance index that an In-house counsel will be measured against would be if he or she is effectively controlling the cost of the legal department.

5. What Is The Difference Between In-House And Practice?

Some Pros And Cons

(a) Cons

Pay: The average lawyer in practice makes more than the average in-house counsel. Please do note though that this is a generalisation comparing the top in-house counsel with the top lawyer in practice.

The prestige: The impression is that lawyers who are in-house counsel are failures in practice. This is, of course, not necessarily true. However, an in-house counsel is not always regarded as highly as a lawyer in practice.

The work hours: Many lawyers think that in-house counsel do not have to work as hard as lawyers in practice. This is not necessarily true. The in-house counsel is employed by the organisation which usually expects its employees to be on call 24-hours a day. If the organisation has operations in different time-zones, you will need to be available at the time-zones of those entities.

Not the star: In any organisation, the in-house counsel is a necessary evil. The in-house counsel does not generate any revenue or profit but is, in fact, a cost to the organisation. The legal department is always a cost centre. As such, the in-house counsel within an organisation will not be given the same treatment as a revenue generator, such as a salesperson or the deal maker.

(b) Pros

Varied work: Generally, in an organisation, especially a sizeable one, the work will be much more varied, and you will get to deal with many different kinds of situations. The work is so varied that throughout my 18 years, it feels as if I have changed my job many times without ever having left the organisation.

Glamour: Depending on the industry of the organisation, there is usually the glamour of traveling far and wide. Many deals and claims require the in-house to be physically present at the location of the claim or where the deal is to be closed. Sometimes, when the in-house is familiar with the operations of the company located elsewhere, the in-house counsel may be able to offer better and more practical advice. I was lucky to work for a company with hotels, in addition to factories and it was very glamorous indeed to be visiting the hotels and the factories as a representative of the parent company. This is in addition to learning about the glamorous life of hoteliers and factory managers.

Exposure: The extensive exposure to the different people, different situations, different environment cannot be described in words. I had the privilege of working with some very experienced Japanese and Taiwanese engineers who were managing plants in Taiwan and the People's Republic of China. They were highly experienced and motivated people. They work very hard and play very hard. They were prepared to spend months away from their families to run factories in foreign countries and train factory workers of a different culture and background. I have had to work on the documentation of a deal involving the barter of goods for real property. I have also had to conduct due diligence of a factory in the middle of winter in Denmark, and the factory was located in a small town surrounded by snow and trees. The exposure to different experiences has taught me to marvel at how entrepreneurs can dream of new ways to grow and expand their business, and work with them to achieve their objectives instead of being negative when something that has not been done before is proposed.

6. Still Going After 18 Years?

I am still an in-house counsel after leaving practice 18 years ago... And I am still enjoying the ride.

CHAPTER 19

INTERNATIONAL MONETARY FUND – MY JOURNEY AS AN IMF LAWYER

Ho Seng Chee

Ho Seng Chee is Group Chief, Corporate Services of Mapletree Investments Pte Ltd, where he oversees all human resource, communications, legal, and administration functions in the Mapletree Group. In his 11-year career at the IMF, he held diverse positions spanning strategic communications, policy planning, investor relations and legal work. Seng Chee began his working life as a litigation counsel in Singapore, first with Drew & Napier and subsequently with Rajah & Tann. He has a keen interest in international affairs and politics, and is a Council member of the Singapore Institute of International Affairs, Singapore's oldest independent think tank.

When Madeleine Albright was the United States' Secretary of State under President Bill Clinton, she reportedly said to an audience: '[In international relations], if you do not like what your lawyer is telling you, you can change your lawyer.' In quoting Secretary Albright, I am not suggesting that lawyers are just hired guns or that one can always find a lawyer who will provide the answer that one seeks. Rather, Secretary Albright's comment speaks to the fact that in international affairs, lawyers are frequently called upon to advise on policy issues which have no clearly right or wrong answers.

Within the realm of international economic policy where the International Monetary Fund ('IMF') operates, the lines between right and wrong could be even more blurred. For a start, all (honest) economists will readily admit that their chosen field is more an art than a science. The very nature of the subject renders it difficult to legislate or codify decisions on economic policy. In this setting, the role of IMF lawyers is not so much to advise on the legality of the institution's policy positions. Instead, IMF legal officers are expected to play both advocate and devil's advocate in testing the integrity of any policy position taken. The elements of fairness and objectivity are the constants that guide a lawyer's daily work in the institution.

Take the area of IMF lending. This is the part of the institution's functions that attracts the greatest public scrutiny and, usually in borrowing countries, widespread scorn. In lending operations, IMF lawyers do not act very differently from in-house legal counsels at international banks. Loan structuring and documentation form the bulk of legal work here. The interesting difference, however, lies in the type of conditions around which loan disbursements are phased. In essence, disbursements are always tied to the borrowing country achieving certain economic targets (for example, a certain level of reserves accumulation or a ceiling on the budget deficit). To ensure fairness and certainty for borrowing countries, IMF lawyers enforce a rule that requires these targets to be specified in a way as to enable their compliance to be objectively assessed ex post. In other words, each borrowing country must be assured that, if it were to do 'A, B and C', it will receive the promised loan tranche in return.

In theory, the rule is simple. Once the targets are met, the loan tranche is pushed out the door. But alas, the art of economics brings many surprises in real life. Imagine, for instance, that all pre-set targets in a country's loan programme are met. Yet, the expected economic outcome of meeting those targets is not achieved. This deviation could be due to unforeseen intervening factors, a worsening external environment, or maybe just bad programme design. Should the loan be disbursed nevertheless? A strict application of the fairness principle would dictate that the country should receive the money, despite the fact that the programme's objectives may not have been met.

At some level, the risk of a mismatch between programme targets and outcomes can be mitigated through careful programme design and target-setting. Therefore, to be effective in lending work, IMF lawyers need to understand some measure of macroeconomics in order to appreciate the objectives of a loan programme. Only through such understanding can a legal officer help structure conditions which clearly anticipate the programme's economic outcomes. This need for clarity in target-setting is also partly the reason why negotiations over loan programmes are always protracted and intense. Debates over loan conditions occur not only between the borrowing country and the IMF, but also internally among IMF departments and staff. For those of us who are keen followers of international affairs and politics, the intellectual stimulation from being engaged in such negotiations is job satisfaction in itself.

The battles over targets and loan conditions, while highly technical, have very real consequences for people who live in the borrowing countries. In all cases of economic adjustment, things inevitably get worse before they get better. Once austerity measures and other reforms stipulated in IMF loan programmes kick in, jobs will be lost, factories closed, and companies made bankrupt. IMF staff know that what they structure as loan conditions will affect lives and livelihoods. For lawyers, the considerations of 'fairness' and 'objectivity' take on added importance when viewed in this context. Indeed, the impact of economic adjustment under IMF programmes can bring down entire governments. Just recall what happened to President Suharto of Indonesia, whose 31-year rule ended amidst a severe recession which, many have argued, was made worse by the IMF programme. For the younger readers out there, you may even ask: 'Suharto who?'

Given the 'blood and gore' inherent in many IMF lending programmes, it is hardly surprising that IMF loans tend to hog the media spotlight as the most prominent of its activities and operations. Yet, within the IMF and among international policymakers, it is the pre-emptive instrument of 'economic surveillance' that receives greater attention. The idea is that, rather than have a crisis occur and then try to use loans and money to resolve it, more resources should be devoted to monitoring economies and diagnosing weaknesses in them before they precipitate full-blown financial crises.

Under the IMF's economic surveillance programme, all member countries of the institution are required, as an obligation of membership, to undergo an annual economic health check. Lawyers help police this obligation by designing and enforcing rules which compel countries to not only undergo this annual check, but to also provide all economic data and information required to perform that check. These rules can be thorny to apply in, say, some of the more opaque economies, many of which are run more like family businesses than sovereign nations. One such case which I handled concerned a publicity-shy oil-producing monarchy's refusal to disclose the levels of its international reserves. Needless to say, the Sultan's men were not amused when advised by IMF lawyers of their obligation to disclose what was, for all intents and purposes, the contents of His Majesty's treasure chest. Years of gentle persuasion and diplomatic taichi were required to get them to comply.

Where weaknesses are identified in a country's economic system, the IMF can help the country address them. In some cases, an ineffective legal or court system may be the cause of these weaknesses. For example, during the 1997/1998 Asian financial crisis, a major constraint faced by some crisis countries was the inability of their bankruptcy and court systems to cope with the sudden build-up of massive corporate debt and bad bank loans. As a result, a good portion of the reforms undertaken in these countries involved the restructuring of bankruptcy laws and court processes to streamline and expedite enforcement actions. In such programmes, IMF lawyers would be involved in designing the changes to the laws and drafting the necessary legislation for the country. While working on one such programme, I had to lead some tense negotiations with senior judges and Justice Ministry officials. Many of these country counterparts were grey-haired senior figures in their national establishment, with a good number of seasoned politicians thrown in. It took more than a few deep breaths to maintain a cool head and to hold my own.

As a former litigation lawyer, I quite enjoyed the opportunity to be in those negotiations. Aside from the intellectual challenge, there is also the incidental benefit of befriending some of my negotiation adversaries from these encounters. This, for me, is my personal reward from working on these programmes. I still keep in touch with many of these individuals, and we always have a nice time reminiscing about the days spent together in the war trenches of IMF programme negotiations. As the Chinese saying goes: '不打不相识' or, according to my severely limited translation abilities, 'from fights will arise friendships'.

Indeed, the chance to meet and forge friendships with people from all over the world is a priceless privilege of IMF employment. For many international civil servants, being part of an international organisation means having the unique opportunity to work with colleagues who hail from all corners of the planet, day in and day out. The IMF actively promotes and celebrates this diversity in its staff makeup, which, during my time there, had over 150 nations represented. With everyone coming from somewhere else and having different ways of working, you learn very quickly to treat each colleague with courtesy and respect. That applies from the mailroom clerk all the way up to the IMF chief. A corollary of that culture is an absence of pressure to fit into any particular mould. I am often asked why I still speak with the same Singaporean accent despite having lived more than a decade in the United States. My consistent reply is: 'Where I used to work, everyone spoke with a funny accent and we had no trouble understanding each other.'

As an IMF staff member, I also had the good fortune of travelling to diverse countries along the entire development spectrum. Every project and new country presented fresh personal challenges and discoveries. In places like Burkina Faso and East Timor, I found myself secretly questioning the relevance of macroeconomic policy planning to the daily lives of the subsistence farmers and petty traders who made up a large part of those economies. In the middle-income powerhouse of Brazil, I admired the professionalism and public service mindset of its highly competent civil service and key political leaders. In the European Union, I experienced first-hand the infamous inefficiencies and red tape of a bloated European Commission bureaucracy. Each project and mission provided different 'takeaways' and lessons. Quite apart from adding to my professional knowledge, these stories can come in extremely handy as conversation gap fillers at dinner parties.

But, jokes aside, there is one consistent thread which flows through these different experiences. It all comes down to people – in particular, the inspiring optimism and strength in spirit of the many individuals that I have worked with along the way. I will always remember the story of my Cambodian counterpart from a project I led around 2001. This man was in his mid-teens when the Khmer Rouge took power in 1975. Being part of the educated elite, he endured four years of starvation and hard labour in a re-education camp. Shortly after the Vietnamese 'liberated' Cambodia in 1979, he fled to Thailand with only the clothes on his back. From there, he was resettled to the United States. Fluent in only French and Khmer, my friend had to learn English from scratch in his new adoptive country. Amazingly, by the time peace returned to Cambodia ten years later, he had completed graduate school and, armed with a US law degree, promptly returned to Phnom Penh to serve in its new government. What a rebirth!

Then, there is the young bureaucrat from an Ivory Coast project I handled in 2004. His country had been in a civil war for a few years, but my African friend was full of optimism that the fighting would end soon. He spoke with pride about his hometown Abidjan being a vibrant West African city, and about how the Ivory Coast was once held out as a rare success story in that region. He was so confident that his country would bounce back very quickly from that war. That Ivorian war did end in 2005, and I imagine he must have been thrilled when that happened. Sadly, as I write this essay, the Ivory Coast is emerging from another political crisis. Yet, I have little doubt that my Ivorian friend remains as strong and forward-looking now as he was then. Whenever I recall these encounters, I am humbled by the stories of the individuals in them.

"Humbled" is also one word that comes to mind when I think back to the intellectual environment of the IMF. The organisation's professional economist staff is made up almost entirely of doctorate holders. The IMF's headquarters on Washington's 19th Street must have one of the highest numbers of PhDs per square foot anywhere in the world – and with all the brand name schools represented. The economists are complemented by similarly well-qualified staff from other professions, e.g., lawyers, accountants, communications specialists, etc. Most are well read, and almost everyone has an opinion on everything. Depending on how you see it, this mix can be exciting, motivating or downright frustrating (and sometimes all at the same time).

Given this professional environment, if there is one character trait I would single out as being common among individuals who have succeeded at the IMF, I would say it is respect for your colleagues. That means having empathy for each person's opinion and point of view, and being able to disagree without being disagreeable. Regardless of the issue, always use polite questioning to gain clarity before responding. Never jump straight to a conclusion with guns blazing – you may be smart, but so are your colleagues and everyone deserves to be heard. Above all, recognise and purge your own biases and prejudices; deal with the issue and not the person (unless, of course, it is a human resource problem and the issue is the person!). From these factors, it does not take a rocket scientist to deduce that a big part of the equation is about having effective communication and inter-personal skills. And there is no better training ground for those skills than the multi-cultural environment of an international organisation like the IMF.

Needless to say, one needs to be able to do more than just listen, talk and make friends to get a job at the IMF. Since one of the aims of this book is to provide some information on how individuals can prepare for a career in the field being described, I will briefly recount how I ended up at the organisation. In that regard, the journey was partly deliberate, but mostly fortuitous.

While I have, for as long as I can remember, always been very interested in public international law and global politics, the thought of building a career around these subjects never really crossed my mind. But things changed about four years after I left NUS law school. I was into my third year as a litigation lawyer, and getting jaded with the daily grind of every junior litigator's life, ie, the mindless photocopying and document-preparation work. I began to wonder what it would be like to work at a place like the United Nations. Through some research and anecdotal due diligence, I concluded that, in order to stand any chance of joining the UN, I would need to do one or both of two things. First, I would have to get a Masters degree. International organisations almost never hire professional staff who possess only undergraduate degrees. Second, I could consider joining the Singapore foreign service as a diplomat.

Since I was not of the scholarly bent to have been chosen for government service in my late teens, I decided to remain a private citizen and to make a bet on a Masters in Law. Numerous application forms and 'what I want to do with my life' essays later, I ended up in New York University's International Legal Studies Masters programme.

While at NYU, the IMF happened to be recruiting on campus for lawyers. In particular, they were interested in candidates who were in their late 20s, had about three to five years' working experience, and were preferably from regions under-represented in the IMF staff (east Asia being one such region). To top it off, the legal department's hiring manager was a Malaysian who had graduated from the University of Singapore law school in 1962. He was able to, at the minimum, interpret my Bs and Cs from NUS as the equivalents of As and Bs in the rest of the world.

And so I ended up joining the IMF in September 1997. Fast-forward thirteen plus years, and I am now back in Singapore in a job that barely resembles what I have done before. Thinking back on my own career choices returns me to Madeleine Albright's point about the lack of clear answers and definite solutions. Aspiring lawyers out there should feel free to explore. Short of thievery or high-sea piracy, there are really no right or wrong career choices. In any case, what you learn in law school will be largely obsolete within 10 years of your graduation, so you might as well start dreaming now of possible alternatives to a legal career. Above all, never let your law degree define what you do in life.

Bon voyage.

CHAPTER 20

TEACHING LAW IN THE UNIVERSITY – SHAPING FUTURE GENERATIONS

Jack Tsen-Ta Lee

Jack Lee is an Assistant Professor of Law at the School of Law, Singapore Management University. He has an LLB (Hons) from the National University of Singapore and an LLM from University College London, and is in the process of completing a PhD at the University of Birmingham. He was in private practice and was subsequently an assistant director of the Singapore Academy of Law before joining Singapore Management University where he teaches and researches constitutional and administrative law.

1. Introduction

'He who can, does. He who cannot, teaches.' It was George Bernard Shaw who gave us this pithy and often quoted and misquoted line ('Maxims for Revolutionists', *Man and Superman* (Archibald Constable & Co, 1903), 230). The statement was partly true in my case, though 'would rather not' is more accurate. It was really a matter of discovering my inclinations and strengths rather than – I hope – any real inability to practise law!

As I write this, I have been a law academic at the School of Law of the Singapore Management University ('SMU') for just over two and a half years. Before that, I was a litigator in a local law firm for about six years following my call to the Bar. After that I was engaged in postgraduate study, apart from a stint at the Singapore Academy of Law. I do not know if this can be regarded a 'typical' route into academia, but hope that my experiences give you some idea as to what is involved.

So, why did I decide to give up legal practice? I did enjoy the variety of work that came my way, but after a few years in the job, I discovered that there were aspects of it that did not appeal much to me. These included the long hours and short deadlines, and handling the administrative aspects of legal practice such as issuing bills and reminding clients to pay them. I had some delightful clients – those who thanked me for helping them and surprised me with small gifts, even though we had not achieved the results we hoped for – but there were also difficult ones. One client called up several times a day demanding to know if there had been any developments. Another one refused to listen to advice from my colleague and me that the case was weak and ought to be settled, and then blamed us for incompetence after the claim was dismissed by a judge.

Ultimately though, I think two things led me to realise that I could not see myself continuing as a litigator for the rest of my working life. The first was that I lived with a constant niggling sense that something might go dreadfully wrong with a particular file – despite care being taken, the filing of a court document might be overlooked, or a key witness might refuse to testify at the last minute. These sorts of risks are inherent in a litigation practice, but I did not see why I had to subject myself to the anxiety they caused. Secondly, I found out I did not particularly enjoy the cut-and-thrust of court work, finding it exhausting rather than exhilarating. The sheen of litigation starts to wear off when you have been on your feet for three hours cross-examining an uncooperative witness who, despite your best efforts, does not break down and start spilling the beans as they are wont to do on television. There was also the uncertainty factor – no matter how prepared I was for a case, it was possible that a witness would start on an unexpected line of testimony, or the judge would ask an unforeseen question.

If litigation work interests you, I hope I have not put you off – I certainly do not intend to do so! I do not regret at all the practical experience that I gained as a litigator, and I feel it has informed my teaching in all sorts of ways. Volunteering with the Law Society's Criminal Legal Aid Scheme and being able to provide *pro bono* representation to accused persons unable to afford a lawyer was particularly rewarding. Nonetheless, I came to realise that the aspects of my work that really interested and engaged me were carrying out research and writing legal opinions. Thus, I felt that I should find a career that maximised these skills and began to consider whether academia was for me.

2. Will Academia Suit You?

Research and Writing

An important factor, therefore, when contemplating academia as a career is *whether you find legal research and writing interesting*. This is a significant aspect of a law professor's job as it is probably the predominant factor determining the prospects for your pay raises and promotion, and whether you will be offered tenure. As a junior academic

I am presently not tenured, which means I am hired by the university for a certain number of years only. During this time, I have to demonstrate my teaching and research ability by generating positive feedback from my students about my teaching skills, and publishing legal articles in reputable journals. If I succeed in this, the university should offer me tenure – an employment contract that has no fixed ending date. I will then be able to work as an academic until retirement age unless either the university or I decide to give notice to terminate the contract.

I find legal writing challenging. When you are working on a paper at school or university, you will score a good grade if you consult a range of sources and summarise them in a clear and coherent way in your essay. If you are able to express some interesting personal views, you may even get an 'A'. However, when you are an academic, this is not enough. You have to make sure you have read and understood the most relevant books and articles relating to your topic. Next, your article has to make a useful contribution towards the field of law you are writing about, otherwise you will find it difficult to get published. For instance, this could mean commenting on a judgment recently handed down by a court, suggesting a new way of thinking about a legal issue, or applying existing rules and principles of law to a different situation. It will not be enough simply to parrot the views of other scholars without adding anything to them. Finally – and I do not find this easy – you need to be able to express yourself in writing clearly and convincingly, and to structure articles so that they are readily understandable. Like many things in life, this takes practice. Despite the exertion involved, it is particularly satisfying to see the results of your hard work in print, and perhaps even to have your opinions cited by judges and other academics.

I often set myself a target to write a paper for presentation at a conference to encourage myself to get some research and writing done, and to have an article I can submit to a journal for consideration for publication. Conferences are also a great opportunity to meet fellow academics from other parts of the world and find out about their research, not to mention the opportunity to travel that they offer.

Teaching

Obviously, another thing to consider is *whether you can teach and enjoy it*. Teaching includes actual class time with students. At SMU we use a seminar system, so law instructors spend three or four-and-a-half hours a week teaching in a classroom setting. Over at the Faculty of Law of the National University of Singapore ('NUS'), classes are taught in a lecture (one teacher in a large class) – tutorial (small groups) style. However, teaching also encompasses spending time reviewing cases and other materials, drawing up reading lists and seminar sheets, preparing for lectures and seminars, meeting students to discuss problems or queries that they may have, setting assignments and examination papers, and of course, marking the answers. I hazard that if you polled academics, a large majority would cite marking as their least favourite part of the job. Unfortunately, it is often monotonous, there is quite a lot of it, and it usually needs to be completed in less time than you actually need. But someone has to do it. Students also appreciate it when you take the time to provide useful suggestions on how they can improve their work.

If you want to be a primary or secondary school teacher, you are required to take a course in education and to do practical teaching stints. On the other hand, when you apply to join a university the main assessment of your teaching ability is a 'job talk'. This is a lecture on a topic of your choice that you deliver to faculty members, who will freely interrupt you from time to time and ask pointed questions. If you get through that, it is pretty much assumed that you are capable of handling students, and little or no formal training is given. You have to take the initiative to improve your teaching skills, for instance, by attending in-house courses and working with a peer coach who will sit in on your classes and give you feedback afterwards.

Responding to requests from journalists for quotes, and writing letters to newspapers and websites are also aspects of an academic's job. One of my colleagues appears regularly as a pundit on the radio and television, and has a column in a daily newspaper. I am mentioning this under the heading of 'Teaching' because I believe it can be seen as part of a law professor's educative function. I know some academics prefer not to engage with the media as they dislike being misquoted or quoted out of context. Unfortunately, this does happen from time to time. Nonetheless, these are ways of making one's research interests more widely accessible by stimulating public discussion of legal issues, and helping the person in the street to better understand what law is about. Speaking or writing in these fora may also help to raise one's profile and that of one's university.

How will you know if teaching is something that will suit you? Well, nothing beats actually trying it out. If you have just finished school or are an undergraduate, giving tuition to younger students may provide you with a sense of what it is like to be a teacher. If you are already working, consider offering to teach university students on an adjunct basis. I gave evening tutorials in public law to students at NUS for a semester, and also taught first-year undergraduates Administrative and

Human Rights law while I was working on my PhD at the University of Birmingham. These experiences helped me to decide that teaching was something that I wanted to make my career. You can also consider penning letters to the press, and making comments on or even writing short articles for websites, about issues that you feel strongly about.

One of the great things about teaching is that it is a two-way street of learning. I teach constitutional and administrative law, and each time I run the course I gain some new insight into legal issues or cases through the discussions my students and I have. This helps to inform my thinking and, eventually, my research.

Administration

Being an academic also means bearing your share of the *administrative work* that needs to be done around the faculty. Among others, I sit on the School of Law's JD Committee, which manages the School's Juris Doctor programme; as well as the Law School Building Taskforce, which examines issues involved in the construction of the School's new building that we hope will be ready in a few years. I am also a member of the Singapore Academy of Law's LawNet Management Committee, which oversees policy matters concerning LawNet, an online legal information portal widely used by law firms, government agencies and universities. My senior colleagues take turns to act as associate deans in charge of research, teaching and curriculum, and external relations.

Supporting school events is very much part of the job. This includes being present at recruitment open houses to talk to prospective applicants and their parents, interviewing shortlisted applicants, and attending convocation and commencement ceremonies. (Incidentally, the terminology relating to these ceremonies has completely changed since my undergraduate days at NUS. Back in the 1990s, my classmates and I were said to have matriculated when we first registered with the University at the start of our programme, and attended a convocation ceremony upon graduating with our LLBs. These days at SMU, one attends convocation to be welcomed as an incoming freshman, and a commencement ceremony when one is graduating. I suppose this is the American usage, but I still find myself having to stop and think in order not to confuse the two! Over at the NUS, they still matriculate, but subsequently commence.)

I also see it as a vital part of my duties as an academic to support students in their endeavours. This ranges from writing references for those applying for internships and training contracts, to judging debating and mooting competitions (which involve legal argumentation), to attending performances and social events organized by them. Another of my colleagues was a former Jessup mooter – the Jessup Moots being the largest and most well known mooting competition in the world – and now trains students for this event and others like it. I am thoroughly impressed by how my students, occupied as they are with preparing for presentations and seminars, writing research papers, and studying for examinations, still find the time to take part in competitions and sports, and produce amateur musicals complete with original costumes, storylines and songs!

Other Considerations

When I was wondering whether to embark on the journey of becoming an academic, I spoke to a number of my former professors at NUS for advice. Some suggestions that they gave me stick in my mind. First, realise that *academia is often a rather solitary pursuit*. It is entirely possible to go through a whole day without seeing any of your colleagues. Everyone's schedule is different, and most academics shuttle between their classes, the library and their offices and do not hang around the corridors or the proverbial water-cooler. This, of course, means that you have to make a bit of an effort to catch up with your workmates over lunch, coffee or drinks in the evening. E-mail is a boon, because you can send a message to everyone to find out who would like to meet. However, if you are the sort of person who thrives on constant interaction with people, then be aware that you are more likely to find this in a law firm or a company than inside the halls of academia.

Another consideration is *pay*. If a handsome salary is important to you, then once again private practice or the government's Legal Service is likely to be a better paymaster than a university's bursar. The salary of an academic is decent, but if you were to compare it with the salary of a lawyer of the same seniority it is very likely to be rather lower. However, that is not the whole picture. Lawyers are paid more because much is expected of them – late nights in the office, higher stress levels and clients who need much hand-holding, for example. While academics are busy during term time, especially when assignments and exam scripts start flooding in for marking, their work schedules are far more flexible. Unless we have classes to teach, students to see or meetings to attend, we may work from home or, presumably, while sitting on a sun-drenched beach.

3. Positioning Yourself

How, then, can you best position yourself for an academic career? I'd say that one of the most important things is to do the best you can in law school. If you try for a university teaching position with a first-class honours or *summa cum laude* under your belt, it is hard to see why your application would not be favourably considered. What if you are only a 'mere mortal' and your law degree does not reach such dizzying heights? You will then have to bolster your academic credentials with further degrees, preferably combined with some practical experience. Though I had a fairly creditable LLB, I was not one of the two students in my year who achieved a first-class honours. If I had been, I suspect a university might have offered me a job fresh from graduation, and might even have agreed to pay for my postgraduate studies. (Whether this is the case at present depends very much on each institution's current policies). I therefore decided that I needed to attain higher academic degrees on my own, and was fortunate enough to be awarded scholarships to pursue an LLM at University College London as well as a PhD at the University of Birmingham which, at the time of writing, I am in the process of completing.

Next, start building up a publication record. When writing research papers during your undergraduate programme, aim to produce work that might be publishable with a bit of tweaking. Local law journals such as the student-managed *Singapore Law Review* and the NUS Faculty-run *Singapore Journal of Legal Studies* accept well-written submissions from students, and you might even try foreign journals such as the *Oxford University Comparative Law Journal*. Ask a professor to recommend suitable journals to submit your work to. In any case, try to publish in peer-reviewed journals issued by established institutions. Reputable journals usually have in place a double-blind review system, which means that your article is submitted to a reviewer with all references to your identity removed, and you are, in turn, not told as to who the reviewer is. This ensures that the article is judged on its merit and not on the person who wrote it.

It is harder to find time to write and publish when you are working in a law firm, but certainly not impossible. When I was in practice, I set myself the modest goal of trying to complete one or two publishable pieces of writing each year. After a few years, I had built up a portfolio of journal articles and contributions to books such as the *Halsbury's Laws of Singapore* and the *Singapore Court Practice*, which I could then cite in applications for postgraduate studies and scholarships, and eventually, for a university teaching position. As I mentioned earlier, try gaining some teaching exposure – this will, in turn, boost your CV.

Your research and writing should help you to begin contemplating the areas of law that you might eventually focus on as an academic. I would suggest not picking too narrow a subject to start with. Try writing on a range of topics that are of interest to you, and after a while you will probably realise which ones appeal to you particularly. Do bear in mind that universities always need academics able to teach core law subjects such as company law, contract law, criminal law, equity and trust law, the law of evidence, legal theory, property law, public law and tort law. If you inform a prospective employer that you are happy to teach one of these subjects, you have a higher chance of being taken on than if your interests and teaching abilities lie only in rather more esoteric subjects!

I am still learning what being a law academic is about, but I like what I have seen so far. It is an opportunity to think deeply about subjects I find intellectually fascinating, expressing my thoughts on them in writing, and sharing and discussing them with others. I also feel that I have been granted the privilege of shaping future generations of judges, legal officers, business people and politicians – perhaps even academics who will one day succeed me in this noble profession.

CHAPTER 21

TEACHING LAW IN THE POLYTECHNIC – LIVING AND LEARNING

Sylvia Lim

Sylvia Lim holds an LLB(Hon) from the National University of Singapore and an LLM from University College London. She joined the Police Force which she left for private practice. She joined Temasek Polytechnic as a Lecturer where she remained for almost 13 years. Sylvia Lim is currently Member of Parliament for Aljunied GRC.

It may seem ironic that I write this piece just as I am about to leave my employment at Temasek Polytechnic ('TP') in order to accommodate my other public duties. However, having spent twelve years on the job, I would highly recommend teaching law at a Polytechnic to anyone who desires a few key things – first, work-life balance; second, a working environment where you can pursue institutional goals in a manner which is interesting to you; and third, and most importantly, the opportunity and challenge of contributing to education, and through it, the building of our society for the future.

1. Work-Life Balance

In 1998 I was in the throes of a litigation practice. While I liked my bosses and colleagues, the prospect of handling trial after trial did not appeal to me. To each their own. While I am aware of some who enjoy careers in litigation, I was getting tired of preparing Bundles of Documents and memorising them for cross-examination. Litigation is strongly adversarial and the acrimony involved in dealing with the opposing party was also beginning to wear me out.

Around that time, a particular feature on the satirical website 'talkingcock.com' struck me as so true – it told a (possibly fictitious) story about how former lawyers were enjoying second careers selling blue DVDs and boasting how they were so much happier, as they no longer woke up in the middle of the night wondering whether their affidavits had been paginated according to the Practice Directions! A polytechnic colleague also shared how as a practitioner in a law firm, he would be in Disneyland with his children queuing up for rides, but replying to client queries on his Blackberry.

So when TP advertised through a Law Society circular that they were looking to recruit a lecturer who, preferably, had police experience, I applied immediately. I commenced work there in October 1998.

Polytechnics are public-sector educational institutions which receive government funding. The students pay subsidised fees. There are no billings to determine one's income. One is assigned a certain teaching load, depending on one's subject expertise, and also appointed to do some committee work, ranging from time-tabling to promoting the Polytechnic.

A civil service culture prevails – five day week, 8.30am to 6 pm. Generally, no after-office hours work is required, unless one is teaching adult learners for night classes (for which there is additional remuneration) or one is working on a project with a tight deadline, eg preparing for a road-show or event (which is predictable for scheduling, and usually once or twice a year only). Going on leave is usually blissful, with no calls from the office. Colleagues are relatively non-competitive and more collegiate in their approach.

The corollary of work-life balance is, of course, a compromise on income. The prevailing recruitment schemes at Polytechnics take into account industry experience, but matching the salaries paid by medium to large law firms is generally not possible. Salary increments are modest compared to the private sector. However, government wage policies apply, ie one is assured of 13th month pay, with annual and performance bonuses following civil service pay-outs each year.

Sole breadwinners with young children or dependents should seriously do their sums. However, one should take a global perspective – whether any compromise in income is made up for by greater peace of mind and more time for the family.

2. Pursuing Personal Interests for Polytechnic's Goals

Polytechnics offer a holistic lifestyle, if one wishes to seize upon the opportunities available.

If sport is your thing, you can compete as a polytechnic representative in staff competitions, or enjoy the facilities on campus recreationally. Going to the on-campus staff or student gym at lunchtime is convenient, and something I enjoyed doing. In my prime (ie not now), I represented TP in inter-tertiary institution and intra-polytechnic cross-country runs.

The more artistic types can also find an appropriate outlet. Those who like to act or sing on stage can find roles in musicals and plays put up for special occasions – I relished occasions to sing with the staff band. Many colleagues find ways to contribute their talents towards fund-raising activities for student aid. For instance, a Law colleague delighted in baking elaborate, almost architectural, cakes for auction to the highest bidder, with proceeds going to our Campus Care Network fund for needy students.

Perhaps more significantly for me, I was able to pursue my passion for criminal justice issues at TP. TP is a leader in providing diploma courses for law enforcement and private security practitioners, with strong support from the major employers in these fields. Due to my past work-experience in the police force, I was in a position to work on curriculum and to forge industry links – to be part of a movement to uplift standards.

When in class as an adult educator, law and practice meet. There is no equivalent opportunity in other jobs. I discussed criminal procedure with police officers who have to apply the rules on the ground. We debated what amounts to an arrest. I battled common misconceptions and engage with orang lama (literally, 'old persons', meaning 'institutional') folklore. Classes are an eye-opener for both the lecturer and student. We discussed best practices from other jurisdictions and this would be considered seriously by those who wished to improve the quality of policework.

3. Contributing to Building Society for the Future

The educational enterprise is a constructive one, and its impact potentially far-reaching. One encounters new students in every new semester of teaching. In my twelve years, I have cumulatively taught thousands of school-leavers and adults. Each student is unique and has different strengths and challenges. The demographic profile of students attending polytechnics cuts across socio-economic classes, with a fair share of those from lower-income families. Anyone who is considering a career as a Polytechnic lecturer would need to have a strong interest in people.

As the full-time students are typically between the ages of 17 to 21, they are going through adolescence and are typically searching for an identity. They are transitioning from the school system, where they wore uniforms and attended classes according to a regimented schedule every day, to individualised time-tables where they might commence classes even in the afternoons on certain days. Some agonise over what to wear. Facebook and other online pursuits have some of them going to bed at

3am. One thing is for sure – you will be forced to keep up to date with the latest fashion and technological trends!

Some students may be grappling with serious family or financial issues. For example, I had a student who needed to commute daily from Johor Bahru, as her family sold their HDB flat to pay her father's business debts. Seeing students falter in their studies in such circumstances is painful. Lecturers need to be very alert for signs of students having difficulties, to spend time counselling them, motivating them and putting them onto various financial or professional help schemes.

As for the adult learners, their life experiences will teach lecturers useful lessons too. The role reversal is enjoyable for the lecturer. For example, the Supreme Court and Subordinate Courts send their staff to attend paralegal diploma programmes at TP. Anyone practicing law will understand how powerful some of the court registry staff are in the day to day running of the judicial system. They are the ones who fix hearing dates (and hence, incidentally, the judges and magistrates too). Seeing them in front of you as students, waiting to be assessed, ie being relatively helpless, is refreshing! Nonetheless, I can safely say that TP has made important contributions to the upgrading of paralegals in both the public and private sectors.

4. Conclusion

A significant proportion our waking hours are spent on the job. Marrying one's passions with a viable career is an ideal state which can be elusive to many. For someone who has always felt the importance of contributing to public service, my twelve years teaching law at a polytechnic were very fulfilling. I got to know and respect many wonderful colleagues – people who want to make a difference to our students.

OVERSEAS PRACTICES

CHAPTER 22

PRACTISING LAW IN THE UNITED STATES OF AMERICA – TAKING A BITE OF THE BIG APPLE

Benjamin Tan

Benjamin Tan is presently an equity partner in a New York law firm on Wall Street, Sichenzia Ross Friedman Ference LLP. He holds an LLB(Hons) from the National University of Singapore and an LLM from the University of London. He started out as a shipping associate at one of Singapore's largest law firms and then went on to practice banking and corporate law at Colin Ng & Partners. In 2000, he left to join a NASDAQ listed company as General Counsel and in 2006, returned to private practice. He presently practices securities and corporate law, with a focus on bringing mainland Chinese companies public in the United States.

1.   Introduction

As I reflect on my journey from graduation from law school to the present day, I cannot help but wonder how different my life would have been if I had not made the move to leave the creature comforts of family and home to venture abroad to seek my fortune. I have known for a long time that I would someday find myself working and living abroad. I just did not know where or how I would get there. Even so, upon graduation in 1995, I found myself seduced into life of a young associate in a leading local firm practicing maritime law, believing, quite erroneously, that I was set for life.

Someone once said that if you spend a day doing something that you do not love, you die a little every day. Without sounding overly dramatic, I knew very early on that the career that I had embarked on was 'wrong', for me at least. I felt like I was 'dying' a little every day. I was uninterested in the practice and it showed. I resented having to be on call, especially during a public holiday, to arrest a vessel. I could not wait to change careers. I switched firms after a year and moved into the banking and cross-border corporate practice with another leading law firm in Singapore, which I enjoyed thoroughly and thrived. I enjoyed working on transactions that involved different jurisdictions, negotiating and drafting contracts and of course, travelling.

For me, understanding how businesses are run, working with management, participating in policy and decision-making and applying the law to achieve the business objectives of the client added flavour to the practice of law. The law is to many an esoteric concept understandable by only a few. However, when it is fleshed out in practice and applied to the business world, it springs to life and is fluid and ever changing. Even though I thrived in my new career choice and experienced the particularly challenging Asian financial crisis which taught me a lot, I found myself dreaming of a life and career overseas and subconsciously went about preparing myself for it.

I started studying part-time by correspondence for my LLM with the University of London. Unlike some of my peers, I was determined to get it without sacrificing my seniority at the firm or spending an obscene amount of money. I obtained my LLM within two years and in the meantime, was admitted to practice as a solicitor in England and Wales. I figured that with a Masters degree from the United Kingdom and admission to the United Kingdom & Wales to practice, more doors would be open to me.

After chalking up over four years of valuable cross-border banking and corporate experience, I started considering my options abroad. Some of my classmates had already left and started working in Hong Kong, which was the natural choice for Singaporeans by virtue of our cultural, educational, legal infrastructure and geographical proximity. I, too, considered and interviewed with a United States firm in Hong Kong but it was not meant to be.

By the end of the 1990s, mainland China was opening up and plans were in the making for China to accede to the World Trade Organisation in 2000. With our Western-style common law legal education and bilingual ability, I saw a unique opportunity to establish myself as a conduit between the East and West once trade doors opened.

2. My Journey to the United States

Opportunity finally came a-knocking when a client of mine from the United States made me an offer to join them as their General Counsel. They were a NASDAQ-listed technology company based in Long Island, New York. At the height of the internet craze and with promises of stock options, I decided to throw caution to the wind and accepted the offer. What enthralled me was not only the chance (and what I thought was the glamour) of working in the United States but also the fact that this was a multi-national, public-listed technology company with interests in Europe, mainland China and parts of Asia. And I was probably one of the youngest General Counsels in the United States!

To be honest, it took a whole lot of soul-searching to decide to leave my career in Singapore for uncharted waters. I was abandoning a career that I worked very hard to establish. If I stayed on, I was on track for partnership in a couple of years. Would I dare risk it all for the chance of a career in the United States? Buddha has a saying: 'There are two mistakes one can make along the road to truth... not going all the way, and not starting.' I knew that if I did not take up the opportunity, I would forever ask 'what if'? If I were to make a go of it, I had to go all the way and make it a success.

I convinced myself that I had nothing to lose. I was relatively young and able. In the worst-case scenario, I could return to Singapore with my tail between my legs and resume my legal career where I had left off. So it was with optimism and much trepidation that I left the security of Singapore and my job and departed for the Big Apple in May 2000.

3. My Life and First Career in New York

It took me a while to get used to my new life. Apart from having to get used to a new working environment, I was also adjusting to a new way of life. Unlike Singapore where everything was easily accessible, it is not so easy in the United States. Getting settled down was not without challenges. Everything which I had taken for granted, from getting a library card to a driver's license, seemed a hassle by comparison. Without the luxury of a National Identity Card, I had to literally prove my identity to everyone. I remember having so much trouble trying to explain to the girl at the Department of Motor Vehicles that the first name in my passport was actually my 'last name'.

Work was no piece of cake either. There were only a meagre six public holidays observed by my company and I had only two weeks of vacation instead of the 24 days that I enjoyed as a senior associate in Singapore. The Americans work much harder and had less downtime than what I had preconceived. But the work ethic that I most admired was that there was a clear demarcation between work and play. My colleagues spend the weekends and major holidays with their family and it was a major transgression to impede on their family time. They worked hard and played just as hard.

Legal materials were not as accessible where I was and when I needed legal research materials, I had to make a special trip down to the district courthouse to use their library. That meant taking a whole morning off just for the trip. Also, I had to get used to the fact that the United States is actually a congregation of different states. There was federal law which governs all states, but each state has its own set of laws. Being General Counsel of a multi-national and multi-state company, I had to be conscious of which state an issue would arise. For example, when the company had let someone go from its California office, we realised that California labour laws dictated that an employer must pay all outstanding dues to the employee on or before his last day, and that the company was liable for damages and interest if it did not do so.

One of my first projects was to restructure my company to take advantage of a tax treaty between Ireland and Luxembourg. This project took several months because, apart from drafting restructuring agreements in-house, I had to ensure that such agreements were legal and valid in each applicable country or state. This was where my experience in cross-border transactions proved very useful. I had to coordinate the timing and execution of each transaction with counsel from different countries and then had to ensure that the new corporate structure was adequately disclosed in the company's filings with the Securities and Exchange Commission (the 'SEC').

My regular duties at this company included drafting quarterly and annual reports. It was a painfully tedious and mind-numbing process which involved thumbing through the Securities Act of 1933 and the Securities Exchange Act of 1934 and their attendant regulations. The former is concerned by and large with the initial distribution of securities. Securities that are offered to the public through the mail or the channels of interstate commerce must be registered with the SEC by the issuer unless the issuer qualifies for some exemption. The Securities Exchange Act of 1934 was enacted to address post-distribution trading. It was later transposed into a philosophy of continuous disclosure and in 1964 or later, extended to securities trading over-the-counter and any class of security held by at least 500 persons and issued by a company with at least $10 million in gross assets. It also provided regulations for the prevention of fraud and market manipulation. This was my first foray into American securities law.

I also had to learn technology and computer terms, and recognise issues which pertained to my company's products. I was involved in several court cases in Massachusetts and Texas and even arbitration in New York. I experienced, for the first time, a trial by jury, which I felt did not mete out the 'right' judgment because it was, in my opinion, swayed by sentiment and loyalty to the plaintiff who was from the same state.

Even the judge acknowledged that he would have delivered a different verdict if there had been no jury.

I must say that lawyers here are indeed far more aggressive and litigious than in Singapore. Oftentimes there is a great deal of chest-thumping and threats in the course of negotiations in the belief that by striking fear in the heart of one's opponent, a better settlement might be wrangled. I was initially taken aback by the lack of courtesy in complaints. It is not usual to see wild accusations of 'wilfulness' and 'disingenuity' and personal digs at the defendant's character in a complaint. In Singapore, complaints are typically drafted in a matter-of-fact style. Parties perfunctorily state their version of the facts, apply the law, make their conclusion and state the damages claimed.

I once dealt with an attorney who obstinately refused to state the legal basis for his claim. He advised his client that he had an iron-clad case and adopted a 'take it or leave it' attitude. I could not ascertain whether he had a good case or not. I could not see why he thought he had a right to his claim and as a result, could not work out a settlement with him prior to legal proceedings. We ended up in court and because, as it turned out, he really did not have any legal basis for his claim, we won the case. In reality though, both parties ended up losers, having wasted a lot of time and significant legal costs. What I learnt is that good lawyers provide good counsel, even in times of dispute. One has to weigh in on the merits of each claim and then proceed to provide good advice. It is very tempting to go with the flow sometimes and give bad counsel in order to appease the client by telling him what he wants to hear. In the long run, such behaviour will inevitably disadvantage the client.

My years in the United States have been tumultuous. We went through the technology and internet bust in 2000 and bore witness to the downfall of Enron and the ensuing requirement of enhanced compensation and corporate governance for all public companies. Most recently we saw how the sub-prime mortgage crisis impacted the entire American and global economy. Amidst all these changes in the corporate environment, there was also the impact of the 9/11 attacks on the World Trade Centre. I was in nearby Long Island and will never forget the day when the boldest attack on American soil shook the foundations of the American way of life and changed the face of history forever.

4.   Bar Admission

I discovered soon after arriving in New York that one has to be admitted to the New York bar to function in any legal capacity. The rules required me to be admitted to the New York bar even if I were to hold myself out as 'Foreign Counsel' and not practice New York law. Fortunately, my law degree from the National University of Singapore was one of a handful of international law degrees recognised by New York State without exception. It also helped that I completed another academic year of legal studies by obtaining my Master of Laws. In other words, I did not have to complete an additional program of study at an approved law school in the United States to qualify to sit for the New York bar examinations.

The New York bar examinations span two days, each about 6½ hours long. It is administered twice a year on the last Tuesday and Wednesday of every February and July. The bar examinations contain two sections, the New York section which is given on Tuesday, and the Multistate Bar Examination ('MBE') which is given on Wednesday. The New York section consists of five essay questions and 50 multiple choice questions prepared by the New York Board, and one Multistate Performance Test question, developed by the National Conference of Bar Examiners.

The MBE is a standardised, multiple-choice examination created and sold to participating state bar examiners. The 200 MBE questions test six subjects based upon principles of common law and Article 2 of the Uniform Commercial Code (covering sales of goods) that apply throughout the United States. The questions are not broken down into sections and the six topics are distributed more or less evenly throughout the course of the exam. Exam-takers generally receive three hours during the morning session to complete the first 100 questions, and another three hours during the afternoon session to complete the second 100 questions. This means that each question can receive, on average, one minute and 48 seconds of the exam-taker's attention, which can make the exam challenging as some questions involve intricate fact patterns.

What I found particularly challenging in the New York bar examination was that, unlike the Singapore bar examination which examines you on a particular topic a day, the New York paper examines you on various topics all on the same day with no clear indication in the question as to what topic you are being tested on. Additionally, one has to distinguish between overlapping and similar federal and state laws when studying for the examinations.

I sat for the examinations at the Jacob Javitz Centre in Manhattan, an exhibition space not unlike the Singapore Expo. I remember being overwhelmed by the literally hundreds of lawyers-to-be sitting for the examination. It was like a meeting at the United Nations. There was probably someone from every nook and cranny of the world sitting for the examinations. Because I was working full-time and could not afford to take time off to attend a BAR/BRI course and prepare for the New York bar examination, I decided to subscribe for an offline course with The Study Group. Back in the days before the advent of downloadable media, I was sent a box of cassette tapes and study materials, which I took home to study in my spare time. Having to juggle the demands of a full-time job and study for a major examination without any prior knowledge of American law and jurisprudence was no mean feat. I found myself constantly tired and stressed out, especially as the examination date drew nearer.

Fortunately, I somehow managed to pass my examinations on my first try without even attending a single formal class. This is the one achievement that I am singularly most proud of. Most of the Singapore law graduates I know who have sat for the New York bar examinations pass the examinations the first time around. One of my ex-classmates who had sat and passed the New York bar examinations said that it would be very shameful for any Singapore law graduate to fail the New York bar examinations. This is probably testament to the quality of teaching and legal training we get in Singapore. Unlike the Singapore bar examinations, there is typically a lower pass rate of between 60–80% for first time takers of the New York bar examinations, with the pass rate usually higher for those sitting for the July examination.

5. Private Practice in New York

With six years of in-house corporate experience in the bag, I decided to return to private practice after concluding that my life as an in-house General Counsel had run its course. By then I was already familiar with the functioning of a US public company and was eager to embark on the next stage of my career. I worked with a couple of legal recruiters to secure a new position in private practice.

As a side note, international students who pursue their post-graduate education here in the hope of securing a permanent position with a New York law firm after graduation may find themselves disappointed. From what I have been told, US law firms are generally partial to hiring their own US-schooled graduates. Secondly, not every law firm practices international law and finally, the bigger firms that hire international graduates do so with the understanding that these new hires will be eventually be sent back to join the firm's counterpart in their respective home countries. As a result most international students eventually return home after graduation.

I was very fortunate to find a permanent position with a boutique New York law firm because of my international work experience and my ability to speak Mandarin. Many mainland Chinese companies were going public in the US and raising capital here. Access to public equity in China and even in Hong Kong had been difficult and expensive especially for smaller to medium sized Chinese companies and they were enticed by the relatively ease of entry into the US capital markets. Conversely, in an era when the world economy was floundering amidst the economic turmoil brought about by the sub-prime mortgage crisis, Chinese companies, with their double digit growth showed amazing resilience and were thus more attractive to US investors.

There was therefore a need to recruit senior, bilingual corporate and securities attorneys trained in the common law. And so began the second phase of my legal career in the US. Ironically, I had never spoken more Mandarin before in my life than here in New York. Almost all my clients now hail from China. Thank goodness for the 'Speak Mandarin' campaign when I was growing up. Arguably one of the advantages that any Singapore law graduate has over our peers from other countries is, apart from an excellent, sound legal education, we are usually able to speak Mandarin.

I presently head the Asian Practice Group of my firm. My Chinese clients instantly gravitate to me when I speak Mandarin to them. Many of my clients explained that they find great comfort in having the ability to speak to someone who 'looks like them' directly without a translator. There is still a general aloofness towards the '*lao wai*' [literally, 'old foreigner'] and reluctance to be too forthcoming with them. I find that my practice involves, in a large part, bridging the cultural divide and acting as mediator between the East and West. Americans are used to a no-nonsense, 'cut to the chase', dogmatic approach while the Chinese are less confrontational and more oblique in their dealings. A recent example could not have illustrated this divide better.

I had a Chinese client who was being audited by an American auditor for the purposes of preparing its annual report. During the course of the audit, in order to verify my client's accounts receivable, the American auditor started calling my client's customers and vendors en masse. The auditor obtained their telephone numbers and addresses from the internet and, without notifying my client ahead of time, made calls to my client's customers. My client received a barrage of complaints from their customers, and was so alarmed that they called me at 2am to complain about the actions of the auditor. Typically in China, an unexpected call from a stranger asking to verify a business relationship or transaction means that the subject company is either undergoing some sort of bankruptcy proceeding or some sort of government investigation. Also, unless anticipated, such calls are generally dismissed with a denial of any business relationship with the subject company.

Because of the cultural divide and as a result of not being cognisant of the way business is conducted in China, the American auditor inadvertently tarnished my client's reputation and caused an upheaval in its business relationships. And to exacerbate matters, the auditor could not satisfactorily verify the accounts receivable as his calls were either unanswered, or his questions met with a denial of any business relationship with my client.

When questioned about their verification procedures, the American auditor retorted, 'I don't care. If they choose to be a US listed company, then they should be bound by US audit procedures. The client should not dictate how and when I can carry out my verification procedures.' The Chinese party, of course, felt slighted at the perceived insensitivity of the auditor. As the go-between, I had to work out a solution between the two parties that would preserve the randomness of the auditor's testing while not interfering with the company's way of doing business and its reputation.

The study of the law does not prepare one for the real problems of today's complex world. In law school, we are presented with case scenarios all neatly summarised and bundled like a gift. In real life, one has to patiently sieve through the iterations of various parties in order to ascertain the facts and then, dispense advice that is practical and, most importantly, palatable to all parties. I also have come to realise that as a corporate practitioner, one has to think outside of the box for creative solutions. Understanding the law and being able to apply it to real life is a given. It is the human quality (or humanity) that sets apart a good lawyer from a great one. I constantly remind myself that I am dealing with individuals, each deserving of a listening ear. I believe that in dealing with problems, reasonable minds will find reasonable solutions and I constantly strive to be a good problem solver.

A multi-million dollar financing deal almost came to a screeching halt when an investor and my client could not reach an agreement on the price of the shares my client would sell to the investor after extensive talks. The financier was only willing to pay $X for a share and the company was not willing to lower the price of its shares. Both parties held their ground and each was willing to walk away. After speaking to both parties, I suggested that the company locate a large shareholder to see if he or she would willing to sell a block of shares to the investor so that the average price the investor would pay per share would be $X.

As luck would have it, the company managed to find such a shareholder and the deal proceeded without a hitch.

Practice in the United States is different than in Singapore in that it is infinitely more varied. There are practitioners that specialise in immigration, environmental, anti-trust and even elder law. There are also those that deal primarily with government defence contracts or even entertainment contracts for Hollywood actors. Even within each field, specialties abound. One can definitely find one's niche in such a wide variety of options in legal practice here.

Having been on both sides of the fence, I would say though that fundamentally, we are probably more alike than different. Legal practice in the United States is probably not very different from practice anywhere in the world. Partners have the same concerns over clients and billings. Young associates share the same anxiety over their career prospects and legal training.

We all have dreams for our lives and careers, wherever we may be. For me, it was to apply what I have learnt in Singapore and be an ambassador of Singapore talent abroad. To my young readers, let me tell you what I know for sure: Be true to yourself. If you can dream it and are willing to work hard, with enough preparation and sacrifice, you too can realise your dreams like I have..

CHAPTER 23

PRACTISING LAW IN THE UNITED KINGDOM – THE WORLD IS NOT ENOUGH

Leonard Ng

Leonard Ng graduated from the Law Faculty of the National University of Singapore in 1994. After a period of travelling, relief teaching and playing music, he returned to complete his pupillage at a Singapore law firm and then studied for a Masters degree in Law at the University of Chicago Law School in the United States. He then joined Sidley Austin LLP, one of the world's largest full-service law firms, and is currently a partner in its London office. The views in this chapter are those of the author's alone; they do not necessarily reflect the views of Sidley Austin LLP.

London has been my home for almost fourteen years now. Yet, cycling to work on a beautiful spring morning, I still sometimes feel like I am on some kind of super-extended holiday. That is a common feeling for people who live and work abroad. Funnily enough, at the time I started writing this chapter, I passed by a billboard in a London airport, saying that over 138 million people work outside their country of birth. What I would like to try and do in this chapter is to give to you, the reader, some insight into what it is like working as a lawyer in the UK.

Naturally, my observations below are coloured by my personal experience. I spent the first four years of my career as a lawyer working on structured finance transactions, but for the past ten years have focussed on financial services regulation as my area of speciality. There are, of course, many fields a lawyer can choose to work in (as the rest of this book attests), so a lawyer focussing on family law or criminal law might have a very different perspective on what I discuss below. In the same way, a lawyer working as a barrister rather than a solicitor, or as a solicitor in a small law firm in Bristol, Manchester or Leeds may have a very different experience to one working in a large law firm in London.

A good starting point would be to explain that the UK (the United Kingdom of Great Britain and Northern Ireland) is actually made up of several different jurisdictions. Although the UK is a single sovereign state, it is made up of Great Britain (England, Wales and Scotland) and Northern Ireland. England and Wales together make up one jurisdiction, while Scotland and Northern Ireland are separate jurisdictions. Lawyers who are qualified in England and Wales are generally referred to as practising 'English law'. Singaporeans who practise law in the UK tend to do so in London or other parts of England and so the majority practise English law rather than Scots or Northern Irish law.

London is in turn made up of two ancient cities – the City of Westminster and the City of London. The City of Westminster is where one is likely to spend time as a tourist; it is where one finds the great theatres, art galleries and museums of London, as well as much of London's famous nightlife. The City of London, also referred to as the 'Square Mile', lies a short distance eastward, with the Bank of England at its heart. It is here that most major financial institutions and law firms traditionally had their offices. Some financial institutions have since moved a little bit eastward to an area called Canary Wharf, although most of the large English law firms have remained in the Square Mile. A 'City lawyer' is generally one who works in a law firm in the Square Mile or Canary Wharf; clients of City law firms tend to be financial institutions (banks, investment firms, insurance companies, investment funds) or companies listed on a stock exchange such as the London Stock Exchange.

Accordingly, the kind of work a City lawyer might be involved in would revolve around mergers and acquisitions, bank lending (for acquisitions of companies, real estate or other assets), financing *via* the capital markets (such as initial public offerings or bond offerings), structured finance (which may involve risk transfer to the capital markets), commercial litigation, financial services regulation, tax and corporate insolvency.

At the same time, unlike the Singapore legal system, in which a qualified lawyer may carry on numerous functions, the English legal system features two types of lawyers – 'solicitors' and 'barristers'. Generally speaking, solicitors advise clients (members of the public, companies and governments) on anything ranging from drafting contracts for acquisitions of companies to advising on how to prepare a will. Solicitors generally do not appear in court (although a few solicitors have such a 'right of audience' to appear in court). In comparison, barristers argue cases in court; barristers receive their instructions from solicitors rather than from clients directly. Apart from appearing in court, barristers also deliver legal opinions on certain complex areas of the law.

Along with New York law, English law is often the law chosen by parties to govern contracts in international commercial transactions, in particular finance and banking transactions. The reasons for this are varied, but they include the fact that English law is considered to be neutral and also fairly predictable in terms of outcomes in case of a dispute between the parties. Also, many international transactions are carried out in English, so the choice of English law to interpret English words and phrases in contracts makes commercial sense. Separately, the English courts are a popular forum for litigating disputes in international transactions because of the experience of the judges and the sophistication of the legal industry (many of the world's largest law firms are either based in, or have offices in, London). In the specialist Commercial Court in London, around 80% of cases involve a foreign party, either as a claimant or as a defendant.

English law also forms the bedrock of the common law system in many countries, including Singapore. As a junior lawyer I spent a year on secondment at the Financial Law Panel ('FLP'), a legal think tank chaired by the late Lord Donaldson, former Master of the Rolls (that is, the judge who presides over the Court of Appeal). An abiding memory of my time there was sitting in our modest little conference room one afternoon, with two judges of the House of Lords and one judge from the Court of Appeal having a free-flowing argument amongst themselves as to the correct analysis on a particularly complex legal issue which the FLP intended to address in one of its papers. These were judges whose legal judgments I had spent many hours as a NUS student trying to dissect (not very successfully!). It was quite surreal for me to sit there and witness first hand how these great legal minds thought about such complex issues and justified their divergent views to each other.

One of the most enjoyable aspects of my life as a lawyer in London is the very international nature of the practice. The clients and fellow lawyers I work with daily are spread out among the United States, the UK, the rest of continental Europe and Asia. Given the time zones involved, it potentially means that I have to work 24 hours a day. On occasion that indeed is necessary (and tiring!), but the saving grace is that the work is constantly exciting. I find myself having to deal not only with legal issues that affect clients in very different circumstances based on local legal and other considerations, but also with people from very different backgrounds and cultures.

By way of example, in 2009 a global financial institution engaged in a public transaction involving the exchange of certain types of shares for other shares in that company. My firm represented a significant shareholder in that company and one of our functions was to determine how the transaction would affect our client's shareholding. A concern that often arises when a company makes adjustments to its capital structure is that certain shareholders in that company might be prejudiced, either because the shares they hold would end up being less valuable than before, or because there is an increase in tax or regulatory obligations for that shareholder.

In many countries, holders of shares above a certain threshold (often around 10%) in regulated entities (banks, securities firms and so on) are required either to seek prior approval from, or file a notification with, the relevant regulatory authority. The reason for this is that a regulator is keen to find out who may have a significant influence on the business carried out by a firm under its supervision. The failure to seek prior regulatory approval or file a notification for such matters is a criminal offence in some countries, so it is critical that the applicable regulatory requirements be properly understood.

Because that financial institution had in its corporate group banks, insurance companies and securities firms in many countries all over the world, it was necessary to work out the regulatory implications of our client's shareholding in that financial institution (which in turn owned the local entities). This meant considering the regulatory regimes in over 100 jurisdictions around the world where that financial institution had a meaningful presence. This in turn required that we work closely with local law firms in those jurisdictions to work out what the local laws and regulations required.

In many cases English was a second or third language for the lawyer working at the local law firm which we were dealing with, so this exercise called for the ability to discuss a complex set of facts in as simple a manner as possible, but somehow with nuances intact in order to ensure that the local lawyers were being asked to advise on all the pertinent issues. More importantly, the exercise required a significant amount of diplomacy and a personal touch, since we had to ensure that the local law firm was giving this matter the right amount of attention. (This type of exercise is often referred to as 'herding cats'). Finally, because the matter involved working with local lawyers in every conceivable time zone, sleep was very much in short supply!

It has to be said, however, that whatever the professional opportunities offered by a particular city or country, and no matter how exciting the work may appear to be, it is likely to be one's personal circumstances that ultimately determine whether to choose one city or country over another. In my case, I had applied to two law schools in the United

States to study for a Masters degree (known as an LLM). This was partly because I had one eye back then possibly on a career in academia, and partly because, having spent a lot of time travelling, I wanted to continue to be connected to the wider world.

Of course, having borrowed a colossal amount of money to pay for the Masters degree (US university education being notoriously expensive), I realised very soon after I started the course at the University of Chicago that I would need to get a position in a good law firm in order realistically to be able to repay my student loan.

I had not necessarily closed my mind to going back to Singapore to look for a position, but when Sidley Austin LLP (then called Sidley & Austin) offered me the chance to work in London, I felt that I would prefer to live in London over Singapore and some other cities in the US in which I had been offered positions. Nebulous factors such as London's vibrant culture, charming old streets and buildings and less high-rise working environment, as well as its proximity to Europe (for travel opportunities) and Singapore (at least compared to the US), made me feel that London might be a better 'fit' for my personality and state of mind at that time in my life.

London also offered me the opportunity to strike out on my own and see if I could 'make it' as a foreigner in a big city (although this would also have been true had I decided to work in New York). I liked the challenge of being a tiny fish in a very large pond. Finally, it was important to me to be in one of the music capitals of the world, as music was (and continues to be) an important part of my life. For another person, the ability to explore London's endless tourist attractions, or to be able to watch Arsenal or Manchester United play in the Premier League every week, or to simply feel the 'buzz' of London Fashion Week, might well be the sole deciding factor!

I am now married with two young children, and I find that life is very agreeable in London because of its many activities for families and the abundance of parks for children to run around and play in. Every weekend and every season finds us with something new to do, whether in London or in the countryside. Meanwhile, Paris is but a short Eurostar train journey away. The downside for us of raising small children in the UK is that there is no family support network of parents and siblings (and no, there are no 'maids') to help out, for example, by babysitting; by the same token the children do not get to see their grandparents and other extended family as much as they would like to.

The education system in England was confusing for my wife and me at first (both of us having been educated in Singapore), but after looking at several schools we found one that we felt would be right for our sons. One of the slightly curious features of our sons' school is that the children address the teachers (even the headmaster) by their first names – certainly not something we ever imagined possible growing up in Singapore! The schools encourage a lot of creativity and responsibility at a very young age and it is always fascinating for my wife and me to see the approaches taken in the education system by way of comparison with what we grew up with in Singapore. There is a notable lack of 'hot-housing' in many schools, although such schools are available if that is what a child's parents desires for that child.

One of the personal aspects of living and working abroad in a big city like London that I find very attractive is that there is truly the ability to live life in a manner chosen by you. There is no pre-conceived 'master plan' as to how you should live your life; you are constantly surrounded by people who have taken a very different path in life to your own. The result is that there is much less social pressure than there might be in a smaller country or city to conform to any particular mould. There is no expectation that you should drive a particular type of car, live in a particular kind of housing, belong to a particular club, hold a particular political view, or spend your time in any particular manner. This is especially true where you are a foreigner and thus come from a different background to begin with – so it is more difficult for people to 'pigeon-hole' you. No one judges me on the basis of what school I went to, what neighbourhood I grew up in, or what I like to do in my spare time. Nor does anyone care what car I drive (a seven-year-old Volkswagen which is falling apart, in case you are wondering). My colleagues and clients care only about the advice that I give as a lawyer at my firm. It is this incredible freedom that I value most of all about working in London.

So surely there must be some downsides to working in London, you ask? Oh yes; let's talk about some of them.

First, you may have to work, as they like to say here, 'bloody hard'. There will likely be those occasions when, after 48 hours without sleep, the main challenge (apart from staving off psychosis) will be to ensure that you do not put into the legal documentation something that could have drastic consequences – for example, an extra zero to the price of a company your client is buying! But then I doubt lawyers in London work any harder than those working on similar matters in any major financial centre, including Singapore. In fact lawyers in London often (justifiably or otherwise) look pitifully at their counterparts in New York, who are presumed to work even harder!

Secondly, one consequence of the size of the economy (and thus the legal industry) in the UK is that it generally takes more time to 'make it' in the traditional sense of becoming a partner in a law firm. In a large international firm in London, it takes an average of nine to eleven years – from the time one qualifies as a solicitor – to become a partner (if a position on the partnership is at all available), while it may take seven or eight years in a large Singapore firm (and in some cases this period is even shorter for the best graduates). It may also be more difficult for a lawyer to get noticed in an international firm of 2,000 lawyers, compared with a firm of 200 or 300 lawyers (which would be a large firm in Singapore). In addition, it can take a total of six years to qualify as a solicitor in England – three years in university, one year on the Legal Practice Course and two years as a trainee solicitor in a law firm. This compares with five years in Singapore – four years in NUS, a five-month practical law course leading to the Singapore Bar Examinations and six months as a trainee lawyer in a law firm.

However, the benefit of a large economy and legal industry is that there are many fulfilling positions for a lawyer who does not wish to take the traditional path of aiming to become a partner in a law firm; as evidenced by the other chapters in this book, partnership in a law firm is but one of a number of options open for a junior lawyer. There are superb lawyers working in the government, in companies, in charities and in academia who may feel that it is far more interesting to work in those organisations than in a law firm. At the same time, the size of the legal industry means that there are very interesting areas of law that one might not be able to practice in a smaller market like Singapore's; examples of such areas include space law, human rights litigation and so on.

Thirdly, the financial crisis, coupled with the rapid economic growth in the BRIC countries (Brazil, Russia, India and China), has meant that financial centres other than London and New York have gained in their importance. There are certainly outstanding opportunities for Singapore lawyers to work in any of these competitor financial centres (including, of course, Singapore itself). Indeed, many large international law firms appear to be opening offices in Asia or expanding existing Asian offices. At the same time, however, it takes a combination of many different factors for a financial centre to be truly successful. These include not only 'hard' factors like physical infrastructure (buildings, technology, airports, roads) but also 'soft' factors such as the openness and transparency of the political framework, cultural and artistic vibrancy and freedom, historical importance, tourist attractions and the absence of corruption. For example, international investors are less likely to invest in a country where their assets may be appropriated by the government during times of political or financial instability. At the same time, in a world of global finance it is almost meaningless to speak of a single financial centre; as a practical matter there needs to be at least one major financial centre in the time zones in which America, Europe and Asia operate. In this regard London is well placed from a time zone perspective; for example, it can serve both New York and Shanghai, when as a practical matter each of those cities is generally closed for business when the other is open. So with the unique combination of its geographical location, the English language, its cultural and sporting attractions and its legal, accounting and financial infrastructure, it seems likely that London will continue to be relevant as a major financial centre for many years to come.

Fourthly, the cold and dark winters do take some getting used to, even for the British. There are days when the cold seems to penetrate through to one's bone marrow. And no one I know likes the fact that it gets dark at 4pm in late December each year. But then there are also those occasional white Christmases and other crisp winter days when you can go sledging down a hill in a park, or go ice-skating, and just enjoy all that winter has to offer. There are also the glorious summers, where the sun is out until 9 or 10 o'clock in the evening, the pretty, colourful springs (sometimes with too much rain!) and the atmospheric autumns. Personally, I love the changing seasons and the variety of the weather, plus the low humidity compared to Singapore.

Fifthly, London can be a very expensive city to live in. As any Singaporean who has been to London knows, it is not a good idea constantly to convert London prices into 'Sing Dollars', as one will constantly be in a state of shock. S$9 for a two-minute Tube (subway) ride! S$18 for a plate of duck rice! S$280 million for a flat! (A flat facing Hyde Park was sold to a Russian oligarch for that price in April 2011). Having said that, a lawyer in a good firm should be more than adequately compensated, even if you should not think about buying Chelsea Football Club on your salary any time soon. One saving grace is that, unlike Singapore, cars are relatively cheap since there is no COE system (which begs the question why I drive an old Volkswagen – as to which see the point above about doing whatever you like).

Before I end this chapter, I think it is worth addressing a question that people sometimes feel a little bit awkward asking, which is: to what extent does one's nationality, ethnicity or accent matter in working as a lawyer in the UK? I am Singaporean Chinese. It may have been that I have been lucky, but in the thirteen years I have worked in London, I have never felt disadvantaged in my career by not being white/British/American/European. It is true that you can feel a little self-conscious walking into a big conference room with lots of lawyers and clients on a large transaction and finding that you are the only non-white person there, but that is not particularly different from the feeling one might get from being dressed in yellow in a room full of people dressed in white. The reality is that most people these days assume that you are there because you have the right qualifications to be there, and could not care less if your skin colour were bright purple. That is particularly true in the world of international finance, where there is, in fact, a great diversity of professionals from all races and backgrounds so the scenario above is, in any event, quite rare.

On the other hand, I am not entirely naive in thinking that absolutely everyone in the UK (even in cosmopolitan London) is so progressive and open-minded. My entirely non-scientific poll of a few Singaporean lawyers that I know in London indicated that some of them had at times felt patronised by some other – typically quite senior – lawyers and clients. However, that kind of patronising person is likely to have prejudicial attitudes not only to ethnic minorities and foreigners, but also to women or, for that matter, anyone who is vaguely 'different' (or even simply younger). One should simply avoid these dinosaurs which are, in any event, fast becoming extinct. There is a significant push in law firms (and businesses in general) to be more reflective of the society they operate in, and so diversity in all respects – ethnicity, gender and sexual orientation – is now taken seriously.

Finally, I would not worry about the fact that you may be speaking with what you might assume to be an unfamiliar accent in the UK. Large numbers of people in the UK – particularly in London – speak English with accents showing their roots in myriad countries. In my Financial Services Regulatory Group alone there is a Russian, a Pole, a British Indian, an American, a Chinese – there is even one white English man!

At the end of the day, if you were to ask for my advice on whether to move out of Singapore and work as a lawyer in the UK instead, I would start not by asking what your professional aims are, but rather whether working in another country would be personally satisfying in the first place and whether the UK might be the 'right' country for you. Working in the UK has turned out to be perfect for me, but it might not suit everyone. At the end of the day, perhaps the most important lesson I have learned, having had the benefit both of living in Singapore as well as overseas, is that one must ultimately try and take one's own path, even if that is completely different to what everyone else expects.

Why, Sir, you find no man, at all intellectual, who is willing to leave London. No, Sir, when a man is tired of London, he is tired of life; for there is in London all that life can afford.'

– Samuel Johnson

CHAPTER 24

PRACTISING LAW IN HONG KONG – WHO DARES WINS IN THE FRAGRANT HARBOUR

Connie Heng

Connie Heng graduated from the National University of Singapore and is qualified to practise in Singapore, Hong Kong and England and Wales. She is a partner in Clifford Chance, Hong Kong and specialises in international securities offerings and structured finance.

The last ten years have seen Singapore transform itself not only into a city state offering a high quality of life for professionals but also increasingly into an active financial centre in a fast developing region, largely sheltered from the economic storm that has shaken Europe and the United States. However, any young lawyer eager to experience a dynamic professional environment which provides an opportunity to be exposed to innovative and high profile international legal work, should consider Hong Kong as a destination at some point in his or her career. Hong Kong, by virtue of its history and its geographical location as the gateway to China, offers a unique and rich professional environment.

Most international investment banks and financial institutions at the moment still view Hong Kong as the principal hub for their Asia Pacific business and I believe this will continue for at least the next five years, unless there is political instability or a drastic slow-down in China's economic growth. Undoubtedly, Singapore has tried to compete with Hong Kong by attracting financial institutions and MNCs with its excellent infrastructure, a highly educated local work force and stable political and business environment. However, Hong Kong's proximity to China, with its relentless economic growth in the past decade, is an important factor for many international corporations and financial institutions. For this reason, many global, and particularly financial, institutions and British law firms have had a long established presence in Hong Kong. In the last few years, we have also seen an increasing number of European financial institutions and US law firms set up their core Asian operations in Hong Kong. The presence of these institutions and firms in Hong Kong means that, despite Hong Kong's strong

Chinese identity, it has a very international outlook and a sizeable expat community. Hong Kong is unique in the sense that although it has a central business district only the size of Singapore's Raffles Place, it is a lot more densely-packed with financial and legal professionals from different jurisdictional backgrounds than any other financial centre in the world. In Clifford Chance where I have worked over the last 10 years, the lawyers come from many different cultural and ethnic backgrounds, including Hong Kong, the US, the UK, Australia, China, South Africa, Singapore, Malaysia, Austria, Germany and India. I have enjoyed working in a diverse and multicultural environment and over the years I have learnt a lot from my colleagues. This diversity has been the key to Hong Kong being a vibrant, interesting, dynamic and evolving city in which to work and live.

Every city, of course, has its down-side and, compared to Singapore, Hong Kong has problems with its worsening air quality and high cost of living, to name but two. The property market in Hong Kong is notoriously fickle and reactive, and although I have, in my 13 years of living and working in Hong Kong, seen some spectacular drops in real estate prices, the market tends to recover quickly. Almost everyone I know, who has moved to Hong Kong for the first time, will very swiftly adjust their expectations and reconsider their rental budgets after seeing the quality and size of the available properties, compared to what they are used to back in their home country. Finding an apartment in any city is always a challenge but in Hong Kong it is particularly so because most people who have just moved to Hong Kong want to live in close proximity to their workplace (often no more than 15 to 20 minutes by foot or taxi). Most financial institutions and law firms are located in the Central area (which is the equivalent of Singapore's CBD) and the closest place to live is in the Midlevels which is also where you find the relatively more expensive real estate on Hong Kong Island. Most newcomers to Hong Kong, especially those who are single without families, will gravitate towards Midlevels. Midlevels is densely packed with toothpick-like residential buildings which tend to make this area feel claustrophobic. However, it is 20 minutes by foot or 10 minutes by taxi to Central and close to the restaurants and nightlife in Lan Kwai Fong and Soho districts. When I first moved to Hong Kong to join an international law firm as a junior associate, it was just after the Handover and property prices and rentals were at a record high. After seeing about 30 apartments, I finally accepted reality, lowered expectations and settled for a 400 square foot apartment on the third floor facing a crowded street in Midlevels. Without any exaggeration, the size of my kitchen was smaller than my mother's 6-seater dining table in Singapore and the living room was so small I could stretch both arms out and touch opposite walls. The joke amongst my friends then was that if anyone wanted to learn to roller blade, they could use my living room. I remember consoling myself with the knowledge that the office was just 20 minutes walk down the famous Midlevels escalator to Central and I was probably going to be spending a lot of time in the office or going out. What also surprised me was the number of families with children living in the same block of flats complete with a helper and sometimes even pets. When sharing a lift downstairs with them, I had to remind myself to feel lucky that in my case I had a flat all to myself. Fortunately for me, the time spent in the cosy 400 square foot cubby hole was not to be very long. One of my best friends from junior college days moved from London to Hong Kong to join an investment bank a few months after I arrived and we decided to combine resources to get a bigger flat. We traded up for a 1000 square foot apartment a few streets and 'levels' up Midlevels. The bigger space meant a 200% lifestyle improvement for us as we now had a proper dining and living room. It was also there that we had some of our best dinner and drinks parties. Fast forward 13 years, after going through a few upturns and downturns, the property market is now back to pre-1997 peaks. For a young lawyer considering a career move to Hong Kong, the cost of accommodation is something to take into consideration as it will probably be the biggest monthly expense.

The landscape for law firms in Hong Kong is quite different from the scene in Singapore. Law firms in Hong Kong can be loosely grouped into international law firms (which include the Magic Circle firms headquartered in London, smaller English firms and US firms), foreign law firms (such as those from the Cayman Islands and Australia), the big home-grown Hong Kong law firms, boutique firms specialising in niche areas and small local firms. International law firms are able to practise Hong Kong law if they have a sufficient number of Hong Kong qualified lawyers and fulfil certain pre-requisites set by the Hong Kong Law Society. Foreign lawyers (such as Singapore qualified lawyers) can qualify in Hong Kong if they sit and pass the Overseas Lawyers Qualifications Exams (affectionately known as the 'OLQE') prescribed by the Hong Kong Law Society. One of the things I did in my first year in Hong Kong was to sit for the OLQE. The OLQE is not dissimilar to the exams at the end of what used to be the Practice Law Course (PLC) – now Part B of the Singapore Bar Examinations – which lawyers in Singapore take when seeking admission to the Singapore Bar. However, the common complaint at the time when I sat for the exams (and I believe, still the common complaint now) was the lack of transparency about where the pass mark would be set on the performance curve. For me, having to work during the day and study for the exams at night and over weekends presented its challenges. Luckily for me, I passed the OLQE on my first try but I have known lawyers who had to take the exams at least three or four times.

With so many international and local firms in Hong Kong, competition at every level in the legal services market is fierce. Compared to Singapore where there are only a few large firms with leading corporate, finance, capital markets and litigation departments, in Hong Kong, particularly in financial services, one often sees English firms competing alongside US firms and Hong Kong firms for the same piece of work. As a result, lawyers (especially partners) and law firms invest time in ensuring a high level of client care and in business development. In Clifford Chance, where I am a partner in the Capital Markets department, we try to stay in touch with clients in between transactions through lunches, dinners, drinks and firm-wide events such as wine tastings, invitations to major sporting events or family days at Ocean Park, just to give a few examples. We also encourage our lawyers of every seniority to participate in business development activities which we organise and to keep in touch with the people they have worked with at the client's organisation. Business development activities range from a cup of coffee to a 'Sex in the City' movie premiere night exclusively for clients invited by senior associates. The lawyers enjoy being given the autonomy to develop client relationships early in their career.

Immediacy is a signature of doing business in Hong Kong: clients expect immediate attention at short notice and often with very tight deadlines to resolve issues as they occur. The practice of law is no different. This sense of immediacy gives the city its vibrant environment both at work and during down-time. Another trait which is special to Hong Kong is the 'can do' attitude which permeates society from street vendors to professionals. To take a simple example, if you are in a basic clothing chain store buying an inexpensive t-shirt and they have run out of your size, the service staff will take the initiative, even before you ask, to offer to check with their other stores and to send it to a store convenient for you to try it on or purchase. No expense is spared in making sure customers get what they want and the shop gets the business done. To a large extent, clients expect their lawyers to adopt the same attitude as service providers. In my role as a transactional lawyer, I have had to learn to provide legal advice and run transactions with commercial mindedness to help my clients solve legal issues and close deals. I learnt quickly that to be successful as a lawyer at all levels of seniority one has to do more than simply know and recite the law to clients. In my role as a capital markets lawyer, clients look to me to help them structure their transactions to avoid legal and regulatory issues so that they can successfully achieve their fund raising plans.

The training that lawyers receive in a firm is important. The international law firms in Hong Kong invest a lot of time and resources in providing ongoing training for their lawyers. In Clifford Chance, we have the Clifford Chance Academy which structures and organises firm wide training globally. Courses are made available online through e-learning and trainers are sent around the network to give training. The courses range from soft skills training to technical topics. In our Hong Kong office, each department also runs lunch-time courses regularly and, on relevant topics, other departments are invited to attend. Lawyers are encouraged to hone not just their technical skills but also their soft skills as we believe in developing well-rounded lawyers.

Corporate social responsibility is also an area law firms have been actively promoting in Hong Kong. This has taken many forms: involvement in charitable fund raising such as hikes and donation drives, dedicating time and labour to accomplish practical goals such as cleaning beaches to running pro-bono legal advice clinics for under privileged/ vulnerable segments of society such as asylum seekers. Increasingly law firms such as Clifford Chance partner with clients with similar corporate social responsibility goals to achieve a more significant impact on the community. These initiatives also have the benefit of building closer relationships between lawyers and their clients.

Since moving to Hong Kong in 1998, I have seen Hong Kong go through a few economic cycles – the internet bubble, SARs, the boom years post-SARs up to 2007, the global crisis in 2008 and the pick-up in the economy in 2009. Two key words, in my view, which best represent Hong Kong are 'reactive' and 'adaptable'. People in Hong Kong react fast to events, adapt and bounce back quickly. As a legal practitioner, being able to react and adapt is critical. As soon as the Hong Kong economy reacts to events around the world and in the region, the reaction is also felt in the work place. In the context of the legal industry, one can look at the example of the China IPO boom over the last few years. The international law firms in Hong Kong reacted to the opportunities by opening offices in Shanghai and Beijing and by building teams of lawyers with the right background, training and language skills to capture the China IPO deal flow. When the global financial crisis hit in

September 2008, the market came to a complete halt. I remember that my office phone suddenly stopped ringing and lawyers in my department went from being very busy and getting by with little sleep to suddenly not having very much to do as deals got put on hold or were aborted. As our capital markets clients started to re-invent themselves, lawyers including myself also had to adapt to the environment and try our hand at new product areas. Due to the crisis, a lot of corporations started having cash flow problems and had to restructure their debt. Very quickly, we had to adapt and transform ourselves into restructuring lawyers to keep busy. Fortunately for us, being in an international law firm meant that we could tap into the firm's know-how and use those partners in our global network who are experts in the restructuring field to quickly get up to speed. At a day to day level, instead of looking at how the Hang Seng Index has been doing, one can get a good sense of how the market is doing by calling up two or three restaurants in Central for a lunch booking. When the market is doing well, it will be impossible to get a table with less than three or four days' notice.

The work day for a lawyer (and most professionals in the finance and banking industry) in Hong Kong is intense and the hours can be quite long, including weekends. But once out of the office, the ease with which one can indulge in activities ranging from wining, dining, clubbing to sports, hiking and the inevitable shopping, sets this city apart from many other financial centres. It is hard to imagine but many office buildings in Central are built above shopping malls. This is convenient but is also dangerous for impulsive professionals who treat their work stress with retail therapy! Over the years, I too have fallen prey on many occasions to the bright and glitzy shops which line the Landmark and IFC on the way to get lunch or a coffee. From October through March each year when the weather is cooler and drier, many people go hiking at weekends in the hills in Hong Kong, the outlying islands or further afield in the New Territories. Hiking is a good way to get some exercise and socialise with friends. Many hiking trails are very green with spectacular scenery and quite different from the concrete jungle of Central. For the keen traveller, Hong Kong is a good base to take long weekends to nearby countries such as Thailand or China. A train runs from Central straight to the airport in about 25 minutes and there is even downtown check-in. If one wanted to visit Singapore for the weekend, he or she could leave work around 6.30pm on a Friday, catch an 8pm flight and be back in Singapore around 11:30pm, which still leaves ample time for supper at a hawker centre!

The professionals in Hong Kong work hard and play hard. It is the place to be for hardworking young lawyers who want to gain a lot of deal experience in a short time and build a network of professional and social contacts from diverse backgrounds. Hong Kong is not for the faint-hearted, but for those who like a fast pace and a real challenge, there is a lot Hong Kong can offer.

CHAPTER 25

PRACTISING LAW IN CHINA – THE RISE OF THE DRAGON

Chong Ik Wei

Chong Ik Wei is resident partner and chief representative of Clyde & Co's Shanghai office. He is a graduate of the Law Faculty of the National University of Singapore, and is qualified to practice in Singapore, Hong Kong, and England and Wales. His practice focus in disputes and investments connected with China, Hong Kong and Taiwan.

Since the turn of the millennium, the People's Republic of China ('PRC') has been a word muttered on the lips of many a politician and peasant alike. Indeed, why not? Its growth in the international arena has been, to put it mildly, astronomical. Currently it is the world's second largest economy, with a nominal GDP of more than USD 4 trillion, the fastest growing economy in the world averaging a GDP growth of 9.9 percent per year, the largest producer of steel, and the top importer of iron ore – the statistics are extremely impressive.

As a result of this exponential growth in the economy of the PRC, there has also been a corresponding acceleration in the need for both domestic and international legal services. In December 2001, the PRC acceded to the World Trade Organisation ('WTO') and committed itself to liberalising its legal services. This resulted in changes in the landscape for the development of Chinese legal services, both within Chinese law firms and international firms in the PRC.

In a global context, it is certainly not an exaggeration to say that the development of a modern Chinese legal profession is still in its infancy. While the PRC has embarked on an intensive programme of reforms at all levels, it is clear that legal reform has only really gained momentum following the PRC's accession to the WTO in 2001. At the moment, there are at least 140,000 registered lawyers in the PRC operating from approximately 12,000 local Chinese law firms.

International law firms have been permitted to open representative offices in the PRC since 1992, and there currently are more than 150 international and foreign law firms with offices mainly in the major legal centres such as Beijing and Shanghai. The representative offices of international law firms are allowed, by the Ministry of Justice regulations, to advise on international and foreign law issues and to also provide advice and information on the implications of the Chinese legal environment. At the same time, international law firms are permitted to form long-term co-operation or 'best friends' relationships with local Chinese law firms.

International law firms are not allowed to advise on Chinese law or appear before the PRC Courts. Should international law firms be required to represent their clients in Chinese Court proceedings, they would need to engage local Chinese firms to do so. In a way, this is quite similar to how most international firms operate on an 'off-shore' basis in Singapore.

For arbitration proceedings in the PRC, international law firms are permitted to be counsel on record and make submissions during hearings. However, it must be highlighted that under the current Ministry of Justice regulations, only locally qualified and licensed lawyers can provide advice and opinions on Chinese law. In other words, should the arbitration proceedings be governed by Chinese law, international law firms will need to work in tandem with local Chinese law firms.

In light of the above, two burning questions must ensue:

(1) How does a lawyer, particularly a lawyer trained in Singapore, involved in dispute resolution work and working in an international law firm in the PRC, find his or her feet and truly engage in the practice of law given the various constraints?; and

(2) In a country where opportunities seem endless and continuing economic growth a given, are sentiments in the legal profession, particularly from the perspective of an international law firm, similarly upbeat?

When we talk about 'The Practice of Law', we need to focus on the words 'Practice' and 'Law'. In other words, to truly engage in the practice of law, one must first understand the legal system and culture of that country ('Law'), and then make use of one's legal skills and commercial acumen to provide the relevant solutions (which often involves not only legal analysis but also a commercial understanding of the existing realities – 'Practice').

I shall first set out a brief introduction on the legal system of the PRC and highlight some of the more significant differences between that and the common-law legal regime, which most of the English-speaking world is familiar with. I will then share my personal experiences and the challenges of practising as a dispute resolution lawyer in the PRC – no day is the same as another, and it may very well be the case that the law states one thing but implementation may prove something different altogether.

1. The Legal System of the PRC

From a political perspective, it is common knowledge that the Communist Party of China ('CPC') is the only political party since the founding of the People's Republic in 1949. The CPC is very much integrated into all levels and departments of legislative, administrative and judicial organs of the country. From the central government to the basic or 'grassroots' levels of local governments, in all ministries and commissions, and in the People's Courts, it is fair to say that members of the CPC hold almost all the key positions, with very few exceptions.

The PRC adopts a civil law system which is very different from the common law system in place in jurisdictions such as the United Kingdom, Hong Kong and Singapore. Concepts familiar to a common-law trained lawyer such as stare decisis and binding case precedents do not apply. In other words, the fact that a local PRC Court has arrived at a particular decision earlier has no or very little binding effect on another Court in the same jurisdiction or elsewhere. Ultimately, the way in which a matter is decided would depend very much on the relevant civil codes and other legislation, and the discretion of the judge or bench of judges.

In the PRC, trials are heard by a tribunal made up of one to three Judges. For some cases, the tribunal may consist of an Assessor (similar to that of a juror in other jurisdictions), who is elected by the local residents or the People's Congress. Whilst, in theory, the Assessor's role is similar to that of a judge, the reality is that he or she is unlikely to have too big a say in the eventual judgment to be handed down by the court. Trials are conducted in an inquisitorial manner, which is in stark contrast to the adversarial system (in common law systems) in which the judge would hear submissions from opposing lawyers.

Structure of PRC Courts

The Chinese courts are divided into four levels. At the highest level sits the Supreme People's Court in Beijing, the ultimate appellate court in the PRC, which is in charge of the administration of justice in all subordinate local and special courts.

People's Courts are the courts of first instance and appellate courts handling criminal and civil cases. These courts make up the remaining three levels of the court system and consist of the High Courts at the level of the provinces, autonomous regions, and special municipalities; the Intermediate Courts at the level of prefectures, autonomous prefectures, and municipalities; and the Basic Courts at the level of autonomous counties, towns and municipal districts.

In addition, it must also be mentioned that there are a number of Courts with specialist jurisdictions, such as the Military Court, the Railway Court, the Maritime Court and the Forestry Court.

The allocation of jurisdiction between the different levels of Courts vary across different regions in the PRC, although, in general, the amount of the claim sought is one of the more (if not the most) important factors in deciding which level of Court has jurisdiction to adjudicate a particular matter.

In contrast to domestic disputes between PRC parties (which are usually brought before the Basic Court), cases involving non-Chinese parties are sometimes commenced at the Intermediate Court level, although the High Court may sometimes exercise first-instance jurisdiction in matters involving large claim or complex issues of law.

Proceedings in the PRC are divided into two levels: the first-instance trial and the second-instance trial (or appeal). A judgment issued by the court of first instance can be appealed to the Court at the next higher level. The second-instance judgment is final and enforceable and cannot be appealed further. The first-instance judgment will become final and enforceable if no appeal is brought within the prescribed time period.

Some Unique Features of the PRC Legal System

Quite clearly, the legal system of the PRC differs significantly from the Singapore legal system (and those of other common-law jurisdictions). I set out below a snapshot of some these key differences:

i.   Documents Required to Commence Legal Proceedings in the PRC

Apart from the Statement of Complaint (which is similar to the Statement of Claim), the other documents required are duly endorsed and signed originals of the Power of Attorney ('POA') and Certificate of Identity of Legal Representative ('COI') and the Business Licence of the Claimant (if applicable). The POA is a document authorising lawyers to commence legal proceedings on behalf of the Claimant while the COI is a document issued by the Claimant company to prove the title and position of the legal representative of the company.

If the Claimant is domiciled in another country, these documents will need to undergo notarisation and authentication in that foreign country. It must be noted that the notarisation or authentication procedures may vary from country to country and would normally take a few weeks to arrange. This requirement by the Chinese Courts has been described by many commentators and practitioners as being overly cumbersome and bureaucratic, particularly when one is faced with the prospect of an impending time bar for the commencement of proceedings, or when urgent applications are contemplated. It is useful to note that the limitation period for, say, a contractual or tortious claim is 2 years from the date the innocent party is or ought to be aware that its civil rights have been infringed, while the corresponding limitation period under Singapore law is six years.

ii. *Presentation of Evidence and Cross-Examination in Court*

Trials and hearings in the PRC are usually conducted in an inquisitorial manner, quite unlike the adversarial system which one is used to in a common law jurisdiction. During the trial or hearing, the primary focus is placed on the examination of documentary evidence. Also, in practice, it is very unlikely for the Court to compel the attendance of a witness in Court for oral examination. Unlike trials in common law jurisdictions which can take up to several days or even weeks as a result of the number of witnesses and experts involved and the complexity of underlying issues, most trials in the PRC do not exceed one to three days.

iii. *Lawyers' Fees*

Party and party costs (ie the legal fees which a litigant pays to the opposing party) are not recoverable from the losing litigant should the matter proceed to trial. This is quite different from the common law system say in Singapore where party and party costs (sometimes up to 60%–70% of lawyers' fees) are generally recoverable from the losing litigant should one succeed at trial. There are very few instances where the Chinese Courts have ordered the losing litigant to bear the lawyers' fees incurred by the winning litigant.

Unlike Chinese Courts, Chinese arbitration tribunals have the power to order an unsuccessful party to pay some or all of the costs incurred by the winning party. These costs would involve administrative fees, arbitrators' fees, and lawyers' fees. Having said that, the award of lawyers' fees depends largely on the discretion of the arbitrators, and amount is usually determined on a broad-brush approach.

iv. *Arbitration Clauses in the PRC*

Unlike jurisdictions such as the United Kingdom, Hong Kong and Singapore, in the PRC, arbitration agreements providing for ad hoc arbitration are invalid. In other words, all arbitrations conducted in the

PRC must be administered by an arbitration commission, for example, the China International Economic and Trade Arbitration Commission ('CIETAC'). Another unique feature about arbitration in the PRC is that it endorses the 'arb-med' procedure – this is a process in which the arbitrator also acts as a mediator in the same dispute. This process is quite common in the PRC. However, this may lead to possible issues of 'impression of bias' of an arbitrator who is, at the same time, acting as a mediator. The flaws of the 'arb-med' process was recently placed in the spotlight when a Hong Kong Court set aside an arbitral award obtained in the PRC on the basis of public policy grounds that there was 'bias' by the arbitrator who was also acting as mediator in the same dispute.

2. Personal Encounters on Dealing with Disputes in the PRC

Enforcing a Foreign Arbitral Award in the PRC – Simply a Matter of Course?

International arbitration has, in recent years, become a growth industry in the PRC, arising from the proliferation of disputes relating to cross-border transactions. The PRC is a party to the New York Convention – it should therefore, in principle, recognise and enforce awards that are commercial in nature and which are issued in a country which is also party to the New York Convention.

Statistics have also shown that between 2002 and 2006, out of 74 applications made in the PRC for the recognition and enforcement of awards rendered by foreign arbitral institutions, rulings in favour of recognition and enforcement were made in 69 of these cases – this represents a success rate of more than 93%. In short, the statistics appear to show that the local PRC Courts, barring any valid challenges against the recognition and enforcement of foreign arbitral awards, adopt a pro-enforcement approach towards foreign arbitral awards.

A matter which we recently handled related to the enforcement of a foreign arbitral award in the PRC which has been the subject of much controversy, largely due to the extra-legal influences which created numerous difficulties in the advancement of the matter. In a nutshell, our clients had obtained a foreign arbitral award and were looking to enforce the same in the PRC. The foreign arbitral award was a commercial one and was issued in a country which is party to the New York Convention. The adverse party (the losing party in the foreign arbitration proceedings) was a subsidiary of a Chinese state-owned company.

Our clients then proceeded to apply for the recognition of the foreign arbitral award before the local PRC court having jurisdiction. The award was subsequently recognised by the Court. The next logical step would be the enforcement of the said award against the assets of the adverse party in the PRC. However, it was at this stage that the matter did not proceed any further. Suffice it to say, our clients faced various hurdles at the enforcement stage, many of them political and extra-legal in nature. The reality was that local governmental bodies and agencies had placed pressure on the court handling the enforcement procedure so that this matter was effectively put on hold. Written representations were made to the Supreme People's Court of the PRC for enforcement, but to no avail. Lobbying efforts were also made via diplomatic channels, although all that garnered was dialogue with the adverse party on how to resolve this impasse amicably, and no practical solution was achieved.

It is common knowledge that the recognition or enforcement of a foreign arbitral award would be refused if doing so would be contrary to the public policy of the PRC. Unfortunately, in reality, it is this public policy limb which is often relied upon by local PRC Courts in refusing enforcement of a foreign arbitral award. Although the Court concerned should strictly not review the substantive merits of the foreign arbitral award but only the procedure leading to the enforcement of the award, the Court often does so on its own volition, and under the guise of public policy or social interests. Legally speaking, enforcement of a foreign arbitral award against a state-owned company should be no different from enforcement against a privately-owned company. Unfortunately, in practice, local governmental agencies may interfere or put obstacles in way of the enforcement of an award, especially if it is against a state-owned company as, amongst other things, the assets involved are essentially state-owned and the employees are civil servants. In short, despite the efforts of the Chinese authorities, local protectionism and political influences still often hinder or prevent enforcement of a foreign arbitral award.

Notwithstanding the prevailing laws and regulations in the PRC and the published statistics, our own experience when it comes to enforcing foreign arbitral awards in the PRC is quite mixed. There have been enforcement proceedings which have basically hit a brick-wall and pending for several years, as allowing enforcement to take place would mean that the local state-owned entity would become insolvent, resulting in the loss of hundreds of jobs. On the other hand, there have also been matters where enforcement was readily allowed and the Chinese debtors then proceeded to satisfy its payment obligations shortly after. The bottom line, therefore, is that no one matter is the same and the eventual outcome for such enforcement would depend on the status or financial strength of the target company and whether sufficient legal or commercial pressure has been put to ensure that its legal obligations are honoured.

3. Conclusion

It is a fact that legal services are opening up in the PRC. More and more international law firms are setting up representative offices in Beijing and Shanghai, and increasingly also in second-tier Chinese cities. With more and more Chinese companies (whether state-owned or private) beginning to focus their minds on overseas ventures and projects of an international flavour, the prospects are fantastic for international and foreign law firms targeting outbound work involving foreign-governing laws and complex international transactions and disputes.

The practice of law in the PRC is certainly not straightforward. Very often, one needs to think out of the box and consider various permutations and options. However, I strongly believe that Singapore-trained lawyers, with their common law background and training, and bilingual skills, would stand in very good stead should they decide to pursue a legal career in the PRC. Instead of looking at the PRC as a destination for a short-term stint to gain exposure to and experience life working in what must be one of the most exciting jurisdictions in the world at the moment, I would also strongly encourage younger lawyers and prospective lawyers amongst us to consider building a long-term legal career in the PRC which I am sure would be rewarding in the years to come.

EPILOGUE

WHAT PRACTICE HAS TAUGHT ME

Adrian Tan

I have been in practice for 20 years. My view of the law as a career?

The pay is unremarkable. A junior lawyer's income is the same as that of a fast-food restaurant manager, when hours worked are taken into account. Because lawyers work all hours of the day (often at great cost to their personal lives).

Despite that, there is hardly any career path to speak of. Most law firms are not very large, so there are just two rungs on the career ladder: associate or partner. There is only one meaningful distinction between the two. The associate who makes a mistake may be dismissed. But the partner overseeing that associate is personally liable for that mistake. Few other jobs offer such risk.

So if you are looking for money or security, then the law is not for you.

In fact, if you are looking for some respect, you should go elsewhere. Lawyers are often sensationally depicted on television and in films. We are shown to be grasping, aggressive and morally ambiguous. And we are the butt of more jokes than any other profession. Only politicians are more ridiculed (but they are merely lawyers in another guise).

Add to that mix the stress that practitioners continually have to cope with. At the start of my career, a senior lawyer told me, 'After a patient sees his doctor, he will still have his headache. But after a client leaves his lawyer, it's the lawyer that has the headache. 'Our' job is to cure a client's headache by transferring it to ourselves. A lawyer's main professional skill is coping with the stress that our own clients inflict on us.

Why, then, do we remain in this profession, year after year?

The poet Kahlil Gibran had the answer. He wrote, 'Safeguarding the rights of others is the most noble and beautiful end of a human being.'

Those of us who continue to practice, year after year, realise this. No other profession is as rewarding. Each day, we are faced with the challenge of protecting a client's rights. Often, clients come to us as a last resort, when everything else has failed. We are expected to resolve long-simmering conflicts, untangle complex issues, or find a comfortable space between a rock and a hard place. And very frequently we have to finish our work as soon as possible. To do all that, we are armed with only three weapons: our knowledge of the law, our wits and the stubbornness of our character. The first may be improved with diligence, but not the second. And it is the third – stubbornness – which distinguishes the good lawyer from the great. The good lawyer advises the client on the state of the law, and the problems the client faces. But the great lawyer chips away, relentlessly, at the problems, until a solution is shaped.

Nowhere is the need for tenacity more important than in the courtroom. In every trial, there are moments when everything seems dark, and the case is doomed. Some lawyers may be tempted to throw in the towel. But the great lawyers never surrender. They soldier on, making argument after argument, asking question after question, trying to push back the darkness and uncover some small spark of light that may reveal their case to the judge. They do this day after day, trial after trial, until optimism becomes a habit.

So practice has taught me to value tenacity. I have learnt to accept that in litigation, as in life, the victor is the one who shows up the next day. And the day after that. And the day after that. Always hoping for the best. Because the ultimate point of tenacity is a belief that things will improve, if only we stay the course.

Practice has also taught me something else: to shun animosity. There is a common image of the lawyer as a combatant, someone who is intimidating and quick to take and give offence. But practitioners know the futility of aggression. I do not know of any situation which has been improved by an insult, malice or by open hostility. The true worth of a lawyer to his clients is his ability to find reasonable and reasoned solutions. So what is needed is light, not heat and smoke.

Practitioners know too that they are part of a community. Adversaries in one case may become allies in another. So they learn to limit, not escalate, conflict. In practice, as in life, there is no value in unpleasantness.

That leads me to the third lesson that practice has taught me. Every society has laws, and every democracy prides itself on having the rule of law. What then is the law? The answer is surprisingly simple. It can be found in the 1932 House of Lords decision in *Donoghue v Stevenson*, which dealt with the question of when a person would be liable for negligence that hurt another. Lord Atkin, in the House of Lords, explained that 'The rule that you are to love your neighbour becomes in law you must not injure your neighbour… You must take reasonable care to avoid acts or omissions which you can reasonably foresee would be likely to injure your neighbour.'

The decision established the tort of negligence, one of the most important areas of law today. It paved the way for patients to sue doctors who botched surgeries, for consumers to sue manufacturers who produced shoddy goods and for anyone who is hurt to sue the one who caused the hurt. What has always impressed me about that decision was its origin: love your neighbour.

In a very real sense, that has always been the essence of law in society. It sets a standard of human behaviour which is consistent with the principle that we love our neighbour. It imposes on us a duty to love each other. Because if there is love, there is empathy. If there is empathy, there is fairness. If there is fairness, there is justice.

Persistence, civility and love. That is what the practice of law has taught me.